THE
BIG
SHOW

THE BIG SHOW

INSIDE ESPN®'S
SPORTSCENTER™

Keith Olbermann
AND Dan Patrick

INTRODUCTION BY
Bob Costas

POCKET BOOKS
New York   London   Toronto   Sydney   Tokyo   Singapore

POCKET BOOKS, a division of Simon & Schuster Inc.
1230 Avenue of the Americas, New York, NY 10020

ISBN: 0-671-00918-4

First Pocket Books hardcover printing June 1997

10 9 8 7 6 5 4 3 2 1

POCKET and colophon are registered trademarks of
Simon & Schuster Inc.

Text design by Stanley S. Drate/Folio Graphics Co. Inc.

Printed in the U.S.A.

CONTENTS

☆ ★ ☆ ★ ☆

INTRODUCTION

What comes to mind when you mention Keith Olbermann and Dan Patrick? Well, I'm no Alex Trebek but let me answer that with a question.

Who are my ten-year-old son's favorite sportscasters?

Correct. Every morning, young Keith (go figure) starts his day with a bowl of cereal and the *SportsCenter* rerun. *Every day!* What does it mean when a ten-year-old kid brings home a report card sporting three "A's" and two "B's", and summarizes the achievement by saying, "Dad, I'm *en fuego*"?

It means that "The Big Show" owns the hearts and minds of a generation. Why? Simple. Patrick and Olbermann. Olbermann and Patrick. Two names. Two voices. One parking spot. (You see, Keith doesn't drive—one of a number of personal oddities which I'll leave to him to detail). Anyway, where was I? Oh, yes. Dan and Keith. Beloved and respected impresarios of "The Big Show"—by now a sports and broadcasting institution. Two guys riding an incredible wave of public adoration and critical praise. I mean, what can you say about these Bards of Bristol that hasn't already been said by every TV sports critic in America?

I guess I'll just have to start at the beginning. . . .

It was March 1976. I'd just finished a grueling triple-overtime broadcast of a Spirits-Squires game, and I was looking to put the day behind me. So, I'm sitting in the bar at the Algonquin, nursing my usual stein of Colt.45 with a Yoo-Hoo chaser (a little trick I learned in the Navy SEALs) when two seemingly underage patrons finesse their way past the maitre d', saunter on in, sit next to me, and order a couple of sarsaparillas. That's how I came to know Keith and Dan. They were taking night sportscasting courses at the Sorbonne, and were still buzzing about that evening's seminar on sport coat selection, conducted by the late, great Lindsey Nelson.

We struck up a conversation, debating, as I recall, the relative merits of Marv Albert and Chick Hearn. I remember fondly our spirited repartee. Still, as one last Boz Scaggs tune played on the jukebox, and dawn sent us traipsing toward the street, I was pretty sure I'd seen the last of them.

How wrong I was. How often do we fail to recognize genius in its nascent stages? (A rhetorical question, actually, so I wouldn't give it all that much thought, if I were you.) Now, as I conjure up the misty water-colored memory of that night, I realize the callow lads were just beginning to develop the chemistry and style that would eventually help redefine sports broadcasting, and earn them a mention anytime the great duos are discussed: Rodgers and Hammerstein, Huntley and Brinkley, Mantle and Maris, Sacco and Vanzetti. And why not? Dan and Keith are state of the art. A complete and distinctive package. Knowledgeable. Witty. Insightful. Irreverent. The models for countless sportscasters across North America. Their influence can be seen everywhere—network, cable, markets large and small.

And that brings me to my point. *What the hell have these guys wrought?* Look, I've got to level with you here. Just because Keith and Dan do it so well doesn't mean that every prompter jockey from Worcester to Walla Walla should be trying this stuff at home. Or in the studio, for that matter.

These days I flip on the set and get an endless parade of people who think *they're* the next Dan and Keith: Wannabes desperately trying to squeeze a Larry Sanders reference in during a kick save by Ron Tugnutt. All I'm looking for is the Cavs-Pacers final, and what I get is something like Open Mike Night at The Chuckle Hut. *"How quickly can I get the A.L. West out of the way and buy some time for my Marcel Lachemann hunk?"* Please. I beg you. Enough.

Of course, if Keith and Dan weren't so good at it, there wouldn't be imitators, would there? And there wouldn't be this surefire bestseller of a book, would there? Not that it's fair to blame the masters for all the unintended consequences. I mean, Ali's not responsible for every trash-talking tomato can who followed him, right? Is Call-Waiting Alexander Graham Bell's fault? Do we blame Dylan for England Dan and John Ford Coley? No, no, and no.

Yeah, I know I sound bitter. I've been this way since the Olympics. Whatta summer. While the Big Show boys are signing a huge book deal, I'm trying to keep a straight face throwing it to Tesh on a tape delay . . . and the indignities don't stop there. Keith and Dan are authors, and I'm on a flight to Kansas City to interview Neil Smith's mother for *Dateline*.

So in closing, I'd like to say, *"Move over, John Steinbeck, there's a pair of new kids on the block . . ."* I'd like to say that, but I can't really, because I haven't read the book yet—except for the one chapter about how they didn't speak to each other for almost two years after Keith tricked Dan out of a date with Toni Braxton. And believe me, if the rest of this thing is even half that good, it'll be worth a read. Or at least a listen once the audio version comes out—read, oddly enough, by Vince Cellini. Personally, I can't wait.

Bob Costas, NBC Sports
Colleague and Admirer

★ ☆ ★ ☆ ★ ☆ **1** ★ ☆ ★ ☆ ★ ☆

HI, HELLO, AND HOW ARE YOU?

Warm greetings and welcome to the *Big Show* book. Alongside my tag team partner Keith Olbermann, I'm merely Dan Patrick.

You're right about that "merely" part—and right at the outset here I think we should mention, Dan, that it's an amazing coincidence that you and I speak in different type styles.

Stop it. Just stop it. We have a very important question we have to answer right away. People kept asking us, "Dan and Keith, barometers of the sports world you may be. Stars of television and radio, sure. But what are you doing writing a book? What exactly is the *Big Show* book going to be about?"

"It's going to be about nine inches high by about four inches wide by about two hundred pages long," we tell them. "That's what the hell it's going to be **about.**" Then we explain that we were selected for *People* magazine's "TV's 40 Most Fascinating Stars" in 1996 and we placed ninth in *TV Guide*'s list of the top ten performers in all of television for 1995 and all the other guys on the list had already written a book—Seinfeld, Oprah, Marcia Clark—and we felt it was our turn to rake in some easy cash. I mean, John Tesh has even written some music.

Well, sort of.

Right. Sort of. Anyway, we thought we could convey our take on the world of sports, pass along that kind of behind-the-scenes stuff of what goes into the making of our show, tell our dreams and hopes and favorite ABBA songs, explain why I can't drive and why it's the New York Mets' fault, and—

And how I invented the word "Gone." People are always asking us where all these catchphrases came from. You know, "Gone" for a home run, "The Whiff," "En Fuego," "Nothing but the Bottom of the Net," and all the other good ones. And of course the ones Keith uses, too. The ones he steals from other people, usually me.

That's right. You invented everything. The whole English language.

"Gawwwwwn!"—give me a break! In ABBA's megahit "Dancing Queen" there's that moment when these two great singing legends pause for a moment. You know. "And then you're . . . **gone**." As old as you are, Dan, I **believe** that song came out even before your brilliant career began. So what if they were just repeating sounds they had learned phonetically and didn't understand a stitch of English? They still said "Gone!" Nothing is new. Not in sportscasting. Not in Swedish disco music.

What's wrong with you? Where did all this ABBA stuff come from? This is supposed to be a book about our show. We're supposed to be explaining the show, and introducing the book, and why you'd want to buy it or read it or maybe just steal it. We're supposed to be talking about all the ballplayers we know and how I got to meet Bill Murray and how Dennis Rodman wanted to write one of our commercials for us. Instead it's microdetails from the career of ABBA. What's next? "99 Luft Balloons?" Have you lost your mind entirely?

Well, we **have** been working together for five years now.

Could we possibly get this back on track? Where was I before you ruined it? Oh yeah. People are always asking us what this book could possibly be about and I tell them it's an attempt to translate the idea that every night we go out there and have fun with the world of sports. We show the highlights and tell the news, of course, but we're there **enjoying** what we're presenting. And, of course, we're doing it almost completely ad-libbed and we're seeing the highlights just as you're seeing them and that lends a certain "without a net" quality to our show that seems to attract people like a magnet. And sure, we have an attitude, we criticize the bad trends and the show-offs and the greedy players and the greedy owners, but we're there to have fun, and that's what I tell them the book's going to be about.

Of course by this point they've either walked away or taken a swing at one of us.

Usually me.

Well, you **look** guiltier.

I **do** look guiltier. Why do you suppose that is? I mean, the number of times you say something really stupid on the show about a player or somebody and then I run into him at a game or somewhere and he blames me for it. Remember that thing with Bob Knight, the Indiana basketball coach? When you showed him grabbing one of his players by the shirt and you said, "At home with the Knight family?" Real good, Keith. I saw him on the road and I thought he was going to put a chair through my thorax.

My point is proved. And it's not like you always defend me or anything, bub. The awards night? When you went up to Eric Lindros of the Flyers at the ESPYs and told him I kept bashing him on the air about not playing every night and he should come over and threaten to kick my ass? I mean, what was the idea **there**? If he'd hit me, I would've been drooling the drool of regret out of my ear instead of my mouth. And anyway, it backfired. We wound up buddies.

Oh, and won't we hear about **that** in the pages to come! It'll be Eric Lindros this and Eric Lindros that and Eric Lindros told me and my new best friend Eric Lindros and on and on and on.

It'll be in chapter 6, dear reader. Anyway, jealousy does not become you, Dan. As ABBA sang, "If I had—"

Enough with ABBA already! We've got a book to start here, and you're babbling on about four singers nobody remembers anymore. Next thing you'll be working the 1899 Cleveland Spiders baseball team into it or what Joe Magrane did in the 1987 World Series or who won the All American Football Conference title in 1946!

It is that kind of historical context that allows you the freedom to express yourself every night on The Big Show. If we don't know our stuff, all the goofiness doesn't matter one whit. And the same goes for the *Big Show* book. High good humor and satire, yes. Without a question. But if there's no knowledge, no awareness of the past still hovering around us like a shielding diaphanous cloud, we are lost—and this book is used by some guy to even out that one short leg on his desk. Historical context. Paramount.

Historical context? Like the time you said it was an outrage that Bill Veeck hadn't even gotten one vote in the baseball Hall of Fame ballot and it turned out that was because he was elected the year before? Is that the kind of shielding diaphanous cloud of history you mean?

It had been a very long week, Dan. You know that.

You're right. I'm sorry. Our dear reader is going to get the impression that we hate each other. In fact, Keith and I have been friends since we worked together, years ago, at CNN. I was even at his going-away party. Keith gave me some very good advice about my career, and to repay him, I've carried him professionally since he joined me on The Big Show.

Oh, now I get it, Dan! We're writing a **fictional** account of the show! Well, let's get the obligatory facts out of the way. We have lots of folks to thank, not merely for this book, but for all the moments in our lives that led up to this book. This is usually the part you skip to get to the good stuff. We'd like to warn you that **this** could be the "good stuff."

Obviously we'd like to thank our editor Pete Wolverton, who put this together, and our agent Esther Newberg, who put this deal together. And of course, Bob Costas and his son Keith for writing such a lovely, and obviously heavily exaggerated, foreword. And also Andy Ward, who originally approached us about the concept.

Andy was promptly turned down by his own farsighted bosses and then had the presence of mind to get out of publishing altogether.

Keith and I would also like to collectively thank a number of our professional colleagues and friends past and present without whom we couldn't have done this book, do our jobs, and/or have our jobs: Dave Albright, Jim Allegro, Chris Berman, Tony Bruno, Jennifer Chafitz, Linda Cohn, Jack Craig, Lenny Daniels, Rick Davis, Tim Kiely, Craig Kilborn, Bill MacPhail, Chris Martens, Kenny Mayne, Peter McConville, Mike McQuade, Danny Meara, Tom Mees, Gary Miller, Gary Parker, Hank Perlman, Gus Ramsey, Ed Schimmel, Howie Schwab, Charley Steiner, Kevin Stolworthy, Mark Summer, Mike Tirico, Rob Tobias, Vinnie Vassallo, Linda

Willhite, and Mary Alice Williams. I'd also like to remind them that these thank-yous are in lieu of free copies of the book, so don't even bother asking.

Not even an injury can break up the team. *(photo by Scott Clarke)*

We get **charged** for free books. My personal thank-yous go first to my broadcasting agent of fourteen years, the impeccable Jean Sage, who has saved me from professional suicide about 206 times (she's ahead 206 saves to 44 suicides), and also to many friends and loved ones, living or living now in my memory and my daily life: Steve Ackerman, Dick Amaral, Mike Aronstein, Nick Bakay, Laurel Beverley, Mike Bogad, Clark Booth, Jay Brachulis, Ronnie Bradford, Christine Brennan, Glenn Brenner, Jim Burger, Barry Carlin, Rick Cerrone, Marie and Victor Charbonnier, Peter Ciccone, Bob Clark, Jon Clark, Eric Cohen, Chris Conangla, Glenn

Corneliess, Dan Davis, John Doyle, Larry and Karen Hasby Epstein, Kevin Ettinger, Beth Faber, Jeff Finch, Andy Fisher, Hal Fishman, Erin Foley, Laurie Freeman Shimizu, Cliff Gelb, Carol and Peter Gibbon, George Goodman, Nancy Gottesman, Ron Gralnik, Gordon Gray, Phil Griffin, Ed Gullo, Brett Haber, Allan Havey, John B. Hill, Marc Hofman, Denis Horgan, Ed Ingles, Jo Interrante, Stan Isaacs, Kristen Jochum, Wally Joyner, Josh Kaplan, Cathy Karp, Jim Katzenstein, Benjie Kaze, Bob Keisser, Mark Keizer, Andy Lavick, Chris Lee, Rob Lemley, Hans Letz, Richard Lewis, Bob Lilly, Bill MacPhail, Joe Magrane, Cal Mankowski, Al Marcus, Don Martin, John Martin, Bill Mazer, Brian McFadden, Randy McNaughton, Tom Morrera, Roger Nadel, Arthur Naething, Mike Nardin, Dan Noel, Roger Norum, Mac O'Grady, Marie and Ted Olbermann, Jenna Olbermann Smith, Eric Orent, Steve Orlandella, Bill Pidto, Stanley Pinsley, Marjorie Plant, Ed Pyle, Frank Raphael, Paige Reyes, Ellen Rice, Milton Richman, Jose Rios, Marcia Rock, Maryellen Rock, Barry Rohde, Mike Rosen, Sam Rosen, Norm Rosenfield, Phil Rosenthal, Stan Sabik, Bob Sagendorf, Rich Sandomir, Jim Savitt, Leslie Sawyer Bascom, Peter Schacknow, Walter Schneller, Willie Schlumbohm, Denis Sedory, Bob Sims, Patricia Sinatra, Buddy and Robin Singer, Barry Sloan, Erik Sorenson, Gil Stratton, Bill Stout, Bert Sugar, Sam Swift, Tritia Toyota, Jeff Wald, Belinda Walker, Lou Waters, Chuck Wilson, Roland Woerner, Stan Wojcik, Rick Wolff, David Ysais, and Bill Zimmerman.

My personal "thanks" list includes: Smokey Anderson, Eddie Arsis, Chris Ballante, Brett Bearup, Artie Berko, Bob and Brian, Britt, Bean and Antman, Allan Brown, Chuck Browning, Zeke Campbell, Stacey Eisenberg, Fishco, Ann and Rob Fosheim, Peg Hayes, Dr. Jim Hays, Jason Hochman, Mollye and Matt Hollis, Jon Hopkins, Kathy Johnson, Jackson Jones, John Kiesewetter, Chris Kubiak, Larry Lain, Steve Leftkowitz, Bob Ley, John Lindesmith, Dave Luczak, Greg McCracken, Steve Mata, Bill Murray, Jeff Neal, Kelly Neal, Tammy Parkhurst, Sue, Jack, Grace, and Georgia Patrick, Ambrose Pugh, Bill and Linda Pugh, Dave and Jen Pugh, Jack and Patti Pugh, Mike and Sue Pugh, Bill Richardson, Dave Ritter, Darius Rucker, John Saunders, Ricky Shine, Sean Sizemore, Jim Sonifeld, Dr. Arthur Ting, Mike Troiano, Sonny and Pam Vaccaro, John Walsh, Jim Walton, The Walton Gang, George and Irene White, Peter and Gina White, Norby Williamson, Florence Wolff, and Tim Wood.

Well, let's get started, shall we? But one more thing first, Dan . . .

What?

You need some more rouge.

Oh, **that's** original.

A SORT OF GLOSSARY OF TERMS

Look, we don't take what we say all that seriously. But apparently we live in a time when the catchphrase is America's primary form of communication and evidently we're a catchphrase factory, to the point that our stupid little sayings are spat back at us at ball games (by players and fans alike), by other sportscasters, and in every darn article that's ever been written about us. The *Chicago Tribune* once devoted an entire column to some of our key sayings. *Sports Illustrated* once ran a six-inch-square, six-color graph analyzing the home run calls of all of us at *SportsCenter*. In '94, Bob Abreu, an outfielder from Aragua, Venezuela, who was playing in the Astros' farm system, told *Baseball America* that, sure, he watched our show for the highlights, but he **paid attention** because it had been "helping me pick things up in English." (Abreu made the majors in September '96. Bob: Repeat after us: "Houston, Hello!")

At the 1995 Super Bowl, Dan was riding the Chargers' team hotel elevator, when the doors opened and Natrone Means and a couple of teammates stepped in.

MEANS: Hey, Dan Patrick, how ya doin'. I'm Natrone Means.

9

DAN: Nice to meet you. Good luck Sunday.

MEANS: Man, say that thing you say.

DAN: Huh?

MEANS: The thing you say.

DAN: What are you talking about?

MEANS: You know, you know, that thing you always say.

DAN: Natrone, I'm on TV five hours a week. I say a lot of things.

ANOTHER CHARGER (annoyed): C'mon. Your phrase. Your thing.

DAN: Which one?

MEANS: The one that begins with "N." Come on!

DAN: Nothing but the bottom of the net?

MEANS (very annoyed): No, no, man, N . . . N Fuego!

We'll spare you the other stories. Very frequent. Very similar. Rush for a plane and somebody wants you to give them a "Hel-loooooo!" Pick up a paper and every two months or so you'll read somebody talking about how they can't hope to stop such and such, they can only hope to contain them. One of us (we won't say who, but Keith's the single guy) was actually asked by a date, at a critical moment, to say one of the catchphrases (we won't say which, but it ends in "Bang!").

The thing has gotten so out of hand over the years that a viewer named Mark Coale, who actually has turned watching the show into an academic pursuit at Bowling Green State University in Ohio, presented a scholarly paper on "The Metatextual Viewing of ESPN's 'SportsCenter' " at the Midwest Popular Culture Association confer-ence in Indianapolis in 1995. Mark explained that we had sur-mounted our "inability to remain insulated within the diegetic world of the program . . . compounded by the frequent interruptions of the narrative by commercials" because the show taps "into its viewers' collective knowledge through use of metatextual refer-ences from not only sports, but also the larger whole of popular culture."

Gosh.

As the comedians Bob and Ray used to say when people would read a message into their humor: "It left here fine. Something must have happened to it when it got to the transmitter." To be fair, some of the catchphrases are intended to make people see sports in a little larger context (we're beginning to sound like our Bowling Green friend, here, aren't we?). But most of all, they're just plain fun. And catchphrases have been with us as long as we've had societies. There's an amazing nineteenth-century book called *Extraordinary Popular Delusions and the Madness of Crowds* by Charles Mackay that tells of a London populated by people going around saying "Quoz" to each other to mean all kinds of insults, greetings, and exclamations, who all of a sudden switched to mocking each other's headgear by shouting, "What a shocking bad hat!" Not exactly "Where's the beef?" but you get the idea.

Truth be told, our catchphrases, and we were shocked to discover there are seventy-six of them still more or less regularly in use, have a practical value. Remember, we're usually ad-libbing the narration of the highlights, and there's nothing better when you're trying to think of what to say about the play in progress, or better still the **next** play we're going to show you, than to turn to a trusty old catchphrase and kill off a second or two while giving your brain the chance to say something—**anything**—that might actually be insightful.

Enough analysis. We promised you a glossary and an explanation of all of these metatextual delvings into semiotic baggage and electronic shadow memory. And as Dan says, when we promise, we always deliver:

A Good Craftsman Never Blames His Tools: *(Keith)* For use when a player breaks a bat, throws one, slams a stick or a racket, or otherwise, well, blames his tool. Keith says he heard this somewhere but can't remember who said it (a likely story).

And a Mighty Roar Went Up from the Crowd: *(Keith)* Usually used to describe players or fans who do not seem to be as happy as they should be following a home run, touchdown, or victory. Often accompanied by Dan making a faint "yay" sound. A paraphrase of a Bob and Ray sketch in which a promoter explains his plans to play team backgammon in the Yale Bowl using refrigerators as dice.

And There Was Much Rejoicing: *(Keith)* See above. Direct rip-off from the movie *Monty Python and the Holy Grail.*

Awinnn Buhhh: *(Keith)* Used only when an athlete or fan is caught in the highlights wolfing down food or drink. This is from a commercial for milk featuring a guy who was a fanatic about the duel in 1804 in which American revolutionary leader Alexander Hamilton was shot and killed by Vice President Aaron Burr. The guy's got a mouthful of food and nothing to wash it down with, and when a radio station calls to offer him a huge prize if he can identify who shot Hamilton, he can only mumble "Awinnn Buhhh." Specialized use: when someone hits a homer off Joey Hamilton, or blocks a shot by Zendon Hamilton.

Berroa Means Good-bye: *(Both of us)* Very specific to Oakland A's outfielder Geronimo Berroa. This is a parody of our colleague Larry Beil's home run call ("Aloha means good-bye"), which, to our credit, we first offered to Larry when Berroa took one out of the yard. Larry didn't use it, so of course we took this to mean he was giving us full rights to use it every stinking time Berroa showed up in the highlights. And you're right, we get real territorial about this junk.

Be There. Aloha: *(Keith)* Used only at the end of promotional announcements shown during *SportsCenter*. It's very simple. This is what the actor Jack Lord used to say as Steve McGarrett when he would narrate the highlights of the next episode of *Hawaii 5-0* on CBS. They cut the coming attractions out of all the reruns, so you have to have been a TV viewer in the late '60s and early '70s to actually get it.

Big Show: *(Both)* Keith started calling it "The Big Show" within a week or two of joining Dan in 1992. Interestingly, this had a very off-putting effect on some of our colleagues who thought we were implying that the eleven o'clock show was "Big" and the other editions of *SportsCenter* weren't. In fact, we were just comparing the hour we put on to the half-hour that CNN Sports put on. Considering that everybody from David Letterman to Ed Sullivan has called his show "The Big Show," we have no flippin' idea how this actually stuck. But it did. And you bought a book titled it, didn't you?

Biscuit in the Basket (He Put the): *(Keith)* Used for hockey goals, and, with the increased advent of soccer highlights, soccer goals. We could also use it for water polo, I guess. A simple steal from a Canadian show that once popped up on one of the monitors in the newsroom in which some announcer used the phrase to describe some junior league player scoring a goal. It also spawned such mutant catchphrases as "If you don't bake the biscuit, you can't put the biscuit in the basket," which can be used to describe a hockey team that doesn't take enough shots on goal. Alternative etymology suggests the phrase originated in the movie *Silence of the Lambs*, but Keith never saw the film and Dan doesn't remember that part.

Brought to You Bah: *(Both)* Also from hockey, to describe a pass leading to a goal, or to list the assists credited after a goal's been scored. This particular phrase represents a fairly familiar etymology. It has a basis in another network's broadcast, was noted by an ESPN person who went around the office saying it, and then Keith stole it from him. The original is from CBS, whose voice-over announcer for commercial sponsorships was a famous New York disc jockey named Rosko. Our pal Bill Pidto became so enamored of Rosko's gravelly voice and elongated delivery that he would march around the newsroom saying, "Brought to you bah . . . ITT . . . and bah . . . Pennzoil." Typical of Keith's ethics, he stole it.

Check Please: *(Keith)* Multipurpose. As an exclamation noting the end of something (a strikeout, the last out of a game, a football player eluding the final would-be tackler), it is simple and effective. Hard to say where it comes from originally, but Woody Allen used it in the next-to-last scene in *Annie Hall* when, over lunch, he couldn't convince Diane Keaton to move back to New York with him from Los Angeles.

Detlef Schrempf!: *(Dan)* You have to say this one aloud to get the full impact. Punch yourself in a tender region as you get to this NBA player's last name and you'll be able to pull off a reasonably good impression of Dan saying it. No mystery here. It's Detlef's name. Dan likes Detlef. Dan's constant use of it led to a friendship with the gifted German. They actually dined together during the 1996 NBA Finals, during which Detlef and his Seattle teammates also experienced the phenomenon of being punched in a tender region.

Drooling the Drool of Regret into the Pillow of Remorse: *(Keith)* Used typically while we're showing you the graphic scoreboard "panel," to make comment on a losing team or a player who did not perform up to par. Keith once explained to a reporter that this was an "anti-catchphrase catchphrase," which sounds a hell of a lot like this metatext stuff. In fact, this was created specifically to get a laugh out of Keith's buddy Rebecca Lobo, the basketball player, who had told him that she had turned several shades of red after she and roommate Pam Webber were shown in a photo in *People* magazine brushing their teeth—and a tiny little bit of drool was seen at the corners of each of their mouths.

En Fuego: *(Dan)* As Mr. Means's annoyance suggests, probably the most famous example of Big Show Phraseology and the one Dan most regrets not having trademarked earlier. Used anytime, any sport, but most typically during NBA highlights. This is actually a twice-revised version of one of the oldest of sports clichés, namely that a player is "on fire." Dan simply got tired of hearing it, tired of saying it, and was (typically) complaining about this during a commercial break when one of the cameramen offhandedly suggested maybe he should try it in Spanish. So, Dan modified it to, for instance, "Detlef Schrempf is absolutely 'El Fuego.' " A high school Spanish teacher from Pennsylvania wrote in not long after noting that Dan wasn't saying Detlef Schrempf is "on fire" but that Detlef Schrempf is "the fire," and offered the correct version. "En Fuego" promptly wound up on T-shirts and bumper stickers and hats and as a special insert series for Pinnacle baseball cards. Dan at least got his own card out of that one, standing there in suit and tie with a bat on his shoulder, and a very dissatisfied look on his face. On the other hand, when the cards first appeared in the monthly *Beckett's Baseball Cards Price Guide*, Dan's was listed as being worth six bucks as opposed to just four for 1995 National League MVP runner-up Dante Bichette.

From Way Downtown . . . Bang!: *(Keith)* For use on three-pointers in the NBA and college hoops. Also, during the off-season, can be used in golf. In 1981, Keith's friend Jim Burger left a slightly inebriated message on Keith's answering machine consisting of his imitation of raspy-voiced, legendary Celtics announcer Johnny Most: "Witherspoon. From way downtown. Bang." The Witherspoon was long-ago Washington Bullet Nick Witherspoon, and Most's original version of the call suggested disappointment and resignation. It stuck with Keith ever since, and after a brief period after Most's death in which it was shelved out of respect, it's a once- or twice-a-night staple.

This has nothing to do with the impression, by the way, but apart from Most's legendary homerism and singularly compelling style, he was most famous for a rather disgusting anecdote. It seems Most went to his doctor once, complaining of headaches and deafness in one ear. The physician got out his scope, looked into the offending canal, and blanched. "John," he said, "have you been on TV recently?" "Yeah," Most growled, in a voice that sounded like it could have belonged to Roseanne's grandfather. "About three months ago." The doctor tried to settle his stomach. "Did they give you one of those earpieces to hear the director with?" Most replied affirmatively. Finally the doctor asked, "John, didn't you remember to take it out?"

While you chew on that image, consider this. There was another version of the story that had Most waiting a **year** before going to the doctor.

Freeze It: *(Dan)* Simple narration for a called third strike. Dan hasn't used it a lot lately. He's often claimed it originated with Dick Vitale narrating stop-action replays.

Frozen Pizza: *(Keith)* Simple rip-off of Dan's simple narration for a called third strike.

Full Extension: *(Keith)* A football or baseball player stretching his body to its limit in pursuit of the ball. Can also be used to mock those players who have stretched their body well short of said limit.

Get a Roll of Stamps, and Mail It In: *(Keith)* An insult. Usually implies a lackluster effort on the part of a player or team, or of all the players and both the teams in a meaningless game. To be fair, before and/or during a show Keith has often said to Dan or producer Mike McQuade, "Get me a roll of stamps."

Gianluca Pagliuca: *(Keith)* An expletive, used to describe an arguing athlete's comments to an umpire or referee, or by Keith to describe his own feelings on a story or something happening on the show. Pagliuca was the goalie for Italy's 1994 World Cup soccer team. One of both hosts' favorite colleagues, Gary Miller, was prerecording the narration for a "Breakdown" segment on the Cup that summer when he tripped over Pagliuca's name and involuntarily spat out an expletive in disgust. We'll spare you **which** expletive. Suffice to say, this expletive has come to be synonymous with poor Pagliuca's name. Curiously, ESPN Radio executive producer John

Martin, a long-ago colleague of both Keith and Charley Steiner at RKO Radio, used to use the name Ahmad Rashad to express the same expletive—before Rashad became whatever it is he has become.

Gggggggh!: *(Keith)* Elementally simple. The gagging sound, originally implying nothing less than an athlete having choked, more recently broadened to describe any error, flub, collision, or otherwise untoward on-field incident. Its origins are murky. Karl Ravech and Brett Haber had long before used an exclamation that sounded like "Guh-yee!" to indicate disaster, and at various times each had said that our former colleague Craig Kilborn had originated it. Kilborn, in turn, said it came from the overenunciation of the last syllable of the word "pumping" in the voting promotional announcement for the first ESPY Awards. Further research has suggested a much more subconscious origin. In their song "Good Morning" on the *Sgt. Pepper* album, the Beatles actually sing the word "morning" several times as "mornin-ggggggh." To go back still further, Keith's father insists that as an infant, he would greet applesauce with a noise of approval that sounded like "goit."

This is more than you wanted to know, right?

Goff: *(Dan)* Golf. Dan sometimes spells it out in case you don't get it, or adds on the explanation that what you just saw was a "goff shot." Became particularly confusing when catcher Jerry Goff returned to the majors with the Pirates in 1993. Probable origin: Scottish founders of the game seldom pronounced the *L* very distinctly.

Goff Shots: Nothing but Goff Shots: *(Both)* Usually used in clips promoting upcoming highlights of golf tournaments (usually the PGA: Pro Goffers Association). Keith introduced this one to both tweak Dan's nose a little and also pay homage to David Letterman's use of the 1980s New York radio station promotional slogan "Love Songs: Nothing but Love Songs."

Gone: *(Dan)* A home run, preferably as it leaves the bat. For simplicity and impact, there's no better catchphrase on the planet. Once again, the sportscaster's sportscaster Gary Miller figures in to its origin. He and Dan, like Keith, were formerly employees of CNN, and Dan and Gary would while away the many down hours in Atlanta by playing Strat-O-Matic Baseball (for the uninitiated, one of the two standard dice baseball games that passed for pseudo-realism in our precomputer childhoods). Since each major leaguer's performance was simulated on his own game card, home runs were instantly evident depending on the roll of the dice. In other words, the action would follow thusly, and this quickly:

1. Dan rolls dice.
2. Dice come up 2 and 5.
3. Hank Aaron's card reads "2-5: home run."
4. Dan and Gary, with different levels of enthusiasm, say "Gone."

Dan adds that they often played this game while actually attending home contests of the Atlanta Braves, which gives you a pretty clear picture of just how bad the Braves were in the late '80s.

Good (Goot): *(Dan)* The basketball and football version of "Gone." Nothing complicated, no funny voice required. Dan heard it once on a Georgia Tech basketball game broadcast by a fellow named Al Ceraldo. As near to perfection as possible. The only risk, of course, is if someone's screwed up the highlight and Detlef Schrempf's shot is **no** good, in which case Dan has to apologize to everyone in the world.

Happy Happy Joy Joy: *(Keith)* Used for narrating celebrations. Direct rip-off from the cartoon "Ren and Stimpy." Former Big Show producer Mike McQuade claims he suggested it. Mike also claims the European PGA tour is interesting.

Have a Seat: *(Keith)* Simple phraseology for a strikeout. No origins cited.

He Beat Him like a Rented Goalie: *(Keith)* The phrase used to describe a goal **after** the "biscuit" phrase has been used too many times. A simple parodying of the colorful, sometimes bizarre radio announcer of the Pittsburgh Penguins, Mike Lange, whose goal-scoring call is "He beat him like a rented mule," which may in turn be borrowed from comedian Jeff Altman's bit about his father when angry.

He's Day to Day. We're All Day to Day: *(Keith)* The Big Show version of this most clichéd of medical reports about injured players. "Day to day" originated in the 1970s and Keith was using his version of it on college radio late in that decade. The Associated Press ran a story about NASCAR driver Dale Jarrett in 1995 in which it quoted him as saying, "I decided I needed to make the move one night when I was watching *SportsCenter* on ESPN. The newscaster—I think it was Keith Olbermann—was talking about some baseball player and said his situation was 'day to day.' I thought to myself, 'Really, aren't we all in a day-to-day situation?' "

Got that right, Dale.

He Hit the Ball Real Hard: *(Keith)* A home run call. Not as elegant as Dan's, but simple, and said with a kind of childish respect for the ferocity of the swing. Another paraphrase from Bob and Ray, who once had a sports report about a hockey player who used to try to hide behind the net during fights. "But the other guys would find me and hit me real hard."

Hellooooo!: *(Both)* Absolutely all-purpose. Can be used at a moment of surprise in a game, or when a ball hits a player in a tender area, or during a collision, or during a fight. The origin is again labyrinthine. Once again, the devilish producer Mike Mc-Quade lurks in the background. Q realized that a certain executive of the company had a habit of answering his phone and greeting folks in the hall with this exaggerated version of the standard greeting. Instigator that he is, McQuade pointed this out to both Dan and Keith. Dan started saying it around the office. Keith started saying it on the air. At its apex, in the fall of 1994, it was virtually a universal form of greeting around the *SportsCenter* newsroom and got so annoying that mass suicide was considered, and Keith backed off to an average of less than one of them per show—whereupon Dan started saying it too, most famously for highlights of goff's Dubai Open ("You say Dubai, and I say 'helloooooo!' ").

Here's the Two-Two Pitch to Mariano Duncan: *(Keith)* Used, obviously, whenever Mariano Duncan comes up, or for almost any Phillies highlights. It's a poor imitation of ESPN Radio's Tony Bruno's poor imitation of Phils announcer Harry Kalas, another giant of the industry. Must be said slowly and purposefully, just like Harry. Of all the announcers we've ever imitated or poked fun at, Kalas was easily the most gracious. Keith went to Philadelphia in 1993 to do play-by-play of a Phils-Astros game on ESPN and Bruno introduced him to Kalas. "Good luck, Keith, I'm sure you'll do fine," Kalas said. "By the way, how many innings of **me** do you plan to do?"

Hockey Term: *(Dan)* Also golf term, basketball term, *SportsCenter* term. A word used to demystify sports-speak. Spontaneously unleashed one night when an overzealous production assistant wrote on his shot-sheet that one NHL player "went top shelf" instead of as simply having "scored." Dan caught the pretentiousness (*SportsCenter* term) and deflated it with rare acumen (literary term).

Houston, Hello!: *(Keith)* Meaningless phrasing that follows virtually every mention of the Texas city, of golfer John Huston, or of basketball's Allen Houston. Origins: again, pure thievery. In the embryonic days of ESPN Radio, Keith's friend Tony Bruno came in and told of falling asleep while listening to a Flyers game on the radio. When he awakened hours later with the radio on, the first thing he heard was Larry King, on his old all-night radio show, greeting a caller with a hearty "Houston, hello!" Tony used the phrase nonstop, all weekend long, and it stuck. In an interview with ESPN Radio a few years later, King said he liked all the *SportsCenter* guys, "even that guy who does me. You know, 'Houston, hello.' "

I Can Read His Lips, and He Is Not Praying: *(Keith)* Used during tight shots of athletes swearing, mostly to take the edge off the obvious profanity for all you lip-readers out there. A direct quote from a rather eloquent New York cabby, who in 1983, with Keith as a passenger, cut off another motorist (there's a shock), turned to look at his vanquished driving foe, and intoned the memorable phrase.

I Can't Believe I Shook This Guy's Friggin' Hand: *(Keith)* For narration of the highlights of hockey's long-standing tradition of the teams shaking hands at the conclusion of a Stanley Cup play-off series, or, more broadly, after any shown handshake. This is a direct quote from Dino Ciccarelli of the Detroit Red Wings, referring to Colorado Avalanche captain Claude Lemieux after the latter messed up the face of Detroit's Kris Draper during the 1996 finals. One of the all-time great sports sound bites.

I Have Nothing More to Say About This That Is Either Relevant or True: *(Keith)* Used, generally over scoreboard panels, when there just isn't anything else worthwhile to say about the game or event in question. Paraphrasing of what British prime minister Winston Churchill claims he thought while staring at an essay question on an entrance exam to the prestigious school Eton circa 1887.

If You're Scoring at Home, or Even If You're Alone: *(Keith)* Follows a baseball double play or other event featuring many players tossing the ball around. A homage to the legendary Dodgers announcer Vin Scully, who would often give the exact sequence of fielders on such a play for the benefit of any listener who was, in fact, keeping score at home. (Keith added the licentious part; Vin has far too much class and élan to have ever thought it, let alone said it.)

It's a Power Play Goal!: *(Both)* Pretty obvious. Describes a hockey goal when the scoring team has a one- or two-man advantage during a penalty. But the subtext is different. Dan intones the phrase as part of an impression of President Reagan; Keith is either impersonating a generic Canadian hockey announcer or is honoring New York Rangers play-by-play man Sam Rosen, who was his first boss in radio in 1979.

It's Deep, and I Don't Think It's Playable: *(Keith)* Another home run call, and another theft. Dan said it around the office. Keith said it on the air. Dan threatened to break Keith's clavicle if he kept doing it. Keith modifies it sometimes to insert Dan's name by way of giving him credit: "It's deep, Dan, and I don't think it's playable." Sometimes further modified to describe a great catch, as in, ". . . but Kenny Lofton does!"

Invisible Gophers: *(Keith)* What hockey players skating on clear ice trip over, what clean grounders hit before hopping over shortstops' shoulders. Keith thinks he borrowed it from somebody but he can't figure out from whom.

Jumanji: *(Both)* An all-purpose, mostly basketball phrase, suggested by our current producer, Gus Ramsey, for the use of Craig Kilborn when both were working on the 2:00 A.M. ET edition of *SportsCenter.* Upon Killer's departure, we both picked it up for the heck of it, and so that neither Craig nor the silly movie of the same name would be completely forgotten around the office.

Lugnuts: Nothing but Lugnuts: *(Keith)* See "Goff Shots: Nothing but Goff Shots." Used mostly for NASCAR races, seven out of ten of which see a driver sent to the pits due to a lugnut mishap.

Mr. Dictionary Has Failed Us Yet Again: *(Keith)* Another means of covering up obvious obscenities in tight shots of pitchers, managers, whoever. A direct rip-off from the frenetic British comedy series *Absolutely Fabulous*.

Niedermeyer: Dead!: *(Keith)* Very specific. Used only when Rob Niedermayer of the Florida Panthers or Scott Niedermayer of the New Jersey Devils shows up in NHL highlights. A tribute to a famous line from the movie *Animal House*. Mike McQuade, having just seen the film on TV and thus having been freshly infused with the anarchical desires it always stirs, not only suggested the line but actually procured hockey trading cards of the Niedermayer brothers and pinned them to the wall next to Keith's desk to remind him to use the phrase.

Not Appearing in Your Picture: *(Keith)* Generalized phrase coming from a specific event. Now connotes action not being seen in the highlights, or taking place out of the camera's view. The specific origin came from a 1992 meeting at Yankee Stadium when the massive first baseman Paul Sorrento, then of the Indians, spotted Keith near the batting cage and came running in from taking infield practice. Keith, already frightened, was about to run himself but Sorrento got there first. This exchange followed:

> SORRENTO: Hi. Nice to meet you. I'm Paul Sorrento.
>
> KEITH: I'm double-parked.
>
> SORRENTO: Hey, about what you said about me.
>
> KEITH: Dan said it.
>
> SORRENTO: No, you said it.
>
> KEITH: My mom's calling me. Hear her?
>
> SORRENTO: In Milwaukee the other night?
>
> KEITH: Honest to God, Paul, I don't remember half the things I say.
>
> SORRENTO: You don't remember "Not appearing in your picture"?
>
> KEITH: (forms Macaulay Culkin's "O" mouth. In Milwaukee the week before, Sorrento had singled into centerfield and tried to leg out a double. But Robin Yount cut the ball off in the gap and threw a strike to Pat Listach at second. When Listach went to apply the tag on the sliding Sorrento, the camera angle was such that Sorrento was not yet visible.

So Keith said, cleverly, "and Yount gets Paul Sorrento—not appearing in your picture." In fact, the play was shown a **second** time later in the same show and Keith said it **again.** Keith mentally reviews his insurance coverage.)

KEITH: Uh, Paul, I'm very sorry if . . .

SORRENTO (big smile): "Not appearing in your picture." That's all we've been saying around the clubhouse since. Funniest damn thing I ever heard in my life.

KEITH: (sigh of relief as big as Sorrento's chest)

For the record, whenever Sorrento does something good in a highlight, Keith now says "Paul Sorrento, **appearing** in your picture."

Nothing but the Bottom of the Cup: *(Dan)* For an unusually long goff putt or better still a hole in one. See below.

Nothing but the Bottom of the Net: *(Dan)* Another inimitable call, for a three-pointer or a long two-point shot in the NBA. Origins murky. Several variants around the sports world, foremost of which is "Nothing but net," which doesn't quite have the je ne sais quoi of The Big Show version.

Nothing but the Bottom of the Standings: *(Keith)* A parody. Used for a team hitting the basement, especially if Dan has just used either "cup" or "net."

Nowwwwwwwwww: *(Keith)* First line of the preshow opening segment we call the "tease." Keith's caricature of famed voice-over announcer Ernie Anderson, who used to begin the Boston newscast on which Keith appeared with "Nowwww, the news of New England . . . . and the World!"

Oh the Pain, the Shame: *(Keith)* Specialty catchphrase used for a shot of an athlete who has just gggggh'd or otherwise humiliated himself. Comes from the smarmy Dr. Zachary Smith from the '60s TV show *Lost in Space.* Dr. Smith was always being attacked by alien robots while he was in the middle of trying to swindle his fellow marooning victims, the Robinson family, out of the mineral rights on the planet Skyron. This happened **every** episode. At the critical moment, just as the robot closed its eight sticky arms around his real estate portfolio, Dr. Smith would say, "Oh the pain! The shame!"

Or, in English: *(Keith)* A self-parody. For a fumble, a stumble, a giggle, a mispronunciation, or other on-air blunder. Averages about one every other show. Always gets a laugh out of Dan.

Organ-i-zation: *(Both)* Keith picked this up from listening to one-too-many hockey players speak of his team, his franchise, his or-gan-I-zay-shin. Canadian émigrés working for ESPN do not find this funny, and nearly all of them say it is a provincial dialect native to one of the provinces they're not from. Related phrases include referring to the confluence of the ice and the sideboard as "the dasher," a uniform as a "sweater," or an arena as a "building," e.g.: "Our organ-i-zation was hurt when Gretzky ripped his sweater on the dasher in our own building."

Out of the Yard in a Hurry: *(Dan)* Another home run call. Variation has a long pause between "yard" and "in."

O-ver-time: *(Dan)* For use originally in hockey, then expanded into basketball and football. Part of Dan's two-phrase Ronald Reagan impression (see also "It's a Power Play Goal").

Premature Jocularity: *(Keith)* When a team celebrates obnoxiously on the field, in the dugout, or on the bench, and then goes on to lose the game. This is tenth-grade, bathroom humor, combining a peculiar word used in an old *M*A*S*H* episode by William Christopher as Father Mulcahy, and a "man's problem" that Dan and Keith have only heard about but never experienced. Never. Not once. Never. Hell, Dan has three kids!

Real Men Don't Strut: *(Both)* For moonwalks, excessive high fives, one-flap-downs, etc. An attempt to police showboating. Also see below.

Real Men Don't Taunt: *(Both)* For dropping the bat and staring at the fly ball, for pointing at the opposition after vanquishing them, for rubbing it in. Variation of the old phrase "Real men don't eat quiche," etc.

Robert Goulet-up: *(Keith)* A layup basket, especially in college, popularized during Robert Goulet's goofy ESPN college basketball advertisements in the winter of 1995–96. Curious history. The aforementioned producer Gus Ramsey dreamed this up during one Big Show while Karl Ravech was substituting for Dan. Gus sent a message in the ESPN in-house computer to Karl suggesting the line. But unbeknownst to either Gus or Keith, Karl had signed on on Keith's computer in the studio and Keith thought Gus's message was meant for him, and not Karl. Unintentional theft by Keith (that's his story and he's sticking to it).

Saracen Pig, Spartan Dog: *(Keith)* For use during highlights of hockey fights, especially ones in which the players don't actually hit each other. The line is from the Woody Allen film *What's Up, Tiger Lily?* in which the Japanese actors continually call each other these two denigrations while kicking, wrestling, or just staring daggers at each other.

Smash, Please: *(Both)* Used for, well, what else, an overhead smash in a tennis match. From the old ESPN2 show *SportsNight,* in which bottom-of-the-hour news updates (the "SportsSmash") were often presented by the eminently imitable Bill Pidto, who would often attach a "please" to the title of the show. To create the sound, widen your mouth as much as possible and then try to push the two words through your nose. And then seek medical attention.

Smidge: *(Dan)* An indescribably small period of time during the show during which we run commercials. The complete phrase is usually "*SportsCenter* continues . . . in a smidge." Apparently a Patrick family corruption of the English word "smidgen" or "smidgin," which *The Barnhart Concise Dictionary of Etymology* claims entered the language as "smitchin" about 1845, as a variation of a Scottish word "smitch," meaning a small amount or a small, insignificant person.

See, you learned something!

Soft as Church Music: *(Dan)* Used for a gentle basketball field goal, usually one taken with seemingly no effort on the part of the shooter and nothing but a gentle shake to the net itself. Dan once heard Joe Dean use the phrase on an LSU radio basketball broadcast.

SportsCenter Is Nexxxxxxt: *(Both)* Last line of our "tease." The word "next" has to be elongated. Neither the line nor the elongation originated with us. But if you want to give us credit, we'll happily accept it.

That'll Happen: *(Keith)* For use in exactly the opposite way the phrase suggests. Precisely when something **shouldn't** happen or **never** happens, you say this. Larry Walker catches a foul for the second out of an inning with a runner at third base and instead of throwing the ball in, he hands it to a fan? "That'll happen." Jose Canseco goes back for a fly ball and it hits him in the head and bounces off of it and over the fence for a homer? "That'll **happen.**" It also became the tag line to a *SportsCenter* commercial in which Keith appears to sever something vital in Jim Harbaugh's knee while he "operates" on the Colts quarterback. Originates from a story Bill Pidto's former boss at New England News Channel, Mike Adams, told Keith, producer Willie Weinbaum, and cameraman Jeff Alred at Red Sox training camp in 1996. Pidto, a lovely, caring, and gifted fellow, is, however, sometimes known for being, to use his own word, **focused.** Adams tells of watching a news story once in which a convict on a furlough from prison took a cab home, had the driver wait, murdered his own family, got back in the cab, and got back to the prison before the deadline at which the furlough expired. Pidto thereupon entered the newsroom, shuffling through in his distinctive gait, not even slowing down as Adams retold this incomprehensible tale of a man willing to kill half a dozen people but fearful of getting into trouble by getting back late to jail. Adams finished the story whereupon Pidto, as if this sort of thing occurred daily or weekly, announced matter-of-factly, "That'll happen."

That's for Alanis Morissette's Pain: *(Keith)* For use whenever a goal is scored against the Toronto Maple Leafs, or when the Leafs lose. The Canadian songstress's first hit, "You Oughtta Know," about a disgusting, abusive, uncaring boyfriend, was allegedly inspired by her relationship with a Maple Leaf player. We'll never identify the player. The phrase may, however, be adjusted because Toronto apparently traded him away.

The Other Team's Quarterback Must Go Down (and He Must Go Down Hard): *(Both)* When the quarterback is sacked, especially if violently so, you will hear one of us, usually Keith, intone this in a pretty damn good impression of Oakland–L.A.–Oakland Again Raiders owner Al Davis. It's a direct quote from a long-running NFL video ad that invariably ran during *SportsCenter* itself in 1992 and 1993. If you're trying this at home, the correct phonetic pronunciation is: Thotha tim's kwaddaback must go dowen . . . and he must go dowen hod.

The Use of Unnecessary Violence Has Been Approved: *(Keith)* A no-brainer for all Belushi fans, used during hockey fights, football sacks, and other moments of mayhem. Of course, the complete line is: "The use of unnecessary violence in the apprehension of the Blues Brothers has been approved."

The Whiff: *(Dan)* Another of the few A +'s of catchphrasedom. Used for strikeouts in baseball (swinging only). The origins are in the backyard of Dan's beatific childhood home in Mason, Ohio. Dan says he said it every time he'd strike out one of his brothers as they played whiffleball. They say **they** said it every time they'd strike him out. Keith has on occasion used the phrase during tennis matches or hockey games, or, once, when a skunk was seen running around the outfield in Jack Murphy Stadium in San Diego.

They're . . . Not . . . Gonna . . . Get Him: *(Both)* Used either to describe a drawn-out defensive play in which a runner unexpectedly beats the throw to the base or the plate (original), or to describe the same play when the runner is actually out. Keith also adapts it for use on breakaway plays in football and hockey. If one of us had to copyright this phrase, we'd be in court for years. During the 1991 World Series, CBS announcer Jack Buck, a favorite of both of ours, said this very phrase, in this very cadence, as Atlanta's Mark Lemke tried to score against the Twins. Unfortunately for Jack, Lemke was out. In Los Angeles, Keith used the phrase throughout the series and then forgot about it. The next year, after we began working together, Dan would say it around the office. Keith would then say it—but you're familiar with the process by now, aren't you? Then **Dan** started saying it on the air. When he did, that technically made this Dan's impression of Keith's impression of Dan's impression of Jack Buck. And if **you** use it, it's a **fifth**-generation impression.

Thisssss . . . Is SportsCenter: *(Both)* Rightfully perturbed that we called our program "The Big Show" more than we called it by its given name, management suggested we try to reverse the ratio. So we started using this phrase (you should almost sing the word "this") before every commercial. Next thing we knew, the entire *SportsCenter* advertising campaign was built around it.

Un . . . believable: *(Keith)* Alternate version for a three-point basket or a home run. Keith's impression of the exasperated way the word is said by one of the world's finest humans, the pride of Madison, Wisconsin, Maryellen Rock.

Unprofessional, That's What You Are: *(Keith)* Introduced during the bleak days of replacement baseball in the spring of 1995 when Keith would finally give up trying to describe a seventy-three-year old center-fielder falling all over himself trying to corral a fly ball hit by Pedro Borbon's great-grandfather, and would burst into this parody of Nat King Cole's beautiful song "Unforgettable." Also contained in this was a hidden tribute to the greatest of the local sportscasters, Keith's professional friend the late Glenn Brenner, who on several occasions sang the song, on the air at WTOP and later WUSA in Washington, about himself, when he screwed something up in his show.

With Authority: *(Both)* Usually used to describe a slam dunk. Purloined from Larry Beil's impression of Marv Albert's slam dunk call. Often modified to the point of giddiness. In one show we transformed this into "without authority," "with port authority," "without any authority," "by whose authority?," "by the authority invested in me," and "with Brad Daugherty." And then we told Larry we were sorry.

World Series of Wet: *(Keith)* Term used to both mock and hype America's Cup yachting. No precedent. Usually used along with references to Captain Ahab, Great White Whales, The Captain and Tenille, Captain Smith and the *Titanic*, and/or the Loch Ness Monster. Variation: World Series of Wheels (Tour de France).

You Can't Stop Him, You Can Only Hope to Contain Him: *(Dan)* For the purpose of expressing respect bordering on fear for an unlikely hero in any sport. When Benny DiStefano of the Astros legged out a game-winning triple in 1992 (he had a total of twenty-five extrabase hits in his five-year big-league career) Dan paid tribute to him by adapting this old football analyst's clichéd observation. Of course, in a newspaper the next week, Keith got credit for the line, which is the story of Dan's life.

You Da Man: *(Keith)* When a goffer's tee shot lands on or near the green, you applaud him in this fashion. From the habit of caddies shouting exactly this at their goffers—hopefully **after** and not **before** they tee off.

━━━━━

We would be remiss here if we didn't throw in some explanations for some of the one-shot wonder phrases, obscure references, and other knickknacks with which we've clouded your brain over the years. Some of them you may have wondered about. Some of them may have made you wonder about us. Here are our favorites:

———————

Anthony!: A reference to the NBA's Anthony Mason and/or baseball's Eric Anthony. Done in a singsong fashion. Stolen from early '70s commercials for Prince Spaghetti, in which Anthony Martinietti lives in the Italian end of Boston. Most days he walks home. But not on Wednesday. Anthony knows Wednesday is Prince Spaghetti Day. (We hear Mrs. Martinietti bellow with a voice that could be heard from Hopkinton to Fenway Park: "ANTHONY!"). How sick are we that we can repeat this commercial word for word twenty years after seeing it for the last time? Destroy your television now! It's alive! It's alive!

Cherokee, I Have a Watch: Anytime Cherokee Parks is shown in a highlight, out comes this one. It's from one of the early *Sports-Center* commercials in which Parks is shown trying to give Dan an expensive watch to curry favor with him. Dan's staccato answer still reverberates around the building. "Cherokee. I have a watch. Cherokee! I have a watch."

City of Merchandise: We trot this one out whenever a sports team unveils a new uniform, or especially an **extra** uniform, in order to sell more souvenir replicas. This is straight from the old Martin Mull talk-show parody, *Fernwood2Night*.

Cody Wants a Pony: Nonsense description of a home run. From the promotional ads run for our ex-colleague Craig Kilborn's show on the Comedy Central network.

Croating off the Dribble: Very limited contribution from the very creative Gus Ramsey. Useful only for plays started by Toni Kukoc, of Croatia and the Chicago Bulls, or during highlights of Croatian basketball teams.

He's Saying Something About a Man and a Cane: Big laughs in the newsroom. Used for manager-umpire arguments. Relates to the legendary ESPN story about a big-league skipper who was less than enamored of one of our producers. The producer happened to be recovering from a knee injury and was using a cane. The skipper suggested what he'd like to see the producer **do** with the cane.

The Gastro-Intestinal Center: Keith's name for the Fleet Center in Boston. A dear friend of his, a medical student, pointed out just before the new home of the Celtics and Bruins opened in 1995 that "Fleet" was also the name of the leading manufacturer of enema products. We didn't want to get that messy. Keith also hates reading brand names. Voila. The Gastro-Intestinal Center.

Hoo Ha!: Dan returned from seeing the Al Pacino flick *Scent of a Woman* shouting this phrase from the film. Skipping his usual steal first, ask questions later policy, Keith asked him if he intended to use it on the air. Dan said no. Keith tried it out for homers. It didn't make it. Of most interest, however, was the reaction of Gary Miller, who was listening to the original conversation about the phrase's potential use. "This is the state of American sportscasting today," Gary said with great disgust. "Two guys negotiating over the use of 'Hoo Ha!'"

Mourning Becomes Eclectic: For use if and only if Alonzo Mourning fakes a pass and takes a shot, or fakes a shot and makes a pass. A pun on the O'Neill play *Mourning Becomes Electra*. Eclectic means selecting from a wide variety of styles or options.

No Soup for You: A regular phrase of Rece Davis's, borrowed, of course, from the character "the Soup Nazi" on Jerry Seinfeld's NBC show. We've modified it to "no hoop for you" and "no scoop for you" and the like. But one night nearly all of us on the various *SportsCenters* used it to the point of inducing nausea. It seems CNN's Vince Cellini had also used the phrase, perhaps before Rece had, perhaps after. But Vince had the bad taste to call up and complain that Rece had stolen "his" line. Said claim was not accompanied by correct complaint form A-273/CP1146, so we bashed him.

Salsa: The power of the meaningless catchphrase. Craig Kilborn was filling in for Dan one night, and he and Keith just started saying "Salsa" after every other NBA basket. We never used it again. The next night somebody at a game somewhere held up a banner reading "Salsa." We became frightened.

Sebastian Melmoth: The most obscure. Utah had a basketball player in 1995–96 named Ben Melmeth, and when he appeared in a highlight, Keith advised the viewers that this was "Ben Melmeth, and not Sebastian Melmoth." Sebastian Melmoth was the pseudonym used by the writer Oscar Wilde after his release from a British prison in 1897.

The Franchise Player of the Colorado Rockies: Actually a retired catchphrase. We both used to use this one every time Dan's buddy Jeff Blauser of the Braves showed up in the highlights. Jeff wasn't doing too well then, and we both guessed Atlanta would expose him to the upcoming expansion draft that would stock the Rockies and the Florida Marlins. Then Blauser blossomed—and the rest is history. Probably coincidental history, but history nonetheless.

Dan gets some wardrobe help from Olympic gold medalist Dan O'Brien. *(photo by Scott Clarke)*

Vincent Eugene "Bo" Jackson: Another retired catchphrase, this one going on the shelf the day Bo did. Dan used to enjoy doing an impression of Dick Schaap, who was forever doing stories on Jackson and referring to him by his full name, Vincent Edward "Bo"

Jackson. Keith started coming up with new middle names for Bo: Vincent Eugene "Bo" Jackson, Vincent Euripides "Bo" Jackson, Vincent Ecclesiastes "Bo" Jackson. Bo wasn't amused. "If he calls me 'Eugene' again . . ." he said after seeing one broadcast. Curiously, he never finished the thought—or his career.

———

THE OFFICIAL TIME-LINE HISTORY OF THE BIG SHOW

MAY 15, 1949: Theodore Olbermann marries Marie Charbonnier in New York. Neither could possibly guess at the havoc they will unleash on an unsuspecting Dan Patrick.

APRIL 1, 1954: Ithaca, New York, becomes the first large community to establish its own cable system. No Ithaca, no ESPN. Keith later attends Cornell University in Ithaca, spending most of his time cutting class and watching cable.

MAY 15, 1956: Patti Patrick of Zanesville, Ohio, tells her husband Jack that her labor has begun. Jack, busy watching a Cleveland Indians game on the television, calls her an alarmist. An hour later Daniel Patrick is nearly delivered in the family car.

MAY 15, 1958: For second birthday, Dan receives thirty-five-inch Rocky Colavito model baseball hat. Indians, learning of gift, begin negotiations to trade Colavito in 1960 and ruin franchise for next three decades.

JANUARY 27, 1959: Keith Theodore Olbermann born in New York City, to startled and consistently head-shaking parents.

Keith Olbermann conserving energy to unleash in later years on the unsuspecting Dan Patrick. *(Theodore C. Olbermann)*

JANUARY 21, 1963: Detlef Schrempf is born somewhere in Germany. If this event does not occur, Dan's catchphrase becomes "Dwayne Schintzius"; history changes.

AUGUST 21, 1964: Dan is taught how to scuff baseballs by his brother Mike.

AUGUST 22, 1964: Dan throws no-hitter for Arizona Sun Shutters Little League team. Feels guilty. Not that guilty.

SEPTEMBER 11, 1966: Keith, who has shown no interest in sports to that point, passes by family living room in which his mother is watching Yankees–Red Sox game on television. Keith hears announcer mention "Fenway Park" and presumes game is being played in open field on adjoining street called "Fenway" in his hometown. He joins Mom to watch telecast.

JANUARY 15, 1967: While watching first Super Bowl on television in family room in Mason, Ohio, Dan is warned by his mother that he's sitting too close to the fireplace. Dan's T-shirt catches fire. Birth of catchphrase "En Fuego."

JUNE 11, 1967: Keith attends first big-league game, at Yankee Stadium. Yankees lose Bat Day doubleheader to Chicago White Sox, 2–1 and 3–2. Jim O'Toole and Bruce Howard are winning pitchers. Just shy of twenty-seven years to the day later, Keith attends Stanley Cup Final game with Royals infielders Wally Joyner and

David Howard—Bruce Howard's son. Keith is also offering his 1967 Bat Day Elston Howard facsimile bat to any interested collector for the low, low price of $500,000.

JANUARY 20, 1968: University of Houston defeats UCLA in first nationally televised prime-time regular-season college basketball game. Dan, aged eleven, cries. Keith, aged eight, calculates it's only two and a half months till baseball season.

NOVEMBER 17, 1968: Keith is only resident of the United States above the age of five to approve of NBC's decision to dump out of Oakland Raiders/New York Jets infamous "Heidi Bowl" game. He mistakenly believes "Heidi" is a show about his future fellow Southern Californian Heidi Fleiss.

JANUARY 12, 1969: While watching Jets-Colts Super Bowl, Keith drops his infant sister Jenna on her head, beginning a lifetime sequence of what he refers to as "unfortunate developments" involving females.

JANUARY 14, 1969: Dan begins cutting pictures from his father's copy of *Sports Illustrated* before his father reads magazine.

AUGUST 5, 1970: Dan begins cutting pictures from his brother Mike's copy of *Playboy* before his brother reads magazine.

AUGUST 6, 1970: Dan's brother and father wait for him at mailbox and beat the living bejesus out of him.

SEPTEMBER 3, 1970: Marv Albert call-in sports show debuts on WNBC Radio in New York at 7:05 P.M. First guest is Jim Bouton. First caller is Keith.

SEPTEMBER 4, 1970: Keith's parents receive bill for $47.50 phone call from Keith to WNBC beginning at 1:17 P.M. September 3.

JUNE 3, 1971: Ken Holtzman of Chicago Cubs throws no-hitter at Riverfront Stadium. Johnny Bench of Reds tries to bunt; is thrown out at first. In stands, Dan protests out call so vehemently he is asked to leave by an usher. Usher's name? Marge Schott.

DECEMBER 3, 1971: Keith reads advertisement in daily announcements at Hackley School in Tarrytown, New York, seeking a play-by-play announcer for school's hockey team and radio station WHTR. Applicants are told to find WHTR sports director Chris Berman.

JANUARY 15, 1972: Keith is published for first time. His article "An Appreciation of Cocoa-Puffs Cereal Harlem Globetrotters Bas-

The young Keith in action. *(Keith Olbermann)*

ketball Cards" appears in trade magazine *The Trader Speaks*. As payment Keith receives a warm note of thanks from editor-publisher Dan Dischley.

MARCH 11, 1972: Dan attends Notre Dame at Dayton college basketball game. Dan encounters Notre Dame coach Digger Phelps and questions some of Phelps's strategy. Phelps replies, "What the **** do you know about basketball?"

MARCH 15, 1972: Dan attends last Los Angeles Lakers at Cincinnati Royals game ever. Gets autographs of Elgin Baylor, Gail Goodrich, Jerry West, and all other Laker players except Wilt Chamberlain. He waits after game for Chamberlain and actually boards Laker bus in pursuit of last autograph. Dan asks Wilt to sign, nearly weeping as he says he'll never see Wilt play in Cincinnati again.

Wilt tells him to "get the **** off the bus." Dan replies, "I always liked Russell better."

MARCH 24, 1972: Dan receives thank-you card from Cazzie Russell of San Francisco Warriors.

APRIL 11, 1973: Dan pitches no-hitter against Springboro High School. He saves ball as souvenir and inscribes it with details of game.

APRIL 12, 1973: Dan's brother Bill gives no-hit ball to family dog. *(Editor's Note: No independent confirmation exists of alleged "no-hitter")*.

JULY 2, 1973: Keith, sitting in front-row box at Yankee Stadium, stands up to catch Rico Petrocelli's foul pop behind first base off Fritz Peterson. Forgetting he is not at his customary tenth-row seat, Keith reaches up and back for ball, which bounces off his hands and back several rows. Keith turns around to see angry Yankee first baseman Felipe Alou staring at him with hands on hips. Petrocelli lines next pitch for first Red Sox hit of game. Peterson gives up no other hits until fifth inning. Keith holds breath until fifth inning.

NOVEMBER 4, 1973: Mike Aronstein of TCMA privately publishes Keith's first book, *The Major League Coaches 1921–1973*. The first press run is 100 copies. Mike still has several if you're interested.

DECEMBER 8, 1973: Dan scores 36 points against Clinton-Massie High School.

DECEMBER 9, 1973: Dan offers services of "a deceptively quick shooting guard from Cincinnati, Ohio," to UCLA coach John Wooden. Wooden does not reply.

DECEMBER 15, 1973: Dan scores 32 points against Little Miami.

DECEMBER 16, 1973: Dan offers services of "a quick shooting guard from Cincinnati, Ohio," to University of Cincinnati coach Gale Catlett. Catlett does not reply.

JANUARY 3, 1974: Dan scores 30 points against Carlisle High School.

JANUARY 4, 1974: Dan offers services of "an exceptionally quick shooting guard from Cincinnati, Ohio," to Marquette coach Al McGuire. McGuire does not reply.

JANUARY 10, 1974: Dan scores 7 points against Waynesville High School.

Dan Patrick (24) shows off his potential before succumbing to the dreaded knee injury that kept him out of the NBA. *(Dan Patrick)*

JANUARY 11, 1974: Dan receives recruitment letter from Notre Dame basketball coach Digger Phelps. In 1995, Phelps will remark, "I was right the first time."

MAY 10, 1974: Keith attends Bob & Ray show at WOR Radio in New York, and leaves studio vowing he will become a broadcaster. Elsewhere, Symbionese Liberation Army and LAPD stage shoot-out for entertainment of Southern California TV audiences.

JULY 22, 1974: Dan attends Cincinnati Reds tryout camp at Riverfront Stadium. Cincinnati scout Chief Bender asks Dan about willingness to play for Reds' rookie league team at Billings, Montana. Dan answers "What state is that in?" Reds tell Dan they'll get back to him.

AUGUST 7, 1974: Eastern Kentucky University wins basketball recruiting war for Dan.

SEPTEMBER 1, 1974: Dan arrives at Eastern Kentucky University. Coach Bob Moelke observes Dan's long hair, dubs him

"Golden Boy," advises him he'll have "best seat in the house" for EKU games.

DECEMBER 11, 1974: During interview with Boston Celtics about possible internship with team for 1975–76 school year, Keith watches visiting Washington Bullets practice. Keith sees a rat leap from Boston Garden rafters, land on fabled parquet floor, turn and wave at him, and then scurry away.

APRIL 9, 1975: Harvard University notifies Keith it cannot offer him a place in its class of 1979. Form letter includes phrase "we know this is our loss." You bet your ass, you condescending swine. Keith instead attends Cornell University. *(Editor's Note: Well, "attends" is something of an exaggeration.)*

OCTOBER 7, 1975: Scheduled to observe sports shift at WVBR-FM, Cornell freshman Keith arrives at station to discover he is actually doing that night's sportscast. Keith's soul leaves his body for the following four hours. He mispronounces his own name on air. Twice.

OCTOBER 19, 1975: Wearied by first five-hour bus ride home from Cornell four days previously, Keith uses adapter plug borrowed from WVBR to attach his studio headphones to a portable tape cassette machine in order to listen to tapes of Bob & Ray on Greyhound trip back to Ithaca, thus inadvertently inventing Walkman. Keith does not notice rest of bus is occupied by Sony executives who all get off at Scranton and fly home immediately.

OCTOBER 9, 1976: During Cornell-Brown game at Ithaca, Keith covers for WVBR-FM and UPI. Chris Berman does play-by-play of game for WBRU-FM Providence. Thirty seats down from Keith's location at Schoellkopf Field press box, Cornell athletic director Dick Schultz takes notes on whether or not to fire Cornell football coach George Seifert.

DECEMBER 11, 1977: Dan informs parents he needs "greater educational challenge" and wants to transfer to University of Dayton. Dan neglects to inform them that his two older brothers, attending school, have told him Dayton is top party school in America.

JANUARY 14, 1978: Dan's broadcasting begins as disc jockey at WVUD, campus station at Dayton. First song played: "Why Don't

We Get Drunk and Screw" by Jimmy Buffett. FCC begins pursuit of Dan; case still considered "open."

JULY 29, 1978: Keith, interning at New York television station WNEW, is at Yankee Stadium for Old-Timers' Day when his friend, vendor Al Marcus, takes him aside and says, "Something's up. Billy's here. He's coming back or something." Keith phones station with tip that Billy Martin, fired/resigned as manager ten days earlier, is at ballpark about to rejoin Yankees and station should send camera crew. Yankees announce Martin will return as manager in 1980. Station announces Keith can have job in 1980. Neither prophecy comes true.

AUGUST 7, 1978: During strike of newspapers in New York City, Keith lands job as sports editor and sole writer for *Our Town*, a free city weekly that attempts to publish daily during the strike. Keith writes four stories and one column per day, each under a different name, for $35 an issue.

AUGUST 8, 1978: Keith starts smoking and vows never to be a newspaperman.

OCTOBER 17, 1978: Keith's father informs him that if he doesn't graduate on time in May 1979, family will not foot bill for any further education. Keith realizes he will have to take the twenty-seven credits in Spring semester. Origin of catchphrase "Gggggh."

MAY 14, 1979: Dan graduates from University of Dayton. He is actually two credits short. He promises he'll come back and make up the difference.

MAY 28, 1979: Keith graduates from Cornell University and sets record with twenty-eight credits in Spring semester. He suffers the first of a series of recurring nightmares that it's graduation day and he has forgotten an entire course and must read ten thousand pages by noon or go back to the third grade and start all over again. Last recurrence of dream: last night.

SEPTEMBER 27, 1979: Dan is hired by WTUE radio, Dayton, Ohio. Paid $4.25 per hour to run religious tapes overnight Saturday and Sunday.

AUGUST 24, 1980: Keith, rushing to catch New York subway "E" train after free-lance photographing members of the Mets and Dodgers at Shea Stadium, leaps on board train, forgetting he is

6' 3½" tall and doors on train are only 6' 2". He briefly hallucinates that his first name is Dan. He will never again be permitted to drive a car, thus denying Formula One of the worst, slowest drivers in its history.

SEPTEMBER 15, 1980: *Sports Illustrated* publishes brief feature on Keith's radio work. Issue sells out in metropolitan New York. On the same day, Keith's savings mysteriously drop from $1,786.42 to $9.42.

APRIL 21, 1981: Keith is again tipped by vendor Al Marcus, this time that George Steinbrenner has recalled and destroyed Yankee yearbook because blotches of red ink appear on his photo making it appear he is wearing lipstick. Yankees deny; angry at story, Steinbrenner later fires PR director, cosmetics director, and Keith.

MAY 14, 1981: WTUE program director Chuck Browning convices Dan he can get into *Guinness Book of World Records* by sitting in a vat of wet spaghetti for sixty hours.

MAY 16, 1981: Thirty-six hours into event, Dan is informed there is no spaghetti vat-sitting record in Guinness book.

JUNE 12, 1981: Stan Isaacs of *Newsday* publishes feature piece on Keith's radio work. Keith suffers hernia carrying forty copies of newspaper into offices of his RKO Radio Network boss Charley Steiner.

JULY 2, 1981: While substituting on Steiner's weekday shift, Keith reads wire account of "fight" in Wimbledon pressroom between British tabloid writers and "an American radio reporter." Keith rushes home to videotape Dick Schaap ABC report on Steiner scuffle.

JULY 8, 1981: Keith loans videotape of fight to Charley. Still awaits its return.

AUGUST 3, 1981: Keith makes CNN debut as fill-in for New York reporter Debi Segura. First interview is with Mets manager Joe Torre. At conclusion, Keith walks away from interview without detaching microphone clip from tie; chokes self. *CNN Sports Tonight* runs only brief "sound bite" of Torre with a two-second shot of Keith nodding. Anchorman Nick Charles, not recognizing Keith, looks into camera with great alarm.

SEPTEMBER 4, 1982: While attending semifinals of U.S. Open tennis, Keith notices that when he turns his head from side to side to watch action, his eyes don't both move at the same time, giving him a Marty Feldman–like appearance. Very worried and in great pain, he goes to see his optometrist, who says he can do nothing for problem and begins laughing. Keith cannot see humor. Doctor says Keith has to see best muscle ophthalmologist in New York. Keith still cannot see humor. Doctor explains this is Dr. Renee Richards, the transsexual tennis player. Keith couldn't care less if the best muscle ophthalmologist in New York is **Keith** Richards. Dr. Richards corrects problem.

MARCH 26, 1984: Keith's last week begins at CNN Sports. His replacement as New York and national sports correspondent arrives from Atlanta: Dan Patrick.

MARCH 30, 1984: At Keith's going-away party at Greenwich Village bar that night, he advises Dan "Bling brrrfff gziupppl and you'll be nftrmnsk." Dan agrees.

APRIL 14, 1984: Climbing circular staircase at his new station, WCVB-TV in Boston, Keith hits his head and bloodies it. He ignores second direct sign from God.

JUNE 14, 1984: Doing feature piece on out-of-town reporters covering NBA Finals, Keith interviews Dan. Dan says he works for Cable News Network. Keith says, "What's that?"

SEPTEMBER 9, 1984: Keith tells WCVB bosses that he wants to resign. They tell him he can, but only if he keeps it a secret and stays until a replacement is found.

OCTOBER 6, 1984: WCVB sources leak story to Boston paper that Keith's ratings stink and he's about to be replaced by Hawk Harrelson, Bud Harrelson, or unknown actor Woody Harrelson.

MAY 11, 1985: Keith's first feature article for a major periodical appears in early editions of Sunday *New York Times*.

MAY 12, 1985: CNN Newswriter Susan White accepts Dan's invitation for their first date. She remarks to a friend, "He's the guy who wrote that wonderful article in the *Times* today."

SEPTEMBER 2, 1985: Keith debuts at KTLA-TV in Los Angeles.

DECEMBER 11, 1986: Dan, low on cash, convinces producer Artie Berko that they should attend Thomas Hearns news conference just so he can get a square meal. Dan has eaten forty-seven pieces of shrimp in ten minutes when Hearns's public relations person tells him Hearns is ready for his interview with CNN. Dan explains his camera crew has been pulled to go cover a story at the United Nations. Dan is lying. Dan pockets 212 shrimp on way out.

DECEMBER 26, 1986: *Los Angeles Herald-Examiner* names Keith its choice as best local sportscaster. *Los Angeles Times* names Keith its choice as worst local sportscaster. Keith is confused.

JULY 14, 1987: Lawrence Taylor of New York Giants is suspended for drug use. Dan asks him for interview. Taylor tells Dan he will kick Dan's ass. Dan responds he'll kick Taylor's ass. CNN cameraman intervenes, suggests drug test for Dan, too.

AUGUST 29, 1987: Dan and Susan White are married in New York.

NOVEMBER 10, 1987: *Los Angeles Herald-Examiner* readers' poll votes Keith as third best and third worst TV sportscaster. Keith is more confused.

DECEMBER 19, 1987: Dexter Manley of Washington Redskins picks nose during interview with Dan. Dan asks him to stop. Dexter replies by wiping his fingers on Dan's pants leg. Dan laughs nervously.

JANUARY 16, 1988: ESPN executives interview Keith in Los Angeles and offer him job as coanchor with Chris Berman on *SportsCenter*. Keith says to agent Jean Sage, "Chris's voice is so loud, I think I'd go deaf."

FEBRUARY 3, 1988: Keith notifies ESPN he will decline their offer to join staff as *SportsCenter* anchor. Panicky ESPN executives ask, "Maybe we can get that CNN guy who had Dexter Manley's snot on his leg."

AUGUST 8, 1988: Keith breaks story of trade of Wayne Gretzky to Los Angeles Kings. In Edmonton, seeing tape of Keith's report, Gretzky has second thoughts about the deal, considers playing hockey in Brazil.

AUGUST 23, 1988: KCBS-TV Los Angeles announces it has hired Keith away from rival KTLA. Deal has been consummated seven months previously.

DECEMBER 20, 1988: Keith makes his film debut as a golf announcer in HBO movie *Dead Solid Perfect*. HBO studios are immediately picketed by PGA, golf club innovator Karsten Solheim, Screen Actors' Guild, Cabinet Makers' Union, and HBO employees.

FEBRUARY 3, 1989: KMPC Radio sports gossip columnist Jim

Healy reports Keith is seen at Thrifty Drug in Hollywood buying cheap underwear. Keith autographs one pair and sends to Healy.

MARCH 4, 1989: Chris Berman agrees to work 2:30 A.M. *Sports-Center* with ESPN rookie Dan Patrick. Halfway through show, Dan says, "Chris, your voice is so loud, I think I'm going deaf." Chris replies, "If you don't like it, go back and work with Nick and Fred." Dan thinks Chris is kidding.

SEPTEMBER 4, 1989: Keith vows on air to shave head if Angels win 1989 World Series. Team owner Gene Autry petitions commissioner's office to buy entire American League and add Kirby Puckett, Wade Boggs, Don Mattingly, and Jack Morris to Angels' postseason roster.

OCTOBER 1, 1989: Keith, subbing for Roy Firestone, makes ESPN debut as guest host of *Up Close*. Within the week his home is burgled and he fractures his pelvis slipping on pavement outside ESPN Los Angeles studios. He again ignores direct sign from God.

MARCH 3, 1990: Keith realizes that legally he is Mike Tyson's cousin. Tyson was adopted by his trainer Cus D'Amato. Cus's niece Geraldine is Keith's aunt by marriage. Learning of family tree, Tyson feels ashamed and foredoomed.

DECEMBER 16, 1991: Keith announces he will leave KCBS to join ESPN. Cable cancellations hit record high.

JANUARY 4, 1992: Keith, Chuck Wilson, and Tony Bruno sign on ESPN Radio Network. A week later, Keith is talked into giving up a two-month vacation to Hawaii to stay in Connecticut to continue to help launch network. National Society of Psychoanalysts convene special convention to analyze.

APRIL 5, 1992: Keith debuts with Dan on 11:00 P.M. ET *Sports-Center*.

APRIL 6, 1992: Keith, exhausted, accidentally verbalizes his thoughts on the length of program. "Damn, Dan, this is one X$%&^@ big show."

JUNE 1, 1992: The Big Show gets its first positive press review. Michael Madden writes in the *Boston Globe*: "Keith Olbermann makes me laugh." Dan and Keith search paper in vain looking for any additional comment.

AUGUST 4, 1992: Given choice between attending hundredth anniversary celebrations of the alleged Lizzie Borden ax murders in Fall River, Massachusetts, and the auction of ball that went between Bill Buckner's legs to decide sixth game of 1986 World Series, Keith goes to auction, bids $40,000 for ball, is outbid by actor Charlie Sheen, who pays $93,000. In Fall River, Keith is also outbid by Sheen, forty-two whacks to forty-one.

OCTOBER 22, 1992: Dan's first son is born. Patricks name him after announcer Jack Buck after Sue refuses to name him after Harry Caray.

NOVEMBER 17, 1992: Keith, Peter Gammons, and Ray Knight anchor live ESPN coverage of Major League Baseball draft. Dan is selected in thirty-seventh round by Rockies. Rockies are then informed draft is only thirty-six rounds long.

NOVEMBER 20, 1992: George Steinbrenner writes fan letter to ESPN management complimenting Olbermann, Gammons, Jon Miller, and Joe Morgan on draft coverage. Olbermann weeps openly, is hired as Yankee manager, and then fired forty minutes later.

DECEMBER 21, 1992: *Sports Illustrated* publishes nine-page feature on *SportsCenter*. Dan is described as "the most popular of the network's anchors after Berman." Keith is shown in the men's room putting on makeup.

FEBRUARY 15, 1993: Two viewers in Midwest notify Dan and Keith that they met, fell in love, and got engaged while watching The Big Show. Dan and Keith repair to nearest church to beg God's forgiveness.

JUNE 28, 1993: Mike McQuade succeeds Norby Williamson as producer of The Big Show. Team of psychiatrists rush to McQuade's side.

JULY 14, 1993: ESPN announces Keith will leave The Big Show to anchor flagship ESPN2 broadcast *SportsNight*. This begins an eight-month period of time of which Keith has no memory whatsoever.

AUGUST 1, 1993: Reggie Jackson is inducted into Baseball Hall of Fame at Cooperstown, New York. In induction speech, Jackson asks Dan to help him "save" baseball. In next fourteen months, Vince Coleman of Mets will be suspended for throwing firecrackers at a crowd of fans in Los Angeles, players will go on strike, season will be discontinued, World Series will be canceled for first time since 1904. Reggie later tells Dan, "Next time I'll ask Keith."

SEPTEMBER 25, 1993: In article in *TV Guide* Keith promises difference between ESPN and ESPN2 will be "some really nice shirts."

OCTOBER 15, 1993: Keith is nominated for CableAce Award as top sports host. Doesn't win.

DECEMBER 7, 1993: *Sports Illustrated* votes ESPN2 the seventh worst thing to happen in sports in 1993, just ahead of Vince Coleman of Mets throwing firecrackers at a crowd of fans in Los Angeles.

FEBRUARY 2, 1994: ESPN announces Keith will leave *Sports-Night* and rejoin The Big Show effective April 3. ESPN2 subscriber total jumps from 1,829 to 24,000,000.

APRIL 3, 1994: Keith returns to The Big Show. Asked if he has missed him, Dan replies, "Missed who?"

MAY 26, 1994: Dan's first daughter, Grace, is born. Patricks name her after Cubs first baseman Mark Grace after Sue refuses to name her after Hector Villanueva.

JANUARY 24, 1995: Connecticut basketball star Rebecca Lobo tells Fort Lauderdale newspaper that her dream job is to cohost Big Show with Keith. Keith faints, tries to fire Dan.

JANUARY 29, 1995: With Dan at Super Bowl, Keith is left alone to host Big Show and traditional two-person lead-in to Plays of the Week is jeopardized. Keith is cloned. Keith II is the one who missed all those meetings and said all those bad things about Bud Selig.

FEBRUARY 13, 1995: Keith and Dan attend second annual ESPY Awards. Dan, forced against will to read ESPY voting "rules," begs audience for applause. Gets smattering. Keith and Dan then brought before assembled reporters at backstage news conference. They are asked no questions.

FEBRUARY 27, 1995: Reds announce forty-eight-year-old former pitcher Pedro Borbon will attend camp as a strike replacement player. Reading story on show, Keith emits scream. Two cameras shatter.

MARCH 23, 1995: Assistant player rep Todd Jones of Houston Astros calls Keith asking if he has any ideas to settle baseball strike. Keith suddenly realizes he's really in over his head.

MARCH 24, 1995: Dan and Keith both nominated for Sports Emmy as top host. Neither wins, but each basks in realization that it's the nomination that counts and their beloved colleague Bob Costas did. *(Editor's Note: Guys, do you think anybody will believe that crap?)*

MAY 3, 1995: Dan and Keith go to Boston Garden to see Celtics-Magic play-off game. Keith visits with former Boston media colleagues and several Garden rats stop by to say hello and offer Dan and Keith some cheese.

JULY 7, 1995: Dan's second daughter, Georgia, is born. Patricks name her after home state of Dan's favorite baseball player, Jeff Blauser, after Sue refuses to name her after birth nation of his favorite German basketball player, Detlef Schrempf.

AUGUST 11, 1995: Dan's three-year-old son, Jack, asks his mother what word "testicle" means. She explains "It's the clinical word for balls."

SEPTEMBER 30, 1995: Dan asks son Jack what he wants for upcoming fourth birthday. Jack answers "Golf clubs, a golf bag, and some testicles."

OCTOBER 1, 1995: Dan and Keith are both nominated for CableAce Awards as top sports host. Keith will win. Dan will "present" him with trophy. Keith will require seventeen stitches.

OCTOBER 29, 1995: Keith "coaches" defending NCAA women's basketball champs Connecticut in scrimmage at Storrs, Connecticut. Keith's team loses by twelve. Keith is expelled from National Association of Pretend College Basketball Coaches.

DECEMBER 29, 1995: *TV Guide* names Dan and Keith as ninth on its list of top ten television performers. First-place finisher Jerry Seinfeld blanches visibly and cancels *TV Guide* subscription.

FEBRUARY 14, 1996: Keith and Dan are approached "about a book." Keith remembers he checked out *Notes on Moby-Dick* from Hackley School Library on November 3, 1974, and never returned it.

MARCH 1, 1996: Before "B" game exhibition between Tigers and Reds at Plant City, Florida, Reds minor league catcher Justin Towle asks Keith for autograph. Plant City police arrest Keith on charge of impersonating an interesting person.

MARCH 12, 1996: Keith and Dan film Jim Harbaugh surgery

commercial. Keith is sued for malpractice. Dan is sued for malprac-tice. Chicago Bears are sued for malpractice for letting Harbaugh go to Colts.

JULY 31, 1996: Keith is diagnosed with "abnormal, irritated brain activity." Dan replies "And?"

AUGUST 29, 1996: Keith and Dan pose for *Esquire* magazine; 51,723 *Esquire* subscriptions are canceled in ensuing two weeks.

SEPTEMBER 10, 1996: Keith nominated for third time for CableAce Award as top sports host. Selects Jack Kemp as running mate. Neither will win.

SEPTEMBER 11, 1996: Keith, Bob Ley, Robin Roberts, and Mike Tirico, walking to a public relations event, are asked by pas-serby on a New York City street for result of previous night's U.S.-Canada World Cup hockey game. They simultaneously answer, "Canada. 3–2. Overtime." Keith adds "Canada was offsides on the winning goal." All four consider committing selves to New York Hos-pital for the Pathethically Insane.

SEPTEMBER 13, 1996: Dan brings son Jack for his first visit to Keith's house. Insurance covers 90 percent of damage.

SEPTEMBER 29, 1996: Mike McQuade concludes three-year stint as producer of The Big Show, during which he has gone from age twenty-eight to age seventy-one. McQuade is immediately ele-vated to sainthood by Roman Catholic Church. Gus Ramsey is dragged kicking and screaming from 2:00 A.M. *SportsCenter* to suc-ceed Saint McQ.

DECEMBER 30, 1996: Dan debuts as guest host of ABC's *Good Morning, America*. World-wide plebiscite immediately held; human race votes to eliminate concept of morning and proceed directly from evening to afternoon.

FEBRUARY 9, 1997: Keith's commercial for Boston Market ap-pears in telecast of NBA All-Star Game. Contest is halted for thirty-seven minutes to allow viewers, fans, and players to recover from shock.

TODAY: You read this. You need to get out more.

HOW WE DO THE
VOODOO THAT WE DO

The old joke about sausages goes, if you like them, don't ever go to a sausage factory.

We're not making any self-deprecating comparisons here, but if you have ever thought us smooth, well informed, unflappable, or infinitely well prepared, under no circumstances should you come to the studio in person and watch us actually do the show. There's no suggestion here that it's a sausage factory, but perhaps the analogy to a Marx Brothers movie might be appropriate. The show itself is conducted amid a chorus of voices, in the studio and the control room, with a thousand last-minute decisions being made and chaos threatening to escape its reins at almost every minute.

Of course, that's only the last hour of our day, the show itself. The rest of the stuff is pretty sedate: We work in an office, we sit in front of computers, and occasionally we get to see some ball games. We often like to explain the job thusly: It's just like yours, with all the hassles and headaches and meetings. Only, **the last hour is on national television.** Perhaps the easiest way to convey how The Big Show gets on the air every night is to take you through the chronology of a typical day:

3:30 P.M.: We start with the "ideas meeting," presided over by producer Gus Ramsey and coordinating producer Ed Schimmel. Gus is the tall, thin one with the innocent look on his face and the devious one-liner in his heart. Ed is the voice of reason (except when it comes to Philadelphia teams) with the mustache, the monotonic voice, and the invaluable capacity to read a hundred facts or more in our script per night, check them all for accuracy, and not lose his mind nor loosen his tie. During the meeting we'll learn what pretaped features are running that night (''pieces''), knock around ideas for the Breakdown segment or other pieces that we or one of the associate producers may be writing particularly for the show (''home-cooked pieces''), discuss in what order we'll do the highlights (''selecting the lead''), and generally get the entire staff of a dozen or so up to speed on what we're going to do and how we're going to do it.

Attend just one of these meetings and you'll wonder why we bother. There are very few nail-biting decisions to be made. You, Dear Reader, could probably figure out the lead story on any given night (after all, we **are** trying to guess which story **you'll** be most interested in), or which Sunday NFL game deserves a feature piece from a reporter on the scene. The ''pieces'' are usually selected well in advance by minds far greater than our own (well, management, anyway), and many are regularly slotted for a particular day. You don't need a meeting to tell anyone that the Sunday Conversation, Plays of the Week, and Today's Best appear on the Sunday night Big Show. The racing news, ''The Fast Lane,'' comes up on Monday. There's no need to fear: ''Inside the Huddle'' will be here on Tuesday. You get the idea. We're both fairly quiet during these sessions, except when it comes to tossing around ideas for Breakdowns or features, or offering opinions on when a particular game might end and whether or not the highlights will be ready in time for when we've slotted them to appear in the show.

One meeting wouldn't seem like much. But often it happens that a comment or a joke or an observation by someone one day will be the wellspring for a great piece the next. Remember the mock-serious Breakdown on Mascot Injuries? For days, the meetings were filled with staffers simply recalling weird pieces of videotape they'd seen involving mascots. A week later we had a two-minute feature, one later nominated for a National Sports Emmy.

And some meetings are epics. We walked into one in 1995 on the day Mickey Mantle died. We found that management, which had been dealing with the story all day in the Sunday morning *Sports-Centers* and all the other shows, had concluded, not without considerable logic, that The Big Show that night should open with reaction from baseball figures to Mantle's death, followed by several segments of game highlights, followed by the official eight-minute-long Mantle obituary piece, followed by more highlights, followed by a special Sunday Conversation made up of Roy Firestone's various interviews with Mantle.

We disagreed. How could we go back-and-forth to the passing of this legendary, almost mythical, figure? We each knew we weren't going to be doing any jokes or any catchphrases during the highlights anyway. We knew in our hearts that the switch from Mantle's death to highlights and back again would be too tough for us, and thus probably too tough for our viewers. We argued, successfully, that the entire segment of the show before the first commercials (''the tens''—stories numbered between 1 and 19) should be devoted to Mantle: the reaction, the obituary, the Yankees game that day. We shouldn't get near the other highlights until after that first break (''the twenties''—stories numbered between 20 and 29). And most importantly, we impressed upon the staff that we had to treat this one show as somberly and as reverently as if we were a religious network covering the funeral of a pope.

4:00 P.M.: The meeting is usually done by now. Associate producers have their assignments, and have gone to search for videotape for pieces or news stories. Gus Ramsey has put the show ''rundown'' into the computer—this is the exact order of stories and listing of what each story will consist. His options are: on-camera segments by either one of us, videotaped highlights (''v/o''—for ''voice-over''), comments from athletes or sports figures (''SOT''—sound on tape), etc. We've returned to our desks, now side by side after years in which we were down the hall from each other, and we begin to write the show.

Don't dust that last sentence so quickly. This remains the biggest surprise to most viewers, many athletes, and even some people in the media. Other than the occasional feature piece written by an associate producer and then mildly tweaked by one of us, we write the whole show. Ourselves. This isn't necessarily a preference—our days would be a lot easier if we had somebody to do it for us. On the other hand, if you don't write your own material, what are you really bringing to your sportscast? How can you even call it **your** sportscast? Many local sportscasters, though not as many as in days gone by, have their shows written for them in whole or in part by producers. And your average beady-eyed local or network news anchorperson is reading stuff somebody else wrote.

It just isn't that way at ESPN. Never has been; likely never will be. The greatest advantage to writing your own scripts is the defense it provides you against chaos. When the TelePrompTer fails or the story changes at the last minute, if you're relying on something somebody else wrote, you may have no idea what to say next. Rework your own writing as your reading it? A lot easier, and a lot safer. The problem with doing it this way, of course, is that it's an **awful lot of writing.** Between what we write, what we ad-lib during the highlights, and all the other sundry stuff we write for the computer or radio networks, we write 10,000–15,000 words. **Per week. Each.** That's the equivalent of this book every five or six weeks.

Right now the deadline of the show still seems far away. We tend to use the 4:00–5:00 P.M. hour to make phone calls, some of them on stories, some of them not (**you** never called a friend, long-distance, from work?). We get enough usable information, however, to justify any phone bill. As the rest of this book, and as every one of our shows, points out, we love to have fun with sports and it's probably our humor for which we are known best. But at heart, however infrequently journalism is actually required in sports, we are reporters. If we don't know what's going on behind the scenes, we won't know enough to write an intelligent script about a story, let alone make a joke about it. As we've suggested elsewhere, we still view whatever acclaim we've gotten as an unlikely gift that could all go away tomorrow (and probably will). But we get very pompously proud of the news stories we've broken on *SportsCenter*—a hundred or more, big and small, in the five years we've done the show together.

And this is the hour when most of the information is sought, or arrives. This is the time when one of us finds out from a source that Mario Lemieux is going to sit out a year to rest up after treatment for Hodgkin's disease and back injuries. This is the time when one of us calls a couple of hoops friends and is told Gary Payton is going to be named to the Olympic Dream Team. This is the time when the unlikely tips come in from people we may know well or may not know at all: like the occasion when one of our top anonymous sources phoned in to say a Major League Baseball manager had just been fired. We asked how he was sure. He explained he was calling from the guy's **office** in the clubhouse and all his stuff was in boxes and he'd just said good-bye to all his players. That's still not the wildest tip we've ever gotten. The day after the verdict in the Rodney King case in Los Angeles, our top source called to explain that the Kings had decided to fire their coach, Tom Webster. Solid enough for a good story. But there was more. In the middle of the meeting to make the change, someone noticed smoke rising from a neighborhood near the Kings' offices at the Forum. The L.A. riots were under way. The meeting, our source explained, was suddenly adjourned (''a vice president said 'let's get the hell out of here!' ''), and as everybody scurried for the door, they confirmed they were letting Webster go, and they postponed announcing it—until after the riot ended! That's just the way we reported it, and that's just the way it happened.

We should point out here that we just don't get a call from somebody and slap something on the air. If one of us has a ''source story'' we have to run it past our senior management, and rare is the occasion that we don't have to go back to the phones and get a second, or even **third** source to confirm what the original one had said. The Lemieux story was touch-and-go for hours. We knew that our guy had an impeccable track record on such stories and direct access to the information he'd given us. But that still wasn't enough. We had to get a second source—on a Sunday night no less—and wound up calling Al Morganti, the network's hockey maven. He had to make a dozen calls himself, and finally got confirmation from an NHL player who'd been told the same thing. The whole process involved literally thirty phone calls and four or five meetings before we got the final OK to run the story—about half an hour before the show began.

Most of the time, the players or teams involved in stories like this will give you a cursory no comment or a ritualized denial. You know they know, and they know you know. Sometimes, however, you hit a nerve that makes a root canal seem like brushing your teeth. Right after the baseball strike in '94, at a time when there were no meetings of any kind going on between the owners and the players, a very plugged-in guy informed us that there'd been a back-channel phone call between Jerry Reinsdorf, the owner of the White Sox, and Steve Fehr, the player agent and brother of the union leader Don Fehr. Reinsdorf was not only conducting "secret" talks, but he'd actually presented a hypothetical to Steve. "The salary cap is off the table," Reinsdorf theorized. "What does the union give up then?"

This was big news. The story getting out was also **bad** news for the owners. If the strike got to the point where the owners went to court and got permission to impose their own work rules, the only things they could impose were the things that were contained in their last offer—like the salary cap. But if Reinsdorf had even hinted, unofficially, informally, theoretically—even just to the union leader's **brother**—that the salary cap was no longer a proposal, the union could argue that it was no longer part of management's last offer. Even if the court let the owners impose everything else, it might have prevented them from instituting a salary cap. Well, we got the necessary second and third confirmations on the story, and we ran it—and all hell broke loose. Reinsdorf not only called us every name in the book, he called newspaper reporters to attack us personally.

A few months later, of course, those same newspaper reporters who had swallowed Reinsdorf's bait were writing up their summaries of the strike—and including the fact of Reinsdorf's conversation with Steve Fehr and the whole business about taking the salary cap off the table. One of them even printed the **date** of the phone call!

The most fun on a source story comes when everybody gets involved. The chronology of our report last November that Lou Holtz was quitting at Notre Dame went as follows (with a few of the details left out to protect the innocent, or somewhat innocent):

Tuesday, 8:00 P.M.: Dan gets a tip that Holtz has met with his bosses the night before and requested a multiyear contract. They've said no. He's said good-bye. Dan makes eighteen phone calls, can't confirm it.

Wednesday, 12:15 A.M.: Dan tells Keith about Holtz. Keith asks why he hasn't said anything earlier. Dan says: "What was your name again?" Keith starts making calls.

Wednesday, 2:30 P.M.: A source with terrific connections to Notre Dame, its board of trustees, and its athletic department tells Keith that whether or not it's over the length of the contract, Holtz is leaving at season's end.

Wednesday, 3:30 P.M.: Chris Fowler calls in with a tip that Holtz has told his assistants that there is "a 90 percent chance" he won't return in 1997.

Wednesday, 9:50 P.M.: Keith's source calls back with more details and Keith writes up the story that "something's going on" for the ESP-NET SportsZone computer service and ESPN Radio.

Thursday, 12:15 A.M.: A Notre Dame football player, cruising the Internet, stumbles across Keith's Holtz story and lets out a shout that rings across South Bend. By morning, every player on the team has read or heard about the column.

Thursday, 11:00 A.M.: The assistant coaches, badgered by their players about the ESPNET column, tell Holtz. Holtz tells them to begin notifying players of a 4:30 P.M. special meeting with the coach.

Thursday, 12:45 P.M.: Chris Mortensen calls in to say he's reached Holtz, asked him about Fowler's tip that "he's told some of his assistant coaches that there's a 90 percent chance he won't be back next year," and Holtz will only answer, "I better talk to some of my assistant coaches."

Thursday, 4:30 P.M.: In a series of meetings, Holtz tells his players he's leaving after the 1996 season. Notre Dame running back Randy Kinder, asked afterwards if Holtz is resigning, tells a Chicago newspaper, "I'm getting all my ideas from Olbermann on *SportsCenter.*"

Thursday, 6:30 P.M.: The "Holtz May Leave" story runs on *Sports-Center* for the first time, on the 6:30 EST edition.

Thursday, 11:00 P.M.: Dick Vitale calls in to say a basketball coach has come up to him at a banquet and told him Holtz has told a friend of his that he's resigning.

Friday, 10:00 A.M.: A source very close to the coach calls Keith at home and tells him, "Yep. He's gone. It's done. And they've already called Gary Barnett." Keith records a commentary for ESPN Radio to be run that afternoon that Holtz will officially resign within the week and Barnett will be Notre Dame's first target—the first national media report that the coach is out.

Tuesday, 1:00 P.M.: Holtz announces he's resigning.

Tuesday, 5:00 P.M.: Barnett announces he's been approached by Notre Dame.

Thursday, 5:00 P.M.: At the moment the story crosses the wire that Barnett will stay at Northwestern, Keith's source calls to say, "Barnett's turned it down. It'll be Bob Davie. Tom Clements is still being mentioned, but it'll be Davie.''

Thursday, 11:00 P.M.: *SportsCenter* reports that Notre Dame defensive coordinator Bob Davie is expected to be named the school's new head coach, within the week.

Thursday, 11:45 P.M.: During the show, Keith's source leaves a message. ''I double-checked. It's Davie.''

Thursday, 11:57 P.M.: Keith's bulletin saying Notre Dame will offer the job to Davie crosses ESPNET.

Sunday, 12 Noon: Bob Davie named coach at Notre Dame.

So how do you mark that down if you're scoring at home, or even if you're alone? Patrick to Olbermann to Fowler to Olbermann to Vitale to Olbermann? Summing it up, that 4:00–5:00 hour can be a lot more important than it looks. Or, we can spend it with our feet up calling old friends from college.

5:00 P.M.: By now, if we haven't started writing, we'd better. Into the computer we go, and we're confronted with something that looks like this:

OE	2	KE/DA	HI/HELLO			2SHT	0:00	0:27
1	30S	KEITH	INDIANS/ORIOLES	41		OTS-VO (2:00)	2:02	2:26
1A			INDIANS/ORIOLES SCORE			SCORE X 2	0:00	0:20
2			TRIBE/O'S POST	42		SOT	0:35	0:35
2A			POW-WOWED			INF Y	0:00	0:19
3	10S	DAN	PADRES/CARDINALS	43		OTS-VO (2:00)	2:05	2:30
3A			PADRES/CARDINALS SCORE			SCORE X 2	0:00	0:11
4			PADS/CARDS POST	41		SOT	0:41	0:45
4A			MYRED NO MORE			INF Y	0:00	0:11
5	30S	KEITH	UMPIRE NOD (SAL PAL)	42		OTS-SOT	2:06	2:26
5A	30S	KEITH	ALOMAR REAX	43		OTS-VO/SOT	0:00	0:30
5B	30S	KEITH	TAG			OTS	0:00	0:26
5C	10S	DAN	RANGERS/YANKEES	41		OTS-VO (2:00)	1:48	2:05
5D			RANGERS/YANKEES SCORE			SCORE X 2	0:15	0:16
6	10S	DAN	PEETE LATEST	41		OTS-VO	0:00	0:28
6A			RAY RHODES REAX	42		SOT	0:27	0:27
6B	10S	DAN	TAG (W/MORT NEWS)			OTS	0:00	0:18
7	10S	DAN	IRVIN CAN RETURN	43		OTS-VO/SOT	0:00	0:14
7A		D/DAN	COWBOYS RECEIVING #S			INF Y	0:00	0:13
9	30B	KEITH	TEASE: CONE/BURKETT	41		CUBE	0:00	0:11
9A		D/KEI	BUMP: SMOLTZ/KEMP/SMITH	48/44		VO	0:00	0:18

This thing goes on like this for sixty-six individual pages. We have to do something about every one of them. And the show from which this rundown was taken, October 1 of last year, was a comparatively simple program.

To explain a couple of technical things here: The number at the far left is the story's page number. The second number from the left is the camera and the type of shot to be used ("1OS" means Dan with an over-the-shoulder graphic, "3CB" at the bottom there means Keith with the "video cube" running behind him, and no number means neither of us is on camera for that page). Next comes which of us is responsible for writing and reading the page in question (if it's blank you just presume the same person who read the last page keeps reading). Then comes the story title or "slug." The next number is that of the tape machine in which the particular tape connected to the story will play. The next is office lingo for what's actually going to **happen** at that particular moment:

2Sht: Be careful with the jokes here. A "two-shot." We're both on camera and we introduce the show. Usually whoever's doing the first story writes the first part of this (Dan: "Warm greetings . . ." etc.; Keith: "Hello good evening and welcome . . ." etc.). Later—often as late as a minute or two before we go on the air—the other will write a few headlines—and then the first one will write a line leading into his own first story.

OTS-VO: That's an on-camera lead-in to highlights of some kind, with an over-the-shoulder graphic appearing, well, over our shoulder (OTS). When followed by the time (2:00) it indicates to everybody from us to the people editing the highlight how long producer Gus Ramsey wants the thing to be. Usually it says something closer to (0:45)—as in forty-five seconds. We write the lead-in as early as possible, and then ad-lib the highlights from a shot-sheet describing what's on the actual highlight tape. This is always, to borrow Bill Pidto's phrase, a dicey situation. We usually haven't seen the highlights before they actually roll them there in tape machine 41 or 42 or 43. We usually haven't even seen the shot-sheets before. Dicey.

SCORE: Just what you'd expect: the scoreboard that follows the highlights. If "X 2" is added, that means we're supposed to go a little longer than usual because the facts about the game placed on the scoreboard are so numerous that there will in fact be **two** scoreboards with different tidbits on them, and we'll be showing them both. Obviously these can't be written very far in advance. The vast majority that are written at all are done **after** 10:00 P.M. Eastern. As likely as not, we're ad-libbing this, off a five-by-seven index card filled with updated facts and numbers by our researcher, who sits just offstage furiously scribbling this stuff. The researcher is clearly the most underrated person involved in The Big Show. We've been blessed with some terrific ones: Vinny ''Vinnie the Statman'' Vassallo, David Albright, and most recently Peter McConville. Without them, we're dead meat.

SOT: Sound On Tape. Usually postgame reaction, and something, obviously, we don't write ourselves. Of course, we have to figure out a way to introduce the SOT, either writing it or ad-libbing it, without doing the following:

> KEITH: ''After the game, Bobby Bonilla said Brady Anderson's leadoff homer made all the difference.''
>
> BONILLA SOT: ''Brady Anderson's leadoff homer made all the difference.''

As stupid as that looks in print, try hearing it on TV. Everybody looks like an idiot. At some point, either because we've actually heard the segment of interview that's going to be used and we've gotten the chance to write something in advance, or because we've just been told seconds earlier what the SOT sounds like, we get to do it the right way:

> KEITH: ''There's still today to talk about, leading off with . . . Mister Leadoff.''
>
> BONILLA SOT: ''Brady Anderson's leadoff homer made all the difference.''

INF Y: That's an abbreviation for the Infinit! graphic system. This is the second kind of full-screen graphic you'll see, the one going in-depth on a particular aspect of the game in question. ''Pow-wowed'' that night simply compared how the top five hitters in Baltimore's lineup did that day compared to the top five hitters in Cleveland's. This kind of graphic can also be written in advance—when the Lord is with us—or it must be ad-libbed.

VO-SOT: Trickiest goober of them all. This is a tape that starts off as just a highlight that we're supposed to narrate. But then, at some point, it becomes a comment from a player or coach. If that ''some point'' happens exactly eight seconds into the tape, we can either write or ad-lib exactly eight seconds of narration. The SOT is going to happen whether we're done or not. There is no room for error. Nine seconds is too long and we get cut off in exactly the same way you'd get cut off if you were talking, not looking where you were going, and walked right into a door. Seven seconds and there's this awful dead spot on the air. You wonder why we each have a lot of gray hair already? Blame it, principally, on VO-SOTs.

NOD, TAG: This one sequence can give you an idea of how complicated this stuff can be. Here again is what it looks like in the computer:

5	3OS	KEITH	UMPIRE NOD (SAL PAL)	42	OTS-SOT	2:06	2:26
5A	3OS	KEITH	ALOMAR REAX	43	OTS-VO/SOT	0:00	0:30
5B	3OS	KEITH	TAG		OTS	0:00	0:26

The term "Umpire Nod" has nothing to do with Tim Welke falling asleep during that pop-up down the third base line in the World Series. This was the week after the Roberto Alomar spitting incident. NOD stands for "News of the Day," and implies we have a reporter on the scene (in this case, Sal Paolantonio, at a courthouse in Philadelphia, covering the umpires' threat to strike the play-offs if Alomar played). We've got to write a lead-in to his report that both sets up what he's going to say **and** doesn't duplicate it. Then we have to follow it up with a little more information—in this case it's Alomar's reaction to the day's event ("REAX"). And after we hear from Robby, we have the TAG, which wraps up the whole story with late information. That night the late information was about how the umps at the Rangers-Yankees game delayed things for ten minutes until the details of the strike-averting compromise were spelled out to them. One more technical term:

BUMP: This is the sequence of two or three snippets of video we show before each commercial in hopes of getting you to stick around for the rest of the show. If the researchers are the underrated humans on The Big Show, the bumps are the underrated components. If we tip our hand as to what's next, and you're not interested, you're gone. We don't like it when you leave. The bump is also a difficult process to pull off. The video has to be carefully selected, edited together—almost always **after** the show has started—and whoever's done that has got to let one of us know as soon as possible what we're going to be narrating. That particular night the bump page in the computer offered us the following information: ":00–:06 iso smoltz walking around in dugout :06–:10 shawn kemp layin and foul reax :10–:17 a smith sack and iso."

That's all we've got to go on.

Now, if we scan down the rundown we know John Smoltz probably has something to do with Bonnie Bernstein's upcoming report previewing the Braves-Dodgers series. And a story in the next segment tells of how Shawn Kemp didn't show up at the Seattle Supersonics camp. But "a.smith sack and iso"? Some phone calls have to be made. Anthony Smith? Of the Raiders? Is he hurt? Was he traded? Why are we showing him? Why isn't there a story somewhere later in the show entitled "Raiders" or "Smith/Raiders"? It turned out he had walked out on the team because he was upset about a rumored trade, and he was fined by the team—fined a lot more than he thought he was going to be fined. And all of this was contained within John Clayton's weekly feature "Inside the Huddle" rather than in one of the stories we were to read. If we don't know that, we can't begin to convince you it's interesting enough for you to avoid going to sleep or watching Letterman or whatever you do when we bore you.

We've gone into such detail because we wanted you to have an idea just how precise all this is. It isn't just "Dan and Keith breeze through the day's highlights and news." It's as complicated and regimented as Tae Kwan Do, or maybe the Macarena. And we haven't even gotten into what has to happen for one of us to make sense of a page like number 6 up there, "Peete Latest." We have to search the Associated Press and SportsTicker wire services elsewhere in the computer to find out the degree of Rodney Peete's injury and the Eagles' personnel response, or make our own phone calls, or, as page 6c suggests ("Tag w/Mort News") get even more information from one of our experts, in this case the well-informed Chris Mortensen.

So the writing goes on all night. We've literally written whole new lead stories at 10:59 for an 11:00 show. We've written stories as late as 11:58 for a show that's going off the air at the stroke of midnight. The night the Los Angeles police finally declared that O. J. Simpson was a suspect in the murders of his ex-wife and Ron Goldman, that news didn't come to us until about 11:15. Three or four different updates were written while the show was in progress—and while, oh, by the way, we were going back and forth from that story (Keith, in Bristol) to Madison Square Garden where the New York Rangers had just won their first Stanley Cup since 1940, to the bar where everybody was celebrating (Dan, in New York).

6:00: We eat. This usually involves phoning in an order to the restaurant next door, walking over and picking it up, and then eating at our desks. While we write. Or make phone calls. Or try to find the script for ''Inside the Huddle.''

7:30: We get to start watching games out of the corners of our eyes. You want the worst possible job in terms of getting to sit around and watch a ball game from National Anthem to final whistle or out? Replace one of us. We have to pay a little attention to almost every single game being televised. This involves a lot of channel surfing. Remember, the record for the number of different game highlights shown in a single one-hour Big Show is twenty-seven. We don't want to disillusion you, but we did not get to see every minute of every one of them.

8:30: Production starts on the Tease—the minute or so of assorted stuff you see before we actually come on and say hello. Depending on the night, the production assistant who'll actually edit the thing together has either himself written a rough script for it, or provided one of us with a list of video shots that look like they'd be good enough to be included and we write the thing ourselves. It's best if it's written and the narration recorded by 8:45 or 9:00. Often it's not done until much, much later. It's also at about this time that we record the narrations to any special features we're doing that night: Breakdown, Peak Performers, or just an extended look at a team, a trend, or whatever.

10:00: We begin thinking about makeup and getting dressed for the show. Disillusionment time again: We're not usually sitting around all day in suits and ties. Jeans and collarless shirts or other easily washed items are our work clothes. Only at this point do the dress shirts, ties, and jackets come on. Then it's makeup. It used to be just what you saw in that most renowned of the *SportsCenter* commercials: We put on our own makeup, in the tiny men's room just off the newsroom— while other people were using the men's room for what you usually use a men's room for. Not pleasant. In the summer of 1995 that changed and we are now professionally painted by a series of very nice makeup artists led by the inimitable Annie Bean. Annie not only erases the bags under our eyes but is also the primary source for news-around-the-office and attends to our psychological needs, gives career and personal advice, and often brings candy.

10:45: Final touch-ups to the script. Late scoreboards can be written. Readjustments can be made to lead-ins if games have gone in directions other than what we've earlier guessed. Wholesale changes often have to be made if the producer has changed the rundown to place breaking news stories higher in the show, or replace outdated ones.

10:55: Head to the studio. This is a comfortable three-minute walk. It can be done in ninety seconds when necessary. We get into our chairs, check to make sure our microphones and earphones work, take a quick mirror-look that is both vain and in vain, and clear our throats repeatedly.

11:00: Time to make the donuts. Basically from here on in it's a roller coaster that never rides the same course twice. Sometimes things go exactly as planned. Sometimes nothing goes as planned. The Tease didn't get edited in time. The TelePrompTer doesn't work. The shot-sheet makes it in time but the tape doesn't. There's a late change in the story one of us is about to read next. The building is hit by lightning and while we're still on the air and the highlights are still rolling, we can't see them—or anything else (this has actually happened).

12:00: Any night of the week except Sunday, we say our final stupid somethings and go home. On Sunday, however, the show will be repeated at 2:00 A.M. and then again every hour from 6:00 A.M. through 1:00 P.M. on Monday. Very often we have to correct technical glitches or incorrect information for the "re-airs." We always have to record a series of new final segments indicating what's next at 2:59 A.M. or 12:59 P.M. This process—The Dreaded Fixes—can take five minutes or ninety-five minutes. And every once in a while, something happens on a Sunday night of a newsworthy nature that makes it essential that we do a large part of the show over again. Legendary is the time that the New York Rangers agreed to let coach Mike Keenan go to the St. Louis Blues—at about 12:45 A.M. Monday morning. One of us had already gotten **home** and had to come back to the studio. We won't tell you which one, but he consequently hates Mike Keenan and he says "Biscuit in the basket" a lot.

We could go on and on about the process. It's maddening, fascinating, and very rewarding, and we've both long felt that its complexity contributes in great part to why we sometimes seem so goofy on the show—we're punch-drunk. But instead of trying to explain **that,** we have an alternative suggestion:

Watch.

"BILL BUCKNER—COULD YOU DESCRIBE WHAT HAPPENED?"

We try hard. Honest we do. The goal, every night, is perfection. We want to make The Big Show flawless in content, flawless in presentation, flawless in entertainment values.

And don't forget **family** values.

Nonetheless, hard as we try, if you're on live television for an hour a night, four or five nights a week, pushing fifty weeks a year, sometimes things don't go **quite** the way we want them to.

For the record, that workload amounts to around eight full twenty-four-hour days. No wonder you look so old.

I have the four kids to deal with.

You only have three.

And you make four.

Rim shot, please. Get back to the point. Screwups.

Sure, people screw up, but everybody screws up. We just wanted to share some of the wilder moments when bad things happen to good sportscasters, for whatever reason.

Mostly courtesy the fickle middle finger of fate.

Or just plain giddiness. And don't get the idea that it's all some production assistant's fault. Sometimes they contribute—a few examples will follow. But we can fall apart by ourselves without anybody else's help. Remember "You a handsome man, Mr. Garrison?"

Oh, Lord. We just got giddy one night and Dan got me started during some White Sox highlights. You just couldn't say the word "mound" and we both started laughing. Then there was a shot in the same highlights of a really overweight guy, sitting there in forty-nine-degree weather. . . .

And I say, "Lots of jokes come to mind here, but I want to keep my job."

So I say, "**There's** your darn **mound.**"

And I start laughing, I just can't speak for a few seconds, and finally I decide, what the heck, it can't get any worse, I'll do the joke I was going to say in the first place. Remember the movie *JFK* when Kevin Bacon says to Kevin Costner in this terrible Southern accent, "You a fine lookin' man, Mr. Gahhhison"? So I said it, or a version of it. "Yo a handsommmmmme mahhhhhn."

And I lose it. There are tears in my eyes I'm laughing so hard. The problem is, as soon as Dan is finished reading the White Sox score, I've got to come back, on camera, and do a lead-in to a piece Tommy Jackson did on the Chargers trying to fire themselves up to play the Broncos. And in it I've quoted Shawn Jefferson saying, "We've got to keep saying we have to kill them! Kill! Kill! Kill!"

So KO collapses completely. He's laughing and coughing and trying to read this quote. It's like, "Kill, ha ha ha, Kill, ha ha ha ha, Kill," and finally he just says, "Never mind, never mind. Here's Tom Jackson with something!"

In college I remember before every broadcast being paralyzed, really gripped with fear, that I'd just start laughing on the air. And I really trained myself not to. But now, I'd say Dan and I laugh uncontrollably on *SportsCenter* maybe once every six weeks or so. If he so much as says, "Yo a handsome man, Mista Olbamon," during a commercial break I've got to fight back the giggles.

Remember the Dona-who incident?

I did **that** all by myself. Terry Donahue had just announced he would be quitting as the football coach at UCLA. I'm reading the story, setting up a sound bite of Donahue as he fought back the tears and talked about how sad he was and everything. First I mispronounced the word legend as if it were "leg end," and then Dan started giggling. Off camera of course. And then I come to Donahue's name and for some damn reason I call him ''Dona-**who**.''

And I'm now doubled over with laughter. Of course, nobody can **see** this except Keith.

And I start laughing again. This time to the point where I just couldn't talk. I just waved at the camera and said, ''Play the tape! Just play the tape!'' We've had lots of those, just incredible moments where it's like Mary Tyler Moore laughing during the funeral of Chuckles the Clown. But you weren't there for the worst one.

Not . . . the disc.

Oh, yes, the dreaded bulging disc. Now I have to set this one up carefully. It was a Monday night and Dan's off and Steve Levy is filling in for him. Steve's very smooth on the air, very good, usually can get through anything thrown at him, probably better than I can. Now on Monday nights during the football season, The Big Show gets very low ratings until the Monday Night Football game ends. When we hear Al and Dan and Giff start to thank their producers, we know the audience is beginning to tune over to us. Sometimes the number of viewers will multiply by a factor of thirty or forty. So we try to get as many commercials and features and whatnot out of the way early in the show so that when these viewers join us, we can give them the big news of the day and maybe go back to the game for a live interview or something.

So anyway, this one night the game's winding down and we're just cleaning up the last of the filler items. Steve's going to do the football injury report from the weekend's games, then I'm going to do a basketball highlight, and then I'm going to do the Monday Night Football highlights, and then Steve's going to throw it out to Andrea Kremer at the game for an interview. No commercials. No breaks. No prerecorded packages.

In other words, no way out.

Exactly. My hair could catch fire and we couldn't take the time to have somebody spit at it. So Steve's reading his story about Maurice Hurst, a defensive back who is now suing the Patriots because they cut him while he was injured. Hurst says he had a neck injury and played anyway and you can't get rid of a player when he's hurt. So Steve's doing fine and he's just finishing up his on-camera about Hurst and preparing to read a long narration of a videotape full of other injuries from the weekend. And that's when it happens. He describes Hurst's back injury. With real force in his voice, he's supposed to say, "Hurst has been suffering from a bulging **disc** in his neck."

Only he doesn't **say** "disc."

Switch a few letters around and you can figure out what he said instead. Well, there's a second or two delay before he realizes it. By this time, the injury tape has started to play. Me, I'm laughing so hard it sounds like I'm getting sick to my stomach. Apparently in the control room the laughter is so loud you can't hear the director talk. Back on the set, I swivel my chair completely around so Steve can't see me coming unglued. And I give him a lot of credit. He's talking about guys with broken femurs and lacerated chins and hyperextended knees and he's laughing a little bit and his delivery is a little disjointed, but he's the calmest guy in the building. The camera people are laughing so hard that their cameras are shaking, for crying out loud!

Now, I'm thinking I have to follow this. I've got to come back on camera in about thirty seconds as soon as the injury tape ends, and I'm just going to lose it. And in my mind I hear Dan saying, "Yo a handsome man," and I'm thinking about all the times in college when my voice cracked and I started laughing, so I think, what the heck, I'm going to humiliate myself anyway, I might as well make a final joke before I fall apart completely in front of all those people just tuning in from Monday Night Football. So, just as the tape ends, Steve pauses, and I say, real loud, "Thank goodness we didn't have any videotape of that Hurst injury." Mean remark, but, why not? He's finished. I'm the one who's going to be on camera, with tears streaming down my cheeks.

Problem was, he **wasn't** finished. There was still a graphic coming up listing all the other injuries. I had **forgotten** about that. So now here's poor Steve, who has struggled successfully to keep himself together for two minutes after this monumental malapropism, and **now** he starts laughing. And **I** made him do it. Sure enough, though, he collects himself and manages to read the first two or three injuries. And then he comes across a guy who has a strained groin. And this time he just collapses in laughter.

So now I'm **really** in trouble. I'm definitely coming back on camera, in about ten seconds, and my eyes are so full of tears I can't even see the TelePrompTer. That's when it dawns on me. If I take my glasses off and just read the basketball lead-in off the script page sitting in front of me, it may look goofy, but at least I won't be able to see Steve laughing or anybody else falling apart. So I take them off and hold the script up halfway to my face and start reading it.

This is the point at which I tuned in, and I'm thinking, why isn't Keith wearing his glasses? He looks **terrible!** What's happened? Is he sick?

Not in the way you thought. Somehow we got through it. Through the basketball highlights, through the football highlights, through the throw out to the stadium, to the commercial. Longest five or six minutes of my life, though.

And it kind of worked out OK in the end. I think Steve got a couple of dates out of it.

Anyway, some of the worst things that have ever happened to us were things you, Dear Reader, never actually saw—and, in fact, are things **we** never saw. Remember the story about Bob Prince, the famous Pirates announcer? He's doing the 1960 World Series on NBC and in the eighth inning of this wild game, they send him downstairs to do the postgame interviews with the Pirates, win or lose. And Bill Mazeroski leads off the bottom of the ninth of a 9–9 tie with the only game seven World Series–winning homer in history. Only Prince never saw it, never heard it, never knew it happened. And he's interviewing the Pirates as they celebrate and who comes up to him but Mazeroski, the hero of heroes, and Prince says to him, "Congratulations, Billy Boy," and Mazeroski says thanks, and Prince suddenly sees the manager about three feet away and he says, "Excuse me, Maz, there's Danny Murtaugh and I think America wants to hear his reaction." Blew Mazeroski off. And we both know how he felt, right DP?

Oh, yes. Sixth game of the 1986 World Series, Shea Stadium. Around the seventh inning, my producer Artie Berko says to me we should probably make our way down to the Red Sox locker room because we want to be in good position and get the postgame celebration of the Red Sox winning the World Series. So, by the time we got down from the press box to the bowels of Shea Stadium it was around the eighth inning. And my only gauge of what was going on was by registering the crowd noise. And it was very quiet at Shea, because the fans were expecting impending doom—that the Red Sox were going to win.

So I'm listening to the game via the crowd for about an inning. We get to the ninth, and I walk back toward the Mets locker room, and I see Dick Schaap and his son Jeremy, who is now a reporter for ESPN but was then just a teenager, and I'm asking Jeremy what's going on in the game. Now, he's a Mets fan, a little down in the dumps, and he's giving me the play-by-play as they start the ninth. I start to walk back to the Red Sox locker room, figuring it's going to be over. Three outs—this is going to be over. Sixty-eight years without a World Series victory and it's going to be over.

I hear a minor roar, so I run back to Jeremy Schaap, he tells me what happened. I start to walk back to the Red Sox locker room. Another minor roar. I run back to Jeremy Schaap. So he's doing play-by-play for me. I figure, I'm going to walk back to the Red Sox locker room one more time. If I hear one more roar, I'm going to get my camera crew and get closer to the Mets locker room. I hear a roar like I've never heard before, or since, at a sporting event. So now I've got my camera crew running back and forth, not sure what locker room we're going in. I run back to Jeremy Schaap to try to find out what happened, and he's so excited, and he's heading toward the Mets locker room.

But my camera crew has gone into the Red Sox locker room. Now, I run into the Red Sox locker room. I have absolutely no idea that they were one out from winning the World Series. I never saw Mookie Wilson's ground ball. I never saw Ray Knight holding his helmet. No clue as to what happened to the Red Sox. Their heads are down, long looks on their faces, very emotional scene. Probably fifteen writers standing around Bill Buckner's locker. My camera crew is over there already, they've got the camera on, and I walk up, and nobody was asking Buckner any questions. So I said, "Bill, can you describe what happened?" and he looks up, and if looks could kill—you know. And he says, "You were there. You saw it." Now I've got fifteen writers looking at me, waiting for my response and my follow-up question. And I couldn't say, "Bill, to be honest with you, I was talking to Dick Schaap and his son Jeremy, I didn't see the play."

We eventually got our interviews. Buckner stayed, in the cross fire, answering the questions as best he could. Finally, a couple of Red Sox players came over trying to shoo the media away so Buckner could try to put this behind him, since they had a game seven to play. So we went over to the Mets locker room, and it had to be around 1:30 before we left Shea Stadium. And I remember walking out of the locker room and grabbing a baseball, and figuring, I might as well do this now if I'm ever going to do it. And Gary Carter was walking out with me and I said, "Gary, can you do me a favor?" and he said, "Dan, no more interviews. I'm just so emotionally spent I don't want to talk about it. I want to get ready for game seven." I said, "Gary, I don't want an interview. I'd like an autograph request." And he said, "You want my autograph?" I said, "Well, not exactly. I'm thinking about getting engaged, and my future mother-in-law is a huge Mets fan. So, if you would write, on the baseball, 'Irene, I think Dan would make a great son-in-law,' it might help me out." And he looks at me and says, "Only on a night like this could I get a request like this." But he signed it, and I gave it to my future mother-in-law, and it all worked out. We lived happily ever after.

Except for Buckner, of course.

Actually, I went to interview him seven years later: 1993, I went up to Syracuse where he was working as a hitting instructor for the Blue Jays' farm teams. I spent about four hours with him, and he was great. He talked about everything, all the things that had happened to him and his family since then. And one of the questions I asked him was, "Do you remember me asking you a question right after the game?" and he said, "Yeah. You said 'describe what happened' and I'm thinking 'that's the dumbest question I ever heard—you **saw** what happened.' " And then I told him, "You know, Bill, I never saw that play. I was down right by your locker room waiting to interview you guys right after you won the World Series." And he **apologized** for that! Seven years later he **apologized** for snapping at me. But I thought I owed him at least that, of trying to explain why I asked him such a dumb question.

I guess it's better that he never really answered that question. We can say it forever: Calvin Schiraldi pitched like crap, Bob Stanley couldn't grip the ball and kept throwing it away, and John McNamara didn't bother to put Dave Stapleton in at first to save Buck's aching ankles like he'd done every other damn game that season.

You're getting off the point. And you're not even a Red Sox fan. The best part of the trip was getting him to do a fake version of our "da da dah" commercials, where the Wilson ball comes at him, we cut to a closeup of him fielding it and tagging the bag and doing the "da da dah" thing. He loved that.

Very cathartic. All because of Dick Schaap. Would you believe I have a Schaap story? I grew up as a huge Yankee fan, and in 1976, when I was seventeen years old, I finagled a media credential for the play-off games at Yankee Stadium. And it's game five and it's tied 6–6 in the ninth and I figure I've got to get downstairs to the locker room area to do my phone report for my college radio station at Cornell, and I've got to be ready to get my interviews. So I'm sitting in the pressroom in the basement of Yankee Stadium and Chris Chambliss comes up and hits a pennant-winning homer off Mark Littell. And am I out there in the stadium itself going nuts with my fellow fans? Am I running onto the field like fifteen thousand other lunatics? No I am not. I am sitting next to . . . Dick Schaap.

It's those lousy Schaap guys. Always the same thing.

We're just kidding. Dick, Jeremy, and I all went to the same college—obviously not at the same time. Heck, Dick's old enough to be Jeremy's **father.** But between us and Bill Pidto and Marc Schwartz, we form a huge on-air alumni association. But I didn't have to go to Cornell to miss things. I've been to perhaps a thousand big-league baseball games and I've never seen a no-hitter. But I **walked out** on one. I was at Yankee Stadium on July 4th in 1983 to do two stories: a thing on the old cliché that the teams in first place on that day always win the pennant, and this feature on this kid hitter from Boston who was tearing up the league. Bagley or Boggus or something. But, I had to get back to the office to do my 5:45 sportscast, so we stayed for an inning and then split. And Dave Righetti went and pitched a no-hitter without me.

Sometimes it's better if you miss the game. I was at the Meadowlands to cover the Jets and Steelers in a Monday night game, and before the game, I was walking onto the field, and from the moment I get out there, this guy in the stands on the fifty-yard line is just yelling at me: "F*** you, Lampley! F*** you, Jim Lampley!" And my producer says, "You know, he's talking to you—he thinks you're Lampley." So I thought, I could either say I'm **not** Jim Lampley, or I could just give him the finger, and then he's going to think Jim Lampley flipped him off. I did the latter. So I'm sure he's telling everybody, still to this day, "Yeah, I was yelling at Jim Lampley and he flipped me off."

Sorry, Jim.

Yeah. Sorry, Jim. Gee, I mean I know the hair's similar but you've got to be eight inches taller than Lamps. I always thought you looked more like David Leisure, the guy who did the old "Joe Isuzu" commercials. Anyway, *that* happens all the time. I get called "Dan" a lot. I was at a baseball card show, must've been 1992 right after we started, and somebody walks up and says, "Chris Myers, how 'ya doing?," and five minutes later it's "Chris Berman! What are you doing here?" Best of them all—at the same show—I stop at some dealer's table and he says, "John Saunders, it's a pleasure to meet you." Never got mistaken for Lampley, though.

It's an experience.

How about this one. Just after my twenty-first birthday I got to cover the Olympics in Lake Placid. An amazing two weeks. I covered the crowds for the hockey games, got to see the win over the Russians and the gold medal and everything. But the real story was, my bosses decided to teach me how to drink. The sports director, Sam Rosen, and our network manager, Stan Sabik, decide to close the bar in the little motel we were staying in. Only, they got to sleep relatively late. Me, they send to covering the skiing. Which starts at 8:30, which means I have to get up at 6:00 to catch three different buses to get to Whiteface Mountain. So somehow I wake up, and somehow I pack up my bag: a telephone, two tape recorders, assorted patch cords, three microphones, an extra package of batteries, a big heavy audio-processing device. And I somehow get dressed in my Nanook of the North outfit. And I somehow get to all the buses on time, and at 7:30 I'm standing on the back of the Snowtrak—like an open-air tank—taking us up the mountain. And I get to the finish line of the downhill race and I remember where our plug is for the telephone and I dig it out from under a foot of new snow, and I'm thinking, "Gee whiz, I can do this while completely hungover." It's snowing, with the wind chill it's fifty degrees below zero, and I feel great.

Until I realize that I don't have any cassette tapes with me. Not one. Nothing to record the interviews on. And I turn around in a full circle just in case there's a Radio Shack up on top of Whiteface Mountain and—guess what—there isn't. But I do see the only other radio reporter who made it to the race. I work for United Press International and he works for the Associated Press and I go to him and I tell him my story. My bosses got me drunk and I forgot my cassettes. Please help me, broadcasting colleague. And he looks at me and he says, "I'm very sorry, Keith. You know that **I** would be happy to loan you a blank tape. But I'm AP and you're UPI and if my bosses ever found out, they'd kill me." And I looked at him and I said, "How in the hell is **anybody** going to find out? We're on top of a frigging **mountain.**"

So I'm going to get fired. Unless I can get Steve Mahre to win the gold, come over to my phone in the snow, and do the interviews that way. And all of a sudden I can feel that fifty degrees below zero. I'm absolutely dead meat. Then I see a sportswriter who's trying to seduce one of our UPI print reporters, and I tell him my sob story and he says, "If you help me get her into the sack, I'll loan you my microcassette machine." So he loaned me his machine, and later I did what I could. ("You know, he sure is a great guy! I don't know about his romantic abilities but he sure gives great loan.")

I get my interviews, and I pack up my stuff, and I get ready to get on the Snowtrak going back down the mountain, and who's standing there next to me but the guy from the Associated Press who wouldn't loan me the damn cassette. And he says, "I'm glad it worked out. And I know you'll tell this story on me forever. And I understand."

And of course, you **have** told this story on him forever.

I left one detail out. His name is Jack Briggs. He was a pretty good sportscaster. The punch line, of course, is that the boss he was so afraid of was the head of AP Radio Sports, Shelby Whitfield, who now runs ABC Radio Sports and has a hand in ESPN Radio. And I told Shelby the story once and he said, "What the hell difference would it have made to me? And how the hell did Briggs think I'd ever find out? Telepathy?"

Nice that you remembered his name, huh?

Something else that once happened to me taught me never to forget a name. In 1994, the Baseball Hall of Fame called and asked if I'd like to go down to New York one morning and emcee this big shindig they were having on the steps of city hall before a big fund-raising dinner that night. There must have been twenty Hall of Famers there—what a thrill that was: Al Kaline stops me and says he watches the show. **Al Kaline**—and I really boned up for this. I tried to find memorable things they'd done on that exact day years before, or great days they had in New York, whatever. It was a hoot, but only after I got through the bad part.

The deputy mayor, a woman named Fran Reiter, was the big fan. She knew every player by sight, she knew me, she asked about Dan, the whole nine yards. And she introduces me to the mayor, Rudy Giuliani. ''Rudy, this is Keith Olbermann from ESPN. You'll make your remarks and then you introduce him. His name is Keith Olbermann. O-l-b-e-r-m-a-n-n.'' And I had to stifle a laugh. She actually spelled it out for him. And he's shaking my hand and looking at her and looking back at me and looking out to see how many people are out there in the park in front of city hall and he's got this kind of glazed look in his eyes. And he and I sit down in the front row, the Hall of Famers behind us, about five hundred people in front of us. And while Deputy Mayor Reiter is making her remarks, Giuliani turns to me and says, ''You're the emcee, right? Your name is Keith Olbermann, right?'' And I say yes and this huge smile comes over his face like he's just thought up the cure for gout or something.

So finally he gets introduced and he goes up to the podium and he starts making his speech. And it's about how wonderful baseball is and how great the Hall of Fame is and how much of a Yankee fan he is and how much of a Met fan he is and how much of a Dodger fan he was and how much of a Giant fan he was, and eventually he's getting around to the point where he's about to explain how he kept the Mets and Yankees from moving out of town and how he invented baseball and how he's ordered up this beautiful sunny day for all of us, when he gets some kind of cue from Fran Reiter and he winds it up. And he says, ''And now, I'd like to turn it over to our master of ceremonies, the great sportscaster from ESPN—and a New York native, I understand—and here he is . . .''

And he goes blank.

Can't remember my name.

He looks over to Fran Reiter—and the microphone for the PA system is the wrong kind and it picks up everything within ten feet—and he says to her, and to everybody in the crowd, ''What's his name? I don't know his name. What's his name?'' And she says, in this great booming voice, ''Keith Olbermann! I told you! Keith

Olbermann.'' And I can hear Benjie Kaze, one of our producers, out in the crowd laughing. So Giuliani recomposes himself and picks up like nobody noticed **any** of this: ''Here he is, our emcee from ESPM, Keith Olbermann.''

Now this next part took only about four seconds but time had slowed for me. I'm thinking, what should I say when I get up to the podium? He's the only one even pretending he hasn't screwed up and forgotten my name. And I'm thinking, ''I'll say, thank you, Mayor Dinkins,'' or ''Thank you, Mayor LaGuardia,'' or maybe ''Thank you, Mayor Whatever-Your-Name Is'' or just ''And you are . . . ?'' And finally I settle on just sitting there for a few seconds and making him squirm. And it works. ''C'mon up, Keith, come on up.'' And he leads the applause and as I go to the podium I can see Al Kaline over my shoulder laughing his head off.

Made me wish they'd gone on strike in April that year, not August.

Oh no, not that. We both covered baseball strikes; 1985, I was covering the short one that year, night and day. So when we heard there was a possibility that there was a breakthrough, that Peter Ueberroth had brought together both sides, that he was the Knight in Shining Armor, that the baseball season was back on, we went to stake out the meeting at a New York hotel. And we were on a floor with only three phones—and two of them didn't work. And my boss at the time at CNN, Rick Davis, said ''Soon as you get word, we're going live with this, with you on the phone.'' So I had my producer Artie Berko, inside the press conference, giving me hand signals of how long the collective bargaining agreement was for, the strike is over—we had all kind of hand signals that we had mapped out.

So, I'm dialed up to CNN and I'm ready to go live and I'm just waiting till I get all the information from Artie. Suddenly, Howard Cosell comes walking out of this press conference smoking this huge cigar. And I'm thinking, ''There are three phones, only one is working—I'm going to meet Howard Cosell.'' He walks up, checks the first phone. Doesn't work. He checks the next phone. Slams the receiver down. So now he's looking at me, and I am just about ready to go on, and I said, ''Howard, I'm sorry, I need to use this phone.'' And he says, ''Young man, do you know who I am?'' and I said, ''Yes I do, Mr. Cosell, and I'm a big fan. But I'm ready to go live on CNN.'' And he says, ''As if the whole world's watching

CNN?'' So he did this about-face, leaving a plume of smoke behind for me to enjoy.

Four years before that I was staking out the talks from the **previous** strike and the players file out during a break and give us all no comments and Howard's there and he says to Reggie Jackson, ''Reggie! Reggie! You've **got** to talk to me.'' And Reggie says, ''No, Howard, I've **got** to go to the bathroom.'' And Howard doesn't miss a beat. ''Then I'm going in **with you!**'' Ah, Howard.

The best.

But you're lucky he didn't hang that phone up on you. That happened to me. Also for CNN, also a strike—but football. And I had been put on this story in May—four months before they actually went on strike. I went to cover negotiations where there were only **four** reporters there. By the end there were four **hundred.** So I had gotten pretty chummy with the head of the players' union, Ed Garvey, and he'd done me favors and I'd done him favors and late in September I go up to cover the talks at the hotel in New York and they don't give me a camera crew.

There's a shock.

I'm fully prepared to do artists' renderings if a fistfight breaks out or something. To be fair, we only had three or four crews back then. So the bargaining session breaks up and the owners' negotiator Jack Donlan goes to one room to hold a news conference and I don't have a camera crew and I know what he's going to say anyway, so I sit down at this table and sure enough, as soon as all of the other reporters leave, who comes out of the bargaining room but Garvey. And he sits down and fills me in and gives me six things he didn't tell anybody else and we just start shooting the breeze about reporters and lawyers and football players, and he reminds me that two or three days earlier, this woman from CBS shows up—we'll just call her Jane—and interrupted all of the other reporters talking to Garvey and starts asking ridiculous questions about some irrelevancy or another.

And, as if on cue, in she walks. She's frantic. She's late for the bargaining session and now, of course, she sees an empty negotiating room and two guys sitting at a table in front of it. Of course, one of them **is** Ed Garvey and she **did** interview him earlier in the week. But evidently Jane's only a backup reporter for good reason.

Her first question is to me: "Has Garvey left?" So I look out over the top of my glasses at Ed and Ed looks out over the top of his glasses at me and we send a telepathic message to each other.

GARVEY: Yep, cleared out.

ME: The bastard.

JANE: Oh, no. I got this tip that he and the players are going back to Washington.

GARVEY: Could be. You can never tell with that guy.

JANE: Could he still be in the hotel or something? I'll bet he's already left for the airport.

ME: No, I don't think so. I bet he's a lot closer than any of us thinks.

JANE: Well, I've got to find him or they'll kill me in the office.

GARVEY: Why? What the hell is he going to tell you anyway?

JANE: What do you mean?

GARVEY: He drinks.

JANE: He **does?**

ME: Like a fish. Never without the stuff.

GARVEY: And the players all hate him.

And this goes on, and on, and on. For ten minutes we hosed this poor woman. We gave her hints that the strike was going to be called off, that there'd been a scuffle in the bargaining room, that Jack Donlan had gotten stuck in the toilet. How we kept from laughing I'll never know. But finally she breaks us.

JANE: Well, guys, it's too bad about me missing him and all, but I really appreciate your help.

GARVEY: It was more of a pleasure than you know.

JANE: Truth be told, I interviewed Garvey just the other day, but I don't think I'd recognize him if he was sitting here at this table.

ME: (bursts into laughter)

GARVEY: Sorry, Jane. **I'm** Ed Garvey, and this is Keith Olbermann from CNN. What can I do for you?

Jane looks straight at me and says, without the slightest appreciation for the humor of the situation, "I'll get you for this."

So a month later we're in Cockeysville, Maryland, for yet another one of these interminable all-night bargaining sessions. And once again, I have no camera crew. I'm on the phone for CNN's late show, actually on the air with Fred Hickman. And who comes sauntering down the hall but Jane. And she comes right over to my phone and daintily extends a hand and disconnects me. CNN gets nothing but dial tone.

We could do a whole **book** on just strike stories.

Not that anybody would **read** it. Just one more: 1981 baseball strike again. It's the night they're finally going to settle it. And it's four in the morning and I've been in this lousy pressroom since three in the afternoon. And everybody's just dead. Lampley is there, sprawled out on the floor, barefoot. All the veterans are slumped over chairs or snoozing on tables. I'm on the floor, leaning up against a post with a phone on it when the damn thing rings. And I'm giddy to begin with so I answer it, "Third base dugout. Billy Hunter speaking." And there's silence on the other end for a moment and then this voice—it's real familiar but I can't quite place it—says, "Is the strike over yet?" And I get mad. If the guy wanted to know, why wasn't he in that stupid room with us? "Listen, buddy, if you want to find that out, get off your ass and get down here. There's plenty of free potato chips." And the man says, "Well, I was told this was the night. Do you see Bob Fishel there anywhere?" And I look around the room for Fishel, who was the public relations director for the Yankees for twenty years, and sure enough, he's in the corner, and I yell, real loud, "Hey, Bob, there's some jackass on the phone wants to talk to you. Says he's been told the strike's over."

So Bob Fishel gets up and he straightens out his pinstriped suit and comes over and takes the phone from me. "This is Bob Fishel. . . . George! Yes, George. Not over yet, George. I'll call you when it is. No, I don't know who the idiot who answered the phone was."

It was George Steinbrenner.

Bingo. I wonder if he remembers.

He does **now.**

You know, it doesn't always matter whether you have a camera crew with you or not. When I was working in Los Angeles, I got a tip from a perfect source the night before the NFL draft that Rocket Ismail of Notre Dame was going to sign with the CFL Toronto

Argonauts, who were then owned by Bruce McNall. Ismail was going to be with McNall at the L.A. Kings game that night at the Forum, and McNall was going to sign him up and then announce it the next morning, right before the draft. So my producer, Ron Gralnik, and I call the station for a camera crew. And the cameraman waits out in his truck in the parking lot, and all through the game we're watching the Kings and watching Ismail up in McNall's box. And early in the third period, the whole bunch of them get up and leave. So Ron, who used to be an usher at the Forum, goes outside and tries to figure out what exit they're going to use. He knows they're not just going to trot out the front door. He starts asking the limo drivers who are parked around the building and sure enough, he recognizes one of them and the guy gives him the scoop.

Ismail and his crew and one Argonauts executive are all going to leave via the side door that the indoor soccer team used for its offices. So the cameraman and I hide behind a big transformer in the parking lot, not fifteen feet from the door. And I tell him: As soon as I see him, you start recording, turn on your lights, and we'll just ambush him. Well, the game goes into overtime. And it starts raining. And some other camera crews come out and we have to pretend we're just standing there in the drizzle for the hell of it. And the game goes into **double** overtime. Finally, I see some activity in the hallway next to this side door. It's Ismail and the executive and three or four other guys. And I turn to the cameraman and I say "Now!"

So he turns on the light and we rush across the fifteen feet and as the door opens I start yelling at Ismail. "Rocket, have you signed with the Toronto Argonauts?" And he's stunned. He doesn't say a word, but the look on his face gives it away completely. "How many years is the contract for?" I shout. "Three?" And he looks freshly stunned and gives **that** away, too. Now he's going to run for the limo. But I **block** him, and I'm thinking, "I can block this guy? Why does **anybody** want to sign him?" And I ask another question: "Did you get a part ownership of the team as part of the contract you signed tonight?" And his look gives it away again.

All this time we're all moving slowly toward the limo and finally the Argos executive grabs Ismail by the arm and just pulls him, the deer frozen in the headlights, away from me. And they all pile into the limo. And my cameraman drops to one knee and starts shooting into the limo where Ismail and the executive are sitting side by side and I yell at the exec, "Is that a Rocket in your pocket or are you just glad to see us?" And at that moment, they slam the door shut and the driver hits the gas and they screech out of sight.

It's one minute of the best story I've ever gotten. I'm the only one who says a word, but they've given away every detail just with their eyes. It went down like we had scripted it, and Ron and I are jumping around and talking about how **other** networks are going to run the tape the next day and we'll be quoted in the papers and the whole silly, giddy, adrenaline-high stuff. And then the cameraman says, "Hold on," and we freeze.

Oh, no.

He says five simple, tragic, words. "I never rolled the tape." The perfect story, the stakeout that pays off for the hundred stakeouts that didn't. And he forgot to press the record button. It's seven years later and Ron and I'll still be talking on the phone and there'll be a pause and one of us will just blurt out, "He forgot to **roll.**"

Good thing one of my cameramen forgot to roll. When I was working in Dayton, we would drive a good hour and a half to get to Riverfront Stadium, so we'd get there early. And the first time I went to a Bengals game, I had a lot of time to kill, so I'm walking around the stadium, just kind of seeing where everything is, and I turn a corner, and I walk right in to where the Bengals cheerleaders are getting dressed. Let's put it this way: They weren't exactly **finished** getting dressed. So I hear a few shrieks, and I felt bad that I'd just walked in on them. Well, sort of bad. I went back and told my cameraman that there was this room back there where they had free sandwiches. I never did apologize to him for doing that.

Gotta watch those stadium doors. I didn't get quite the view you got, but I had time to kill out at Belmont Park one day doing a preview of the big race, and I decided to have a look around the place, just like you did at Riverfront. And I turn a corner and there's a door, and being an idiot, I open it and walk right through. And I'm on the roof of the grandstand. And it quickly dawns on me that the door is probably self-locking. And just as I reach for it, it closes shut. And it sure is locked.

So there I am, half an hour away from an interview with some trainer or somebody, it's four hours before the park opens, my camera crew's out away from the stadium shooting videotape of the horses in their barns, there are no catwalks, no stairs, no other doors, and for all I know I'm going to starve to death out there. They'll find my body the following November or something and even when they do, nobody watched CNN in those days—they'll never know it was me until they check my dental records. Five minutes go by. Ten. Fifteen. Not a soul in sight. Finally, out in a parking lot about a hundred yards away I see some guy just walking and I start screaming at him. "Hey! Hey! I'm locked out on the roof! Help! Hey!" And the guy starts walking slowly toward me until he gets to the fence of the parking lot and he looks up at me and he shouts, "Aren't you that guy from CNN? Keith Olbermann?" We probably had one damn viewer in New York State in 1982 and **he** was the guy who found me out on the roof like the idiot I am.

Did they get you down?

Well, there's the silliest question since you interviewed Buckner.

I'm just trouble with doors. I hit my head on a subway door. I walked right into the studio door at *SportsCenter* one night. In fact the first time I was ever in a press box, I was humiliated by a door. I had finagled a press pass to a Yankee spring training game when I was sixteen years old. And I didn't belong there, and I **knew** I didn't belong there. And so, instead of going in the main door to the press box atop the stadium in Fort Lauderdale, I decide I'll go in one of the side doors. And I turn the knob, and push, and the thing isn't locked, but there's resistance. So I push harder. And with that, the door swings open and the twenty folding metal chairs they had stacked on the **other side** of the door come crashing down and everybody in the press box turns around and stares at me. I couldn't talk for a week.

Speaking of which. Or **not** speaking of which. When we moved *SportsCenter* into the new studio in 1994, I kept warning the stage crew that the microphone cords were too long, that some night I'm going to roll over it with my chair and yank the cord off. I'd been saying this for six months, because I knew I was going to do it. So sure enough, one night, we do the customary mike test before the show, and everything's fine, and then I back my chair up to read the computer or something, and I roll over the cord and pull my mike off. Nobody knows that I don't have a microphone on. They'd already done their mike check—it sounded fine. We come on camera, and I don't have a microphone on, and it's obvious.

You have one on. It's just buried in your jacket down by your belt.

But it's not obvious to me. I just keep reading my part of the opening hello, and then I start reading the first story, a lead-in to some Orioles highlights.

And at home it sounds like you're speaking from under a pillow. So the producer talks to me through my earpiece. "Dan has no microphone. It's dead or something. Give Dan your microphone." So I take my mike off my tie and start to give it to Dan. But I'm going to finesse this thing. I'm going to bring my hand in just under the range of the camera's vision so nobody sees I'm doing this. And very slowly, I take my left hand and inch it close to his lapel. Closer. Closer. Closer. Only I've misjudged the whole thing.

What the viewer at home sees is this hand coming in from the left of the screen.

Like the murderer's hand with the knife in the horror films. I put the mike on Dan's lapel and just as slowly pull my hand back—all of this extremely visible to the dear viewer at home.

All this time I know there's something wrong with my mike but I don't know what. Some technicians sneak up behind me and they're sitting on the floor of the stage working on the mike cord and trying to figure out what happened, and all the while I just keep trying to do the highlights, and finally the Orioles highlights are over, and then the Tigers highlights are over, and, as usual, I finish reading the scoreboard and I say, "Keith?"

And my face pops up on camera and I look at the camera like I could kill somebody and I look at Dan and he's wearing **both** our microphones and he's just realized it and I just say nothing. I make a little gesture with the first two fingers of my hand.

And I say, "Would you like your microphone back?"

And I make the gesture again. And now he hands me back my microphone and I take it and as slowly as I can, I unbutton my coat, and I put the mike clip back on my tie, and I rebutton my coat, and I smooth out my tie, and then I look back up at the camera and do a

Rudy Giuliani and pretend nothing's gone wrong. "In the National League, meanwhile . . ."

So, for one night, for about three minutes, we had one microphone between us.

Which is better than the one night Bob Ley and I had only one **name** between us. We're coming back for the last section of the show and the producer says to me, you've got ten seconds and you've got to mention this thing and that thing. And the commercial ends and the producer starts counting us down: "Ten . . . nine . . . eight . . ." And I'm trying to keep my head clear so I can get these stories out and then say, "I'm Dan Patrick along with Bob Ley. Good night." So I get the stories in somehow and then I say, "For Dan Patrick, I'm Bob Ley. Good night."

Rudy Martzke, the TV critic for *USA Today,* labeled that the "Oops" of the year. I'm still scarred by that.

Heal thyself, Dan. Do you know how many people did that? Or something like that? Walter Cronkite once called himself "Crankcase" on the air. The first show I ever did I mispronounced my own name. My friend Andy Fisher, a great radio newsman who now writes for NBC News, once filled in for the sportscaster on WNEW and said, "I'm Chip Cipolla—no I'm not! I'm Andy Fisher **for** Chip Cipolla!" I had a friend who free-lanced for like three radio stations at the same time and used a different name on each one of them and one show he finished off, "That's the news, I'm . . . I'm . . . I'm . . ." He just forgot which one of him he was on that particular station. You're in fine company Bob. Uh. Dan.

So far everything you've read in this chapter has been our fault. I think it's only fair if we start sharing. Sharing the experience. Sharing the memories.

Sharing the blame. We won't use any names here. You wouldn't know most of them anyway and it would only serve to embarrass them. Besides which, most of them are young people, just starting out in this business, who work dreadful hours for paychecks that look more like the refund you get when you buy a twelve-pack of soap. So these things happen. We don't blame them. Not after the first hour or two of anger subsides, anyway. We won't use any names.

But if you write us, we'll give you their names, addresses, and phone numbers.

And the times they're most likely to be asleep. We have to start with Blow Doll.

We're in the first commercial break. The second section is going to start with Keith doing a couple of highlights and then me doing a couple of highlights—I start with the Tigers game. Only there's no more than a minute left in the break and I still haven't been given the shot-sheet describing the Tigers highlights. Finally, this new production assistant rushes in, hands me this shot-sheet, and says, "This is very important, Dan. The Tigers' starting pitcher was C. J. Nitkowski but he got hurt."

Dan's saying, "Yeah, yeah," trying to get the production assistant to get to the point. Meanwhile our director, Linda Willhite, is talking to us in our earphones. "Forty seconds."

So the production assistant says, "The Tigers brought in this rookie to replace Nitkowski. A very unusual name. Blow Doll. **Ben Blow Doll.**" And I turn to the production assistant and say, "Blow Doll?"

And this is where I come in. "I don't think so." And then the production assistant, trying to impress us, says, "Oh, no, I watched the game. That's the way they were pronouncing it on the broadcast. It's spelled B-l-o-m-d-a-h-l. Blow Doll."

And now Linda Willhite is saying "twenty seconds." And Keith says to me, "Don't say it. It may not be Blomdahl but it certainly ain't Blow Doll."

I mean, if it **was** "Blow Doll" don't you think we would have heard of him before that moment? Or take it the next step. If his name really **was** pronounced "Blow Doll," don't you think he would've changed it? Or that his parents would've changed it?

So now the production assistant starts backing away from our desk and says, "Well, can't you have them check it for you?" And Keith says, "Who's **them?** You, me, and Dan—we're them!"

And now Linda Willhite is saying "ten seconds." And I yell toward our researcher in his alcove around the corner from the set. "Paul Kinney! Do you have a *Baseball Register* in there? An *American League Red Book?* One of them has pronunciations, I can't remember which."

So Linda's counting us down. "Five . . . four . . . three . . ." and Keith looks at me and says, "Don't say it. Skip it or look it up. It ain't Blow Doll!" and a split second later the red light comes on and he says, "We're back. The Boston Red Sox . . ."

And I'm just waiting for the train crash. I'm reading my introduction to the Red Sox highlights and then there's another set of highlights and out of the corner of my eye I'm seeing Dan and Paul Kinney frantically thumbing through at least three baseball guides and I'm not even paying attention to my own highlights. I'm just thinking, "Blow Doll. Blow Doll. Blow Doll." And I'm trying to stretch out the last few things I have to say to give Dan and Paul an extra second to find this guy's damn name in the book and finally I have to throw it to him. And he does his Tiger lead-in and I'm guessing he's just going to skip the name.

But I **can't** skip the name. The production assistant has edited the tape in such a way that you actually **see** C. J. Nitkowski walking off hurt, and Ben Blomdahl coming in from the bull pen. Fortunately this disaster-movie scene pays off.

Dan comes to the name and says, "Starter C. J. Nitkowski comes out with a sore shoulder. And the Tigers bring in another rookie, Ben Bloomdahl."

And I'm thinking "If people only knew what went on in those last sixty seconds, they would never get in this business." Another night, an enterprising young production assistant was working hard, trying to get some hockey highlights done, trying to get the shot-sheet with all the information. But instead of putting down the name "Garth Butcher," the production assistant writes "Garth Brooks." So I'm reading this for the first time on the air and I see the name "Garth Brooks," and I say something like "Garth Br . . . utcher. Not to be confused with Garth Brooks."

These things—and something like this happens at least once a night—seem to be inevitable. Everybody's rushing against incredibly short deadlines. A production assistant who's never seen a hockey game in his life may come to work and get nothing but hockey games for a week. **We** don't know everything so we can't expect everybody else to. But these events certainly do shorten our lives.

There have been times when we've actually come on the air and the guys in the control room have the tape of the highlights and **think** we have the shot-sheet for the highlights, only we don't. And there have been times when I will say, "I have no idea what's going on in this highlight." I figure it's better to be honest than try to fake it. So there have been a few times when one of us has said, "Just fill in your own names, because we have no clue.'' One Monday night this happened during the Vikings-Packers highlights. I didn't have a shot-sheet. No information. So halfway through the highlight, after stumbling and bumbling, I said, ''If you would like to apply for my job, please send your résumés right now to ESPN.''

I've always wanted to just not say anything. Not even try. Just make it Viewer Participation Night. ''This is your chance at home to pretend **you** host *SportsCenter*.'' We play this game of Russian roulette all the time.

Maybe that's why we call them **shot**-sheets.

I can remember coming on during the Stanley Cup play-offs with a huge Rangers-Flyers game as the lead story and we've already finished the mutual hello, and they've cut to me for the lead-in to the Rangers-Flyers, and I **still** don't have the shot-sheet. And finally I see the production assistant standing, off-camera, to my right, holding it. And I'm looking straight ahead, trying to read my lead-in, all the while frantically waving my right hand at the guy trying to get him to give me the shot-sheet. And this particular time the tape had actually started and he **still** hadn't given me the shot-sheet so now I have to stand up from my chair and grab it out of his hands—all the while just saying whatever I can remember about the game.

But perhaps the worst is the dreaded missing page.

Oh, God, is that funny. A short highlight can be described on a one-page shot-sheet. Most of them take two. Some of them take three. One night, the Texas Rangers are playing the Tigers in Detroit and I get a three-pager. And I'm going along, and I finish page one, and I go to page two and I notice that in the upper corner it reads ''page three.'' And there's no other page. The production assistant has given me page one and page three—but no page two.

Now there's a way you can cheat when that happens, if it's baseball. You can listen very carefully to the background noise playing on the tape itself, and the recorded play-by-play will at least give you a clue or a name or something to go on. But not this time.

It was a succession of walks. Not homers, not strikeouts. Walks. And the announcers on the tape were dead silent. I swear I heard crickets on that tape. And this is 1994, I think, when the Rangers had several guys who all looked the same: Jeff Frye, David

Hulse, Rusty Greer, Doug Strange—and damn but if they all aren't playing in this game. So all I could think to say was, "There's a walk to a small white guy on the Rangers . . . and there's **another** walk to **another** small white guy on the Rangers." Dan's trying to help. He's whispering, "I think that's David Hulse. No, no **that's** David Hulse." It was horrible.

Other stuff can go wrong, too. I was off the night that you did the longest, most painful stretch since Harmon Killebrew ripped his hamstring at the 1968 All-Star Game. But I was watching. What was it, game one of the '95 ALCS?

Oh, Lord. Bob Wolcott. This virtually unknown pitcher starts the first game for the Mariners against the Indians. Now, I know the basic Bob Wolcott story and I write the lead-in to the highlights with some stuff about him. But for some reason, just before we went down to the studio to do the show, I decided to stop by the research room and just read up on him. I don't know why I did it—some kind of sixth sense, I guess, or just an accident. So I open up the Mariner media guide and there's all this stuff on him I didn't know, like he was recruited by Stanford but didn't go there, and the Mariners called him up from the minors and had him pitch the exhibition game at the Hall of Fame induction ceremonies one year, and all manner of useless stuff like that.

And the game runs a little long, and something, as they say, comes acropper in the editing room, so the highlights are a little late. In fact they're already about five minutes late when we go to a commercial. And during it, somebody runs in a shot-sheet of the highlights. So I get on the intercom to Mike McQuade, producing in the control room, and I say, "Are we going to do these?" And he says yes, the tape is on the way. And then this is what you saw and heard on the air, taken from an actual tape of the show and what McQ and I can piece together of what he was telling me.

ON-AIR: advertisement for auto parts.
MCQUADE: The tape will be there.
ME: Are you sure? I mean, I got this shot-sheet five minutes ago.
MCQUADE: It'll be there.
DIRECTOR: Five seconds.
ME: It'll be there?

MCQUADE: It'll be there.

ME: OK.

ON–AIR: advertisement ends.

ME: If you were watching the Mariners and the Indians, we welcome you to *SportsCenter*—and that's our subject.

MCQUADE: The tape isn't there. Stretch.

ME: He was not only thrust virtually from the stands to the mound for game one of the American League Championship Series; he was not only the least experienced pitcher ever to start an American League postseason game; but Bob Wolcott was also the first rookie to start an LCS opener since Jim Beattie of the New York Yankees in 1978 against the Kansas City Royals. (This was the end of what I'd written for the lead-in.)

MCQUADE: Tape coming. Stretch.

ME: That's the same Jim Beattie who is now the Mariners' farm director and was, this season at least, Bob Wolcott's boss.

MCQUADE: More stretch.

ME: The guy who decided whether or not he'd pitch in the major leagues or in the minors.

MCQUADE: Stretch.

ME: Wolcott, who was once a top prospect at Stanford—they wanted him, they didn't sign him—in fact signed with the Mariners three years ago.

MCQUADE: Stretch. We'll have it.

ME: He pitched their Hall of Fame exhibition game against the Phillies in 1994.

MCQUADE: Stretch.

ME: He was on the roster, as you know, until September 30th when he was removed . . . as . . .

MCQUADE: Forget it. Do the score panel.

ME: We're going to have to give you the final score.

ON–AIR: Pause. No score. Keith looking nervously into camera.

ME: Let's see the score.

ON–AIR: Score appears.

ME: It's a final! The Mariners beat the Indians three to two and guess what! Bob Wolcott, who we were **talking about**—he

just happens to get the victory; Seattle, in a tremendous
performance by Wolcott, certainly comparable to . . .

MCQUADE: Stretch.

ME: The surprising performances of pitchers like Babe Adams of
the 1909 World Series, Howard Ehmke, and others . . .

MCQUADE: Stretch. Putting the tape in the machine.

ME: He had a marvelous game.

ON-AIR: Highlight tape begins.

ME: And he had a sort of start like we just did! Wolcott facing
Kenny Lofton . . .

What you can't convey on paper or even on the air is the painfulness
of this. If you're being told you just have to stretch a little bit and everything'll be all right, and then it isn't, it's like, I don't know, holding your
breath. How long can you hold your breath? After you run out of air,
how much **longer** can you hold your breath? How much longer after
that?

It was supposed to be about twenty seconds from the moment
that commercial ended until the highlights rolled. It was actually a
minute-seventeen. I stretched for a full minute about a guy who
had just pitched the eighth game of his career. Any more and I
would've been talking about how he likes to hunt and fish, and
what his grades were in the fifth grade. Agony.

This stuff doesn't happen all the time, and when it does it's usually
nowhere near this bad. But once a year is enough to scar you for life. And
of course there's even more inside stuff that people never see. Stuff that
gets fixed before you see it at home. Sometimes fixed by us as we go.

The way we write the show, what with deadlines and all, it
often happens that we have to decide how we're going to narrate a
particular piece of videotape long before the tape has actually been
edited, or sometimes even before it's been selected. This often happens with the "bumps," the little five- to ten-second snippets you
see just before a commercial, during which we promote what's
coming up later in the show.

One Sunday night in September of 1995, I was doing exactly
this—"writing blind," we call it—for a bump promoting what we'd
been told was the "Wild Kingdom Edition of the Plays of the Week."
This particular theme saluted the old TV show in which affable but

slightly dense host Marlon Perkins would always describe the action and mumble something about their sponsor, Mutual of Omaha Life Insurance, while his trusty but mildly frightened assistant Jim Fowler would actually handle the wild animals.

Kind of like the way we do **our** show, Keith.

Only both of **us** are slightly dense and mildly frightened. Anyway, saluting dear old Marlon, I write this: "Coming up, the 'Wild Kingdom' edition of the Plays of the Week. Watch Jim as he's swallowed whole by the giant boa constrictor. Hope he's paid up on his Mutual of *SportsCenter* life insurance.' That's next, this is The Big Show." Now, I know that's not what the video's going to look like. It could be a great catch or a football play or whatever. I'm just goofing on the theme.

About half an hour later I get a phone call from the young man whose responsibility it was to actually edit the videotape for that particular bump. "Uh, Keith," he said with an evident quaver in his voice, "about the Plays of the Week bump? I don't have that shot of the player being swallowed by the boa constrictor. And the producer says there's no shot of a player being swallowed by anything in the plays themselves. Or am I reading this much too literally?"

And again, we're not trying to bash anybody here. These people try really, really, hard. Sometimes the time constraints just get the better of them. Sometimes they try so hard they make a mistake out of something that's correct.

My favorite didn't even happen on **our** show. When the Browns were moving out of Cleveland, they did a piece on the reaction of famous fans of the team. Cleveland sportswriters were in it, and Martin Mull, and the comedian from ABC, Drew Carey. Now whoever was preparing the graphic supers (when it says "Martin Mull/Actor" over Martin's face while he was talking) looked at the name Drew Carey and knew it was a mistake. Who the heck was Drew Carey? So over the shot of Drew Carey, big chunky guy with a crewcut and impossibly thick-black-rimmed glasses, comes the graphic "Drew **Barry**/6 Points Per Game."

Rick had a **lot** of kids. You remember the night with the TelePrompTer?

Another spot filled by a production assistant. Used to be the first thing they'd have them do. And in the studio, the TelePrompTer machine and the operator sit up on a balcony to the right of the set. And if you don't know how to run the machine, or where to find what we've written in the computer, or how to control the speed at which the words go by, you might as well be trying to fly an aircraft or control a roller coaster. But one night, about a minute before the show started, we heard this plaintive cry from the balcony. It was the new guy at the TelePrompTer.

"Ummmm . . . Does anybody know how to turn this **on?**"

Dan and Keith's Top Ten Weirdest Things Said by Athletes:

1. **"I looked at the bitch and I said you're it."**—Mrs. Bernard Freeman, 1989 Westminster Kennel Club dog show judge after choosing the Doberman "Royal Tudor's Wild as the Wind" as Best in Show. This frail, elderly woman had been asked if the winner, as apparently so often happens in the world of dogdom, had looked at the judge and told her "I'm it." Sounds more like Mike Tyson.

2. **"I don't need no press, man. I'm going to be M.B.P. this year."**—Rickey Henderson, to Dan, after his trade to the Yankees in 1985. Who knows, maybe he **was** M.B.P. that year. Nobody has any idea what the M.B.P. is.

3. **"Coach told me to be amphibious."**—Charles Shackelford while at North Carolina State, explaining why he had shot with either hand during a game.

4. **"Never mind the past. We're here in the future now."**—Bobby Hull, to Keith, after a Winnipeg Jets–New York Rangers game in 1979. There's something spooky and time-travelly about this.

5. **"I can't believe I shook this guy's friggin' hand."**—Dino Ciccarelli of the Detroit Red Wings after the decisive game of the 1996 Stanley Cup, referring to Colorado's Claude Lemieux, who had nearly beheaded Ciccarelli's Detroit teammate Kris Draper.

6. **"If Larry Bird was black he would be just another ballplayer."**—Isiah Thomas to a crowd of reporters, including Dan, at Boston Garden in 1986. And this guy became a general manager?

7. **"Just because you guys are perfect assholes, I don't know why**

you're making such a big deal about this. My problems are all behind me."—George Brett, to a crowd of reporters, including Keith, while being questioned about his attack of hemorrhoids during the 1980 World Series.

8. "I'm always going to survive. Only reason I can't survive is if I'm dead or something."—Mike Tyson, August 1996. Can't really argue with him, huh?

9. "Rip those country c**********s! Rip them like you rip the f****** players!"—Cubs manager Lee Elia, 1983. Unfortunately, he's referring to the fans at Wrigley Field.

10. "I know your work. I don't respect it, but I know it."—New York public relations man, to Keith, 1983. The feeling was mutual.

GOOD GRIEF, WE'RE FAMOUS, SORT OF, PART-TIME

It was a big event in my hometown.

It's not a barren place. We have electricity. We have sewers. We even have the occasional sidewalk. But it's still the wilds of Connecticut, half an hour outside of Hartford. My front door is the halfway point of a long four-hour drive from Times Square in New York to Copley Square in Boston. So when a national franchise chain opens a new restaurant in the center of town, it's news. The first Friday the place was open, my friends Tony Bruno and Beth Faber from the radio network and I decide to go eat there. And we're welcomed with open arms. "It's nice to see you here, Mr. Olbermann. We'll be happy to serve you. The wait will only be seventy minutes."

Keith's not complaining about the service. He's pointing out the odd fact that ESPN, "the Worldwide Leader in Sports," is located in the least media-conscious place on the East Coast. We're protected, and also isolated, from what is commonly referred to as "fame."

Sure, occasionally some restaurant hostess will shave ten minutes off the wait. We get an autograph request now and then at a Hartford Whaler game. But I can walk the streets of my hometown all day and never get a hello or a look from anybody I don't know

93

personally. Just like you. I consider it a blessing. But it's a blessing like the weather was when I lived in Los Angeles. It's terrific until you take a trip to New York in February. All of a sudden you have no defense against the cold, or, in this case, the fact that a million people or so see us on TV every night. We're not complaining about either truth—people who watch the show almost invariably say nice things (well, nobody's ever hit either of us with an egg), and also it's nice to have a place to hide. But when we're outside of this little cocoon of ordinary workaday life, it's a shock. People actually **watch**? They know who we **are**? We're—gulp—**well known**? You wanted to read . . . a **book** . . . about **us**?

Why?

The point of this chapter is that we don't want you to think we're boasting about all this. Don't get me wrong. Dan and I worked very hard to get here, and we work very hard to do the show right, and we think we do it as well as it can be done. Just to assume somebody's going to listen to what you say on television requires an ego as big as all outdoors—but an ego about how you do your **job,** not **who** you are. Professional pride does not make you think of yourself as a celebrity, even with a small "c." Everything we wanted to tell you here is written with a sense of—there's no other word for it—shock.

We were sitting in Keith's dining room going over this stuff, and every once in a while we'd remember something that happened—even four and five years ago—and we'd just stare and then laugh and find ourselves not believing it actually happened. A couple of years ago, I was trying to get ahold of Jerry Seinfield for The Sunday Conversation and I got ahold of a number for him and I left a message and just figured, ''I won't hold my breath waiting for the callback—like he knows who I am.'' And while we were on the air that night, he called back and left a message, which was enough of a shock, and then I called him and he said, ''I want you to know that I've been ripping you off for the last year. Every time I leave our set I say, 'As Dan Patrick would say—I'm **gone.**' '' And that was the first time it truly dawned on me that we were reaching a little bit more of an audience than just the average rotisserie sports fan.

OK. Impressive, but this man is our contemporary. I mean, I knew Jerry Seinfeld in Los Angeles when he was a comic you'd see once in a while on talk shows. I used to see him in the parking lot of the Hughes' Supermarket at Beverley and Doheny doing bits for his friends. Given our ages, I'm much more impressed by the ongoing relationship you have with Bill Murray . . .

Yeah, but Bill's a die-hard sports fan.

But this guy **we** saw in our formative, drunken, college years on *Saturday Night Live* or in *Caddyshack*. This is a generational thing. This is Carl Spackler telling us *we're* almost cool. Where does this Murray thing come from?

The Sunday Conversation. How to win friends and influence people. I had arranged a meeting with him in New York, and he showed up forty-five minutes late, and he was very funny, he was "on," and then we started to do the interview. He couldn't get focused, he kept blowing everything as far as the lines, he was out of control, he had to just be goofy. And finally, just to get him to be quiet, I gave him a putter, and he was putting a golf ball around while we were doing the conversation—and it was the only time I could get him to give straight answers.

And since then, he calls. He calls all the time now. He leaves messages. He notices every little thing in the show. He is **the** true sports fan, who wants justice served. If you're saying something wrong, he'll complain. Gary Miller criticized Darryl Strawberry once, saying he was playing in this minor-league game, minor-league team, no pitching in the league, and he hits "X" amount of home runs—well Bill calls me to tell Gary that if Darryl was hitting crappy pitching in Minnesota, was he hitting crappy pitching in Columbus, and was he now hitting crappy pitching in New York?

Wait. Wasn't Bill a part owner of the team Darryl had been playing for in Minnesota?

Yeah, but that's a small thing.

Small thing? Part owner of the franchise calls up to complain and he's a true sports fan. I get calls from full owners all the time! I've got a handwritten note from Bud Selig from when he stopped by ESPN one day saying he was sorry he missed me because he'd hoped he'd get a chance to "defend himself" to me—and you don't see **me** holding Bud Selig's hand at the ESPYs!

There's always next year.

And it's not like I **planned** that hand-holding thing with Bill. Let me explain that.

Your wife and children and America are waiting.

At the ESPYs in 1996, we conned Bill into being onstage one more time. He didn't want to do it, but he said he'd do it one more time—**if** I went on with him. So we get there for rehearsal: Bill doesn't show up. They call me in a panic. Like I was keeping him in my motel room or something. Finally, half an hour before you and I are supposed to go on the air with the "pregame show," I get the call: Bill's arrived, we have to do a rehearsal. I get there and Bill is just goofing around and he just doesn't know what he's going to do out there on the stage. More than that, he doesn't even want to **talk** about what we're going to do out there—he wants to talk about everything else. So finally I say to him, Bill, we're going to be interviewing Michael Jordan **live** and we have to give him the comeback player of the year award and we have to kind of plan this out. And Bill's answer is, "Yeah, yeah. Let's get something to drink."

So we're getting something to drink and I ask him again and he says, "I'll bring it up next time." And I say, "You don't know what we're gonna do up there, do you?" and he says, "No, but as soon as I figure it out, I'll let you know." This is literally five minutes before we go on, and the Alan Jackson band is up there and we're on right **after** the Alan Jackson band. So now I try it this way. "Bill, could you just clue me in on what you want to ask Michael?" And now he says, "C'mon, let's walk." And we walked for about two hundred feet, and he pushes open this door, and I see this plume of smoke coming up—and we're in David Letterman's dressing room.

And I'm thinking, "Oh, my God." I'm a big Letterman fan. I'm also onstage with Bill Murray and Michael Jordan in three minutes and I have no idea what we're going to do. And Bill wants me to meet David Letterman.

Not later. Not after your bit. Right then.

Right then. And Bill says, "David, this is Dan Patrick." And Letterman says, "Dan—big fan. Bill! You know this thing about golf? Why do I have to **putt**? It took me that long to get to the green, why do I then have to putt? I mean, I shot a 135. Dan? What's ESPN3? Is that, like, live televised random drug testing?" So all of a sudden I'm the straight man in a Bill Murray–David Letterman routine and I say to Dave "No. It's **not.** Bill! The song's **ending.** What are we doing with Michael Jordan?" Bill looks at Dave and just shrugs and Bill and I walk out to the stage and as we're being introduced Bill says, "I'm just going to grab your hand and follow along."

(photo by Anita and Steve Shevett)

Oh, **I** see. Bill wasn't doing **anything** with Michael Jordan. **You** were.

This is what is dawning on me as we walk out onto the stage at Radio City Music Hall and Bill Murray is grabbing my hand. And we get through it somehow, even though Bill asks Michael if he thinks it's fair that **he** got the comeback award when Monica Seles got **stabbed** and **she** didn't win it. And we walk offstage and Bill says, "Now you know what it was like to be on *Saturday Night Live!*" and I told him I never wanted to go through that again in my life. And he got the biggest kick because he loved doing it that way, and he loved putting **me** through it.

Which is the theme of all of our brushes with genuine celebrities. They want me to coach first base against the Twins in an exhibition game. They want to see me hit by a line drive. They want me to coach the Connecticut women's basketball team in a scrimmage just to see how funny I look in a suit on a bench. But apropos of what happened with you meeting Letterman. *The Today Show* asked me to come in one morning to be the sports guy for their "Year in Review" segment. And that meant, basically, no sleep and a two-hour dash in a car to Manhattan after one of our shows. And after I get done with my bit with Bryant Gumbel, one of the NBC pages says, "You know, if you want to stick around, Letterman's coming over to tape some stuff with Bryant, if you want to meet him." So I can't resist—he's been to ESPN several times to watch his beloved Formula One races but always at times when I haven't been there, so I've never met him. And for me, this is another Bill Murray thing. This is a guy with the staying power of Winston Churchill, for crying out loud. He's been doing his show since I was such a novice that I was overjoyed to get a raise to $26,000 a year. Not our contemporary. Not Hootie & The Blowfish. Not Seinfeld. Jesus with a cigar, maybe.

So a little after nine, Dave is pacing up and down in one of the alcoves next to the set, furiously smoking his cigar in the hermetically sealed, no-smoking bastion of Rockefeller Center. And I can't resist. I go over to him and I say, "Excuse me, David, could you come back to ESPN and smoke your cigar in **our** hallway so I can smoke **my** cigar in **our** hallway?" And he looks up and gives me the big smile and says, "Keith? What the hell are **you** doing here?" And I just answered him straight, I was on with Gumbel doing the year-in-review stuff, and he says, "Nah, nah. You're just making that up to impress me." And I was too frozen to say "Why would **that** impress you?" I'm just thinking about my anonymity relative to this guy, and now he starts talking about how good the show is, and how often he watches, and now I'm getting frightened by the whole process that somehow, someway, we caught up close enough in some kind of race that David Letterman has some idea who I am and what I do and he actually seems impressed to meet me. And as big an egotist as I am, I'm still amazed by all this stuff.

At the Super Bowl in Tampa, my wife and I were walking through the back of the hotel. And there were about thirty fans there and they started yelling catchphrases and stuff, and if you don't know the catchphrases, which my wife doesn't, really, these guys sounded like the start of a mob, like the folks who pull people out of cabs and leave them standing there in their underwear or something. And my wife is concerned, and she says, "What are they **saying**?" And I say, "It's just stuff I say on the show . . ."

In your other life. Blowing your cover to her that you really work at Home Depot.

Exactly. And all these guys wanted to do was come up and ask me if I thought the backup center for the Bills had a chance to be an all-pro in 1999 or something. But she didn't know that. So there are these little flashes of contact that can floor you or the people you're with.

Last spring, I'm in Chicago at a bar in Wrigleyville meeting some friends, and the place is absolutely packed, wall-to-wall guys, and I'm trying to wend my way through the crowd looking for my friends. And all of a sudden, maybe forty of these people in the bar recognize me, all at once. You can see the lightbulbs going off over their heads. And they all take one half step toward me. And if they had taken a **full** step toward me I'd have been crushed. And nobody means any harm, and it's really nothing to worry about. But then you start thinking what happens to **real** celebrities when it isn't thirty fans at the Super Bowl or forty guys in a bar, but three **thousand** people and they all take a half step toward you. I mean, coming out of Yankee Stadium last year I stopped to sign an autograph and out of nowhere there was this swarm of people around me . . .

Half of them thought you were Jim Leyritz.

No, half of them thought my autograph could be resold. But the point is, it gives you just enough of a glimpse of what life is like for the **real** celebrities that you can't help but be a little more sympathetic to them and how much of their lives are lost—just gone—because they're so recognizable in public.

I'm still amazed that anybody ever asks for an autograph. Or when they ask. I'm at the Super Bowl three years ago, and at halftime I go into the men's room, and the guy standing next to me—at least trying to stand—looks over, looks away, looks over, looks away, looks over . . .

Where are you going with this? Do I really want to hear this, Dan?

Relax. We're both doing what you're supposed to be doing at a urinal, and finally this guy says to me, "Hey, you're one of them *Sports-Center* dudes, aren't you?" And then he turns to me—still doing what you're supposed to be doing at a urinal—and says, "Dah dah dah, dah dah dah." So I tried my best to not Lorena Bobbitt myself jumping out of the way of this guy.

Did you give him an autograph?

No, but he nearly gave me his, if you know what I mean.

Rim shot, please.

The other time was when my first daughter was born. There was the doctor, two nurses, and an intern. Well, the intern had been dying to talk sports with me, but he really couldn't find the opportune time where you're going to be talking about the New England Patriots in between contractions. Finally the doctor says to my wife, "You can start pushing now, your baby's ready to be born." So my wife is getting ready to deliver my daughter. And **now** this intern leans over to me and he whispers, "Dah dah dah, dah dah dah—I guess this is your *Sports Center* moment." Fortunately my wife didn't hear him. I would have hated to read the headline: "Wife of *SportsCenter* Anchor Gives Birth, Then Kills Intern."

I have no story like that. As Hawkeye Pierce said, "I'm still my only child." But the one that still floors me is the *TV Guide* phone call. Remember?

I thought—honestly—it was a joke.

We got this call from our public relations guy at ESPN, Rob Tobias, just before Christmas in '95, and he said, "*TV Guide* wants to talk to the two of you together," and I thought, that's nice, they're going to put a little thing in there. "Dan and Keith are a little bit better than watching the Prevue Channel, or Dan and Keith combined are half as good as one Jim McKay. But not in his prime." Something like this.

And this guy gets on the phone and he starts out by saying "Congratulations."

And I said, "Dan! We got free subscriptions! Wow!" And then it was "congratulations for what?" and the *TV Guide* guy says, "Didn't they tell you? You're in our Top Ten for 1995."

I thought he meant the Top Ten from ESPN.

Here are the top nine TV stars and, as a bonus, these two idiots selected randomly from among everybody else in the country. At least we were among forty in *People* last year.

Closer to a "Where's Waldo" thing.

Dan and Keith in the guest appearance in a Hootie & The Blowfish video. *(photo by Patrick Flynn)*

But I am still surprised Helen Hunt hasn't sued us for cheapening her honor as the top person in their poll. And what the hell were we doing in a music video? They'd finally run out of scantily clad women?

That still amazes me. Hootie & The Blowfish asked for us, and Chris, and Charley Steiner, and Mike Tirico. And the next thing I know, the video's out and it's a couple of months later and we're at the ESPYs and their lead singer, Darius Rucker, comes up to me and says, "To hell with Bill Murray! We sold thirteen million albums—why aren't you hanging out with us? If you cared about us, you would go to Europe with us to start our tour in April. If you cared about us, you'd go with us for a week." So I begin to think: I turn forty in May. This is my fortieth birthday present. So I showed up in Dublin, and I spent a week on the road with those guys, and played golf, and they let me onstage, and they would let me play whatever instrument I wanted to. They didn't care. They would have let me sing.

Oh, that would've been good. "Irish Hootie Fans Boo 'Singer'; Trash Arena."

But they are die-hard sports fans and their drummer, Sony, I went to his wedding. And they would readily trade jobs with us. And I said, "Let's go."

I had Darius on the radio network once and I said that was great, but who would show up to a "Dan & The Blowfish" concert.

Two or three of them were comm arts majors in colleges. Darius really wanted to do this. I suggested to him he's better off the way things are.

This stuff outside of the sports world is silly enough but the things that the ballplayers themselves do to us is just amazing. I can still remember the day you called in from the NBA Finals about Jordan. And you were so not yourself. You were so uncool. I got to hear what you sounded like when you were fourteen.

Yep. 1993. He had this media embargo going. He was not going to talk to anybody. So, we went to the practice that day, and there were probably sixty to seventy media members there, and all the camera crews, and just before the Bulls practiced, everybody descended on Michael— and he just waved everybody off. I stayed away, because John Paxson had told me Michael just wasn't going to say anything. I stayed all the way to the side of the court just to avoid this mess. But the reporters kept pushing toward Michael, and Michael kept walking, walking, walking; the next thing I know, he's standing right next to me. He looks down at me and smiles and says, "Dan Patrick? How are you?" Well, that's the **only** thing he said all day. And of course, by accident, my camera crew was recording it. And that was my exclusive with Michael Jordan.

And we **ran** it.

"Michael says hi to Dan"—film at eleven!

Defining television news in the process. Doesn't matter **what** he said. He said it to Dan. It's a story.

Last year, he actually said to me, "When you show up, I win titles. That's why I'm doing interviews with you after games."

But it's worse, isn't it? On Monday mornings, he and Pippen

and Harper and a couple of the other guys blow off an hour of practice and sit there and watch The Big Show.

The other Bulls call them "The *SportsCenter* club." It's phenomenal. It's like we live in a cordoned-off city here in Connecticut and these guys, the real stars, are much more impressed with us than we are.

When there were still Cleveland Browns, and Bill Belichick was still the coach, I ran into him at a banquet in Washington and I'm about to introduce myself and he beats me to it. And he says, "Unless we're still in the air flying back from a game, I always watch you and Dan on Sunday night," and I thank him and I start to ask him something about the Dawg Pound and he interrupts me. "And then I wake up at six on Monday morning and I watch you again. And then when I'm on the treadmill at eight I watch the show again. And then I drive into the office and I do a little work. And then at ten I call a meeting with my coordinators and **we** watch you. And then at noon I have the whole coaching staff in for lunch and everybody watches you." And I ask him if he isn't a little bored of this stuff by now, and he says, "No, no, it's like watching game films—of everybody, all at once. Besides which, by noon I know when all the good jokes are coming and I can beat you to the punch line."

But **you** don't get this stuff at games. I get to go out and cover stuff more often and they don't just want to talk. They want to make me perform. Like Dan Majerle when he was with the Suns.

Here I must point out, Dear Reader, that my tag-team partner firmly believes that were it not for his knees, he would have been one of the great athletes of all time. Inducted, by now, to the Basketball Hall of Fame. Me, I played catch with Joe Magrane in spring training one year, and he had the human decency not to tell anybody that I throw like a girl, and that's as close as I'm ever going to get. I got to be Bill Robinson's assistant manager for the Reading Phillies of the Eastern League one game, and I got thrown out of it by the home plate ump, I got run by Harry Wendelstedt's son Hunter, so I'm one for one. Thrown out of my only professional baseball game. A record that can never be broken. But that's it. You—you think you're going to stop by the Seattle Supersonics shoot-around one game and get signed to a ten-day contract.

That'll happen. Early in the '92–'93 season, the Suns had been in

Hartford to play the Celtics, and I had gone to see the game and Dan Majerle came over beforehand and he asked me if I wanted to come out and shoot. And he and Cedric Ceballos and I shot three-pointers for fifteen minutes. Majerle beat me, but I beat Ceballos. So I kept saying, "I need a rematch."

So eight months later at the finals, the Bulls have already practiced and the Suns are just ready to get started. And I see Majerle taking some money from his teammate Frank Johnson, and it turns out he's been taking money from everybody in three-point shooting contests. And I'm in my full suit and tie and dress shoes and Majerle says, "Do you want a piece of me now?" In front of everybody on the team. "Do you want a piece of me now?" In front of Dr. Jack Ramsay, who is as respected in basketball as anybody is in any sport. Now **Jack** says, "Go ahead." And I say, "Well, I've got my suit and tie on . . ." And Jack cuts me off. He says it just like he does on the air: "Dan, great shooters can shoot no matter what they have on." Then Paul Westphal, the Phoenix coach at the time, says if I want to shoot against Majerle, he'll **hold up practice** and the whole team will just watch.

You are out of options here, Dan.

No choice. I give Dr. Jack my coat and I loosen my tie and I tell Majerle he has to give me ten shots to warm up, and he says, "You get **five.**" So I shoot my five, and Majerle offers to let me go first, and I tell him, no, you go first. So Majerle makes eight out of fifteen. My turn: I make seven out of fourteen, and before the fifteenth he says, "If you make it, you tie, and nobody cares. If you **bank** it, it counts as two, you win. What's your decision?"

But to be fair, you didn't have anything to lose at that point. You had already hit seven, so even if you lost, you lost by one basket to one of the top professionals, and anyway, you have these horrible, crippling knee injuries. You have **five** knees and they're all hollow, you can keep your change in them, you're Joe Namath and Tony Oliva rolled into one. Holes in your knees like the gaps in the parquet floor at Boston Garden. So you've got an age factor going, you've got a comparatively out-of-shape factor going, you've got a shirt-and-tie factor going, you've got an amateur versus the pro factor going—you've already **won** this.

You see through all this. Majerle didn't. I didn't want to **tie** Majerle, but you're right. Nothing to lose. So I went for it. I went for the gusto.

And I bank it in. And Charles Barkley erupts, gets right into Majerle's face and says it's the greatest thing he's ever seen. And I'll always have this on Dan Majerle. Majerle called it the most devastating moment of his career. Every time I see him, I remind him. So the next guy I take on is probably Deion. I can score a touchdown on him. If my knees were good . . .

Before you get to outrunning Michael Johnson, don't forget the punch line on the Majerle story.

The next night Majerle goes out and sets an NBA Finals record with eight three-pointers.

The only thing I have on you is that all your stuff happened in practice. I've got the day I coached at UConn. Coached the unde-feated defending national women's champs in their first in-uniform game the following year.

This is going to be like the *Penthouse* Forum now, isn't it? "I never thought this would happen to me . . ."

Oh, very nice. Well, I did get to go in the locker room at half-time. And I told them I'd never had players do such a uniformly lousy job in any game I'd ever coached, and the women were all gracious enough to laugh. But what an education, to sit there on the bench and watch from that angle. The women's game may not be the same as the men's, but it's just as fast. Get some distance from it and you can see the strategy. This pick is designed to send this player to that spot, and this player cuts to get that pass right over here. But on the bench, ten inches from the court, it's like watching a bunch of wild horses run past you one way, and then turn around and run past you the other. Jen Rizzotti—who is as amazing a ballhandler and as tough a player as any guy—was on my team for part of this scrimmage and I told her, "You've heard of the expression 'I want you to be a kind of coach on the floor'? Forget the 'kinda' part. You be the coach. If you see me do anything, if you see me make any kind of gesture, just ignore me." And Sarah Northway, a fine player and a strikingly beautiful woman with a great sense of humor, says, "Just like our regular games with Coach."

That was the best part. At halftime the **real** coach, Geno Auriemma, takes me into his office next to the locker room and he explains how he plays with their heads. "If we've had a good first half, I only wait a couple of minutes in here and then I go right in and talk to them for thirty seconds and that's it. But if they've been sluggish, I yell a couple of times and then go in. And if we're losing, or they're just not doing it right, I use props.'' And at this point, his chief assistant, Chris Dailey, hands him a tray, and he wings it against the wall that adjoins the locker room. And Auriemma says, ''And when I'm **really** ticked off I'll stand right next to this wall and scream and pound on it.''

So I didn't do any actual coaching, of course. I sat there and looked good. I mean, I looked as legitimate as Pat Riley out there. I made all the faces at the refs and I folded my arms at the right time and they get these fantastic pictures of me—and all I was actually doing was sitting there in amazement as these wild horses ran up and down the court. Of course, I did call a time-out that still rings through the rafters of Gampel Pavilion.

And nobody was injured.

Well, I hurt my uvula calling that time-out. But I continue to do my rehab.

I have a history with women's hoops. I was in Dallas last year, and Nancy Lieberman Cline, one of the greats, saw me and said, ''You're always talking trash about how great you are. Let's see what you can do.'' And Ken Norton Jr. was there playing hoops with a big crowd of guys and I said, ''Nance, I don't want to embarrass you.'' She says, ''C'mon, we'll play to five.'' So she's dribbling, I steal the ball, I shoot a jumper, I make the jumper, and she mutters, ''God damn it!'' And now I say, ''Nancy, I will kick your ass.'' Well, she comes in, misses her shot; I got it back, made my shot, and it's 2–0 and I said, ''Nance, I don't want to embarrass you'' and she said, ''OK, we'll pick this up some other time.''

Little did she know that I was out of breath. I couldn't continue, let alone make another shot.

You had gone to that ''I don't want to embarrass you'' one time to many. But this was a bluff game you were playing with her. This was poker.

Exactly.

The rest of it would have been the wild horses running up and down the court past you.

Correct. She is truly a great player. But I knew, for five minutes, I could kick her ass. I'm a **great** five-minute player.

Six minutes?

Dead. Stretcher time. Of course, I can last longer in golf.

I was wondering when we'd get to Pebble Beach.

I was at the Super Bowl, in Phoenix, and I get a call from Bill Murray. "Dan, I just talked to your boss. It's OK. You can have next week off. Why don't you come out and play in the Pro-Am with me at Pebble Beach. Do you have your golf clubs? Do you have long pants? Do you have clean underwear? I'll pay your entry fee." So I told Bill I didn't want to hurt anybody, I was afraid I'd kill somebody. And he talks me into it, so now all I have to do is convince my wife. And she says, "Do you **have** to play?" and I tell her, "I'd hurt Bill's feelings if I didn't."

Now you're playing poker with your **wife.** It's "I don't want to embarrass you, Nancy" time again.

So I go out to Pebble, and I'm not in my element. Pro golfers are pro golfers, and I'm an amateur, and I'm not very good. And I show up, and Bill says, "Don't worry, you're going to have a good time." And I'm **not** having a good time. I'm just scared to death. The first thing they ask me for when I go into the players' tent is my insurance policy number. "That's not a good **sign,** Bill," and he says not to worry about it. So I'm about to tee off on the opening round and I'm telling people on the left side of the fairway to back up, get out of the way. So they announce my name, and all of a sudden, I turn around and I see Arnold Palmer racing down to the tee. And now I'm thinking, "This is **great.** Arnold Palmer is going to welcome me to Pebble Beach!"

Now the crowd's getting excited, because it's somebody they care about. Arnie comes down and he's got his driver in his hand, and I'm ready to swing, and I stop. And Arnie says, "Am I on this tee?" and I said "No, you're not." And the marshal says, "Arnie, you're on another **course** today." And Arnie swears, and turns around, and takes off. Well, (a) I am interrupted, not sure where I am or what I'm doing or what I should be doing, and now (b) the crowd is **against** me because they think I'm the reason Arnie isn't teeing off. So of course, I hit the ball into the gallery on the left side.

So you're thinking 115. Instead, you have this marvelous round, you shoot an 89, and then you turn *SportsCenter* on that night . . .

And I got crushed.

Brutalized. And it's still the last remaining point of contention between us. We've resolved all of our other issues. And you still think it was some sort of deliberate attempt to mock you. Rather than thinking that we spent two minutes on our show showing you playing at Pebble Beach . . .

You **could** have shown the good highlights.

I **did** show the good highlights.

No, you **edited** highlights. "Here's Dan hitting into the ocean. Dan hitting into the trees!"

Well, we did do that. We took good highlights and made them bad highlights. You're right about that.

I played very well. While I was scared to death.

And we pointed that out. Admittedly only briefly.

And I was thinking, of all the people who will be on my side—there's you. And I tune in and I'm thinking, "What did he do? Why did my friend do this to me?"

Don't you see? You **ruined** it by playing well. We **needed** you to play badly. The **audience** needed you to play badly, because ultimately, if you had to pick one reason that we appeal in some way to the viewer, it's that we appear to be . . .

Drunk.

Drunken visionaries. From the future. No. We appear to be somewhere within the spectrum defining the average sports fan. And one of us sports fans might **dream** of going out to Pebble Beach and shooting an 89. But we can't actually **go and do it!** That ruins the whole thing. I mean, once we finished with all the mocked-up shots of you hitting a seal or losing your ball in a submarine, we put up that graphic that showed how you did better than a bunch of pros, and how many pars you had, but of course by that point you'd already switched over to CNN *Sports Tonight*.

I was watching Nick and Fred. They were showing better highlights of me.

Well, they had a better satellite feed. But you got me back.

The night you coached first base against the Twins. Very witty remarks about how it was too bad they couldn't find a uniform to fit you, and what the "paunch line" was to the joke you were telling the first base umpire.

But seriously, you know I had that same feeling you did at Pebble. Of having absolutely no business being there. I wanted to apologize to Kirby Puckett. Hell, I wanted to apologize to Scott Stahoviak. Like I had crossed some imaginary line, like Burt Lancaster in *Field of Dreams*. Players—over here. Sportscasters—stay well behind the yellow line, please. Hell, I couldn't coach first base in **high school.** My playing career in high school was getting put in as a pinch hitter for one game and getting hit in the ass with a pitch.

It's as uncomfortable a feeling as when we interview them, I guess. A good learning experience, a good reminder to try to make these guys feel a little more at home. I mean, I have even greater admiration for professional athletes than I did before. Very useful walk-a-mile-in-my-shoes lesson.

OK, what else? What other stupid things have we done?

I dunked at a UMass practice once.

I got banned for a season by the Los Angeles Clippers.

Bet that hurt. Made you the envy of every reporter in the business. I hit grounders to John Kruk at the 1993 World Series.

I'm in a song lyric. Group called "Throneberry." "We'll watch ESPN—with Keith Olbermann."

I was mentioned in a line of dialogue on *Beverly Hills 90210.* "Who do you think you are, Dan Patrick?"

I interviewed Paulina Porizkova on CNN when she was the cover of the *Sports Illustrated* swimsuit issue, and then went and had drinks with her.

I interviewed Elle MacPherson on CNN when she was the cover of the *Sports Illustrated* swimsuit issue, and then went and danced with her.

This was before you met your wife.

Thank you.

But back to can-you-top-this. I wrote the backs for three sets of baseball cards.

I'm **on** my own baseball card.

I was in a movie. Played a golf announcer, of all things. *Dead Solid Perfect*. Randy Quaid, Jack Warden, Katherine Herrold, Mac O'Grady, Peter Jacobson, Me.

I **caddied** for Peter Jacobson in the par-three at the Masters. And all his clubs fell out of his bag when I picked it up wrong.

Advantage, Dan. I give up. You've gotten to do more neat stuff than me. But I ruined your big homecoming! Remember Midnight Madness at Dayton? You just cannot leave me back in the office to sweat it out while you go out in pursuit of admiration.

We're kicking off the Dayton Flyers season, and I'm the guest emcee. Obviously they couldn't get Jim Paxson or Johnny Davis or Donnie May. I'm figuring, "I'm back home! Love me fans! Love me!" And as soon as I get out there, five thousand people in the stands suddenly hold up Keith Olbermann masks right in front of their faces. And I was like dumbfounded when I saw it. He got me again.

It wasn't my idea. I was a very willing participant, officer, but it was not my idea. But you're always ready to seek revenge. Eric Lindros at the ESPYs. You set me up to have my flipping brains beaten in.

For various reasons, I am out there at games more than you are. So if you say something that ticks somebody off, I hear about it. In person. I've taken the heat for you, I have taken the fall for you. So I see John LeClair and Eric Lindros of the Philadelphia Flyers standing at the bar after the ESPYs and LeClair says, "Hey, the guy you work with is just beating up on my boy."

It was nothing bad, really. He had missed a bunch of games with some nagging injuries and we had a shot of him looking at his hand and I said, "Eric Lindros examines the hangnail that'll probably keep him out for three weeks." And when he finally did play two consecutive games, I said, "Lindros is now just 2,128 games behind Lou Gehrig's streak."

So I said to Lindros, "You want to get back at him? Go up to him and say, 'Look, you say anything more about my injuries, I'll kick your ass.'" And LeClair says, "Yeah, yeah, you should," and Lindros says, "Well, maybe I shouldn't. I don't really know this guy." I said, "Hey! You say to him 'I'm gonna kick your ass.' I want to see how he reacts to it. He's never there to back it up. I'm always out in the public. I meet you guys. You vent towards me." And then Eric says, "All right, all right, I'll do it."

I didn't see it when you finally met him. Next thing I know you two are arm-in-arm leaving the party to go to some after-hours club. I can't win.

Well, I went over to the bar to say hi to Geno Auriemma and there's Lindros and he looks at me and raises his hand and says, "Look, Keith, no hangnails," and I laugh like hell and he laughs like hell and the next thing I know he's buying me a beer. And then he goes to the bathroom or something and LeClair grabs me by the arm and he says, "Your partner was over here trying to get Eric to take a shot at you. So we told him we would. But Eric's not mad at you and I'm sure as hell not. Hell, I should be saying 'thank you.' " And now I'm really confused. So LeClair says, "He really didn't know the difference between injuries that hurt that you play through, and injuries that can get worse if you continue to play. And he saw what you said about him and he started thinking he was getting a reputation for being soft. So: thanks. You're an honorary member of the Legion of Doom."

Damn.

No, **doom.** Well, Lindros comes back and we start talking and we just hit it off. And remember, in Canada, when this guy was ten years old people were already comparing him to Gordie Howe. But he says to me, "You know the only thing I wanted to do? I just hoped that maybe, maybe I'd be able to make a million dollars." And I looked at him and I could see it in his eyes and I said, "For your whole career." And that's what he'd meant. Everybody else had these expectations about him and he was just hoping to play seven or eight years and make a **total** of a million dollars. Now this reminds me all of a sudden of myself . . .

And your partner.

And my partner. So I'm seeing this guy in a totally different light now. I'm seeing **all** athletes in a totally different light now. And we keep talking, and talking, and eventually he and LeClair and Dan Quinn shanghai me and take me to this bar in their limo and Lindros can't stop talking about what a hero Mark Messier of the Rangers is to him. So who's the first person we see when we get to this place? Messier. And you had another chance to get my head bashed in for me.

You have made certain unkind comments about Messier's hair. Or lack thereof.

I have suggested his hair is "close cropped." I once had a shot of him holding the League Presidents' Trophy and I said he'd just won the award for having the closest cropped hair in the NHL. So now I'm figuring, I've dodged one bullet with Lindros—this one has my name on it. Mark Messier is going to tune me up.

And Lindros takes me over to him and he **bows** and calls him "Jesus," and he begins to introduce me and Messier interrupts him.

"Oh, I know this guy!" and he raises his hand and I know I'm going to get clocked. And instead he rubs his hand across his head and says, "Close cropped, eh? What it is is, I'm bald, is what it is!" And I start to apologize and he laughs—and he has a classic, head-tilting all-the-way-back laugh—and he says, "Close cropped is a compliment!"

I am outraged.

So the evening wears on, and hockey players are the most convivial people in the world. Lindros hands me a beer. Messier hands me a beer. Quinn hands me a beer. I've got so many bottles cradled in my arms, I have to start handing them out to passersby. Lindros comes back with eight cigars he's found somewhere and starts passing them out. LeClair takes me over to some women and introduces me as "the greatest writer in television." It's beyond belief. And now it's pushing four in the morning and these guys have practice in seven hours—in **Philadelphia**—and LeClair starts rounding them up for the ride home. And Lindros begins to shout about how happy he is he won the hockey ESPY.

Guy won the Hart Trophy as MVP at age twenty-two and he's excited about the ESPY.

Exactly. So he starts to stand up, and he's a little unsteady, and he knocks over his own chair as he does. So he reaches for another chair, and that one goes down, too. And now he starts to get up on the table to dance. And LeClair shouts at him, "What are you doing, you big baboon? That'll never hold your weight, you tub of lard!" And Lindros gets no further than planting the edge of one shoe on the table and he stops and says, "Oh, Johnny, what am I thinking? I've had one too many tonight. Let's get the hell home." And he walks over to me and gives me a hug, and LeClair gives me a hug, and I'm figuring I've got four broken ribs.

And the point of telling this love fest is what, exactly?

The point is that two days later, on the gossip page of the *New York Post*, there's a picture of Lindros and a story that reads that "to the horror of revelers including Tim Robbins, Mark Messier, and Herbie Hancock, Lindros started kicking around chairs and eventually jumped up on top of a table for a victory dance. When the stogie-chomping skater refused to get down, security escorted him to the big penalty box outside." And **that's** the point of this story. I

Keith interviewing hockey legend Gordie Howe. Gordie would soon show Keith the finer points of the crosscheck. *(photo by Scott Clarke)*

was furious. I **saw** this. Tim Robbins left right after we got there. If Herbie Hancock was there he was invisible. Messier stayed an hour after the Flyer guys left! And I saw Lindros accidentally knock over a couple of chairs, start to get up on a table and then realize how stupid it was, and leave of his own accord. And I thought of all the stories we see on the wire services or in the newspapers that are simply distortions of what happened, and I swear, I have never read one on the air since in which I presumed the athlete was in the wrong.

And I thought, it's very nice to be famous, sort of, part-time.

Amen.

HOW TO BE A SPORTSCASTER WHEN YOU GROW UP

Every American male, and thankfully now every American **female**, realizes at some date that he or she is not going to become, or not going to remain, a professional athlete. I figured it out at age eight, after one beanball, and one good look at softball immortal Eddie Feigner striking out every one of my teachers. Dan?

I had a pretty good idea when I was twelve; I knew it for certain at nineteen, about the time I discovered I could make a sound like popcorn popping with my knee.

But there does not appear to be a similar moment of epiphany about the subject of becoming a sports broadcaster. Between us we get at least a dozen letters a week from would-be colleagues—the youngest was probably writing a letter for the first time; the oldest was a bank vice president. The job, from a distance, looks ideal: a paid vacation of sorts, watching sports, going to games, meeting players, getting lots of money, getting fame. Like anything else, however, part of the job is making it look like it **isn't** a job. There is often sheer chaos unfolding in front of us and it's our job to smooth it over nicely, like the story of the notorious labor boss Jimmy Hoffa having been allegedly buried in the end zone at Giants Stadium. You

115

didn't see him get there, you didn't see him dumped there, you didn't see the concrete being poured—you only saw them celebrating the touchdown.

There is also the inevitable disillusionment. You can hold on to a few elements of your fandom—I still get all warm and gooey about memories of the Cincinnati Royals, and Keith still collects his baseball cards. But did you ever see the "Tank McNamara" comic strip? One storyline was of Tank's brother-in-law getting a job watching and logging games for an all-sports network. He couldn't wait for the job to begin. A week after being **forced** to watch games not just when he wanted to, not in front of his big screen at home with his feet up, not of only his favorite team or his favorite sport, not just in the early evening or on weekends but sometimes at 3:17 A.M. on Christmas morning—after a week of that, he was begging to go back to plumbing or cement work or whatever. It's just unavoidable—if you're lucky, as we've been, you can mutate from **a** fan of **a** sport or team into a kind of pan-fan, drawing enjoyment or entertainment out of a lot of different games and players, or at the very least enjoying the process.

But there are two appropriate food analogies here. One: As I said before, they say if you like sausage, never go to work in a sausage factory—once you've seen how they're made you'll never be able to eat one again. And, two: Maybe you like ice cream. Can you imagine being **paid** to eat ice cream for a living? Great. Every day? All day? Not just butter pecan but also that new experimental spinach-salsa crunch?

Trust you to come up with the food references.

Also, this is a very strange business. Full of strange people. Talented, sometimes visionary people. But still strange ones. You have to be prepared for weirdness.

And at all times! Not just in the beginning stages, either. I had been in TV for nearly four years when I went to Los Angeles to audition for KTLA Television in 1985. They asked me to write a script and then read it several different ways. With my horn-rimmed glasses, with wire-frame glasses, without my glasses. Oh yeah, and with and without my mustache. They asked me if I'd be willing to do three audition takes with the mustache, then shave it off, then do three more.

Are you serious? Did you do it?

I wasn't going to. Then the news director said, "We also want you to do the auditions wearing a blue jacket; it'll show up better against the background of our set." And I said I hadn't brought one with me. And he said, "We'll buy you one." And I thought, "Hmmm. I can grow the mustache back. I don't think I can grow a jacket." So I did it.

You still wear the jacket on the show, right?

Ha-ha. Wait, there's more to this. I got the job, and after a few months they let me grow the mustache back. So now, three years later, I'm going to change stations and work at KCBS. And I've decided I don't like the mustache after all—beginning a lifetime pattern of indecision about facial hair—so I shave. And my new boss calls me one day and he says, "Our research shows that people recognize you with the mustache and don't recognize you without it. Would you grow it back?" So from the KTLA audition I'm wise to the thing and I say, Gee, I'm really happier without it, and he says, "It would mean a lot to us," and I say, Gee, what about that signing bonus we talked about and he says, "You know, those two things could become connected."

He didn't!

He did. I got $25,000 to grow the mustache back and keep it for at least a year.

And you, of course, asked him how many mustaches he'd like at that price.

I told him I could grow one on my forehead and one from either ear, and I'd cut the price to $20,000 per.

How much for a Wolfman look?

Shut up.

Also, as we look back on our careers, there are uncountable breaks and circumstances without which somebody else would be writing this book. Moreover, there were men and women, as talented, as driven, often more so, who didn't get those breaks, or who didn't stay in the industry for whatever reason. The Big Show is also hardly representative of the industry as a whole. KO?

I broke in at United Press International's radio network a month after I graduated from Cornell in 1979. My starting salary was $8,870. This was for a national radio network, based in New York. Often on nights off I would take a dollar and a half and buy two subway tokens to go out to either Yankee or Shea Stadium or Madison Square Garden because the free meal and the entertainment allowed me to save about two bucks off the price of dinner at Burger King. And the one overriding thought in my mind at this time was that I had it **easy;** that somewhere there was that other equally talented guy working some horrible shift in some horrible place with absolutely no hope of getting anywhere unless something extraordinary happened.

That guy, of course, happened to be Dan.

I got out of the University of Dayton a week after Keith graduated from Cornell, and, like nearly every other communications arts student, I announced, "OK, where's my job?" Nobody wanted to hire me, and when I finally found employment months later, my first job was running the religious tapes on a rock-and-roll station. I'd get in there at 2:00 A.M. Sunday and till nine, I just sat there making sure the tape didn't break and the revealed word kept being revealed to the five listeners whose dials happened to be broken on our station. For six months, my entire on-air career consisted of saying, "You're listening to WTUE, Dayton's best rock and roll," every hour on the hour. The first two hundred or so times anybody ever heard me on professional radio, I said exactly the same thing—the station ID. Apart from the meager paycheck, the most practical value the job had was that it gave me a great line at parties. "What do I do? Why—I'm on radio. I work at T-U-E."

One blessed Sunday morning, as "Dayton's best rock and roll" station belted out the Mormon Tabernacle Choir, my boss tripped over me and asked me if I'd ever done news before. I said yes. I was lying. Oh, and did I ever pay for it. They put me on doing the morning drive newscasts, and the first name I ever had to pronounce in morning drive was the Ayatollah Khomeini. I turned it into something that sounded like the lyrics to that annoying "Macarena" song ("Aya yaya Tola Tola Coma Niney").

This, at about the same time I was announcing on UPI that USC had beaten Southern Cal. See, on the surface these grinds were different but at the core it was the same: bad hours, learn–as–you-go, hope the boss didn't hear the big mistake, and just enough money to know that you were just short of what you really needed. Moreover, that kind of grind wasn't limited to rookies like us—something else we got to discover firsthand on our first jobs. My first boss at UPI was a wonderful, eminently good-humored and generous man named Sam Rosen, who has graduated from a kind of living-in-a-blender existence to being the play-by-play man on television for the New York Rangers. But in 1979 and 1980, when I worked for him, Sam's **jobs** consisted of the following:

1. Sports director, United Press International Audio Department. Sam was responsible for administering a three-man staff. He sought out and booked "stringers" to cover every game in every city the network wanted postgame comments from. He had to make sure—every day—that the right games were covered and the stringers were all set. He had to make sure they got paid. He had to stay within a budget. He had to listen to tapes of would-be announcers.

He had to deal with **you.**

Correct. Me at the age of twenty, no less. He even had to share a room with me at the Olympics in Lake Placid. That was worth half his salary right there.

2. Those were just the off-air jobs. Sam was also **on** the air, on a radio network servicing a thousand stations nationwide. Sam wrote and announced four, live, two-minute sportscasts, one per hour, every morning, starting at 6:45 A.M. Before that, of course, he had to physically edit the audiotape fed in from the games the night before. **After** that he had to put together a three-and-a-half-minute feature on some athlete—edit the tape, write the thing, record it, hand the tape to an engineer. He also had to be the engineer for at least two of the network's hourly **newscasts.** While he was doing this, he'd make all his calls to his stringers and brief his afternoon sportscaster on what to expect. This generally had him working from 3:30 or so in the morning until noon, or 1:00, or 2:00 P.M. And if anybody got sick, he was the last line of defense to cover their shift. And if something big happened, he had to come **back** to the office at night to help cover it.

A month after I was hired by UPI, Thurman Munson was killed in that horrible private plane crash at the Canton–Akron airport in Ohio. I was the guy on duty when the story became known at 5:45 P.M. Eastern. By 7:00, Sam—who had worked his full shift that morning and had only left the office around 1:30—came back in to put together a special report on Munson's life, to dig up the home phone numbers for Lou Piniella and Roy White (I got to make the calls—boys, did I feel like human garbage) and to make all the arrangements for getting someone to cover the funeral, etc. Nobody **told** him to come back. This was an expected part of his job.

It is not surprising, therefore, that I once saw Sam fall asleep, standing up, an audiotape-editing razor blade in one hand, a cup of coffee in the other, as he played back one of his feature pieces to make sure it timed to exactly three minutes and thirty seconds.

Exhausting? Given up the idea of becoming a big-time sportscaster? Wait—there's more:

3. Sam was also backup play-by-play man for the Rangers on radio;
4. And on television;
5. And he was the backup play-by-play man for the Knicks on radio;
6. And he did fill-ins on the Saturday morning news broadcast on WNEW Radio in New York City;
7. And he was the regular Saturday **afternoon** newscaster on radio station WFAS in the New York suburb of Westchester County;
8. And he was the play-by-play announcer for the old soccer team, the New York Cosmos. Very often Sam would finish his sportscasting shift at UPI, hop a plane, and check in with me in the early evening from his broadcast booth somewhere in a North American Soccer League stadium (Me: "Where are you tonight, Sammy?" Sam: "Tulsa, Oklahoma. Nope. Edmonton. Sorry, Keith. Got confused.")
9. And he got hooked up with ESPN very early and did hockey for them and features and eventually he was doing the Thursday night fights for them, **driving** to Lancaster,

> Pennsylvania, then driving back just in time to go back to
> step one on the list; and
> 10. Sam was thought to be doing very well in this business.

Now, if you haven't already dismissed the idea of going into this business (hell, if you haven't run wretching to the bathroom yet), we are prepared to share with you rather a lot of thoughts about how to get into the business. The first one has to be that the earlier you make up your mind the better. It happens now and again that someone with a good voice, a keen interest in sports, and a lot of luck, wanders in from some other line of work at the age of thirty, but nine out of ten sportscasters at every level of this business **intended** to do this by the time they were in college. If you can tailor your education to match your intent, you have a tremendous leg up. Before we get into specific educational or vocational steps, let's look at what a would-be sportscaster's goals should be: perfecting as many of the following skills as possible. Extra strength in one area will often compensate for a weakness in one area, but not always:

First: Writing ability. We write and ad-lib 10,000–20,000 words a week. That's **each.** That's the equivalent of—we'll say it again—rewriting this book every five weeks or so. You have to write well. You have to write quickly. Even if you wind up doing play-by-play or talk radio, where writing is not a vital portion of the job, the mental skills honed by writing are essential.

Second: Knowledge of sports. Not just your favorite sport. Not just Michael Jordan. Not just today's stars. You have to know a little bit about everything, past and present, and in those areas you don't know, you have to know who to ask or where to look it up.

Third: Communication skills. You have to have a reasonably trained voice, no overwhelming accent, no major speech impediment, and the ability to read aloud. You do **not** need to be, whether male or female, gorgeous. You **do** need to avoid being very unpleasant looking (almost everybody can achieve this—even Keith has—most of the time).

Fourth: Interpersonal skills. Nobody does the job by himself. If you can't work with other people, forget it. I know. Dan's tried.

Look who's talking! Save that for the next book, huh, KO?

Fifth: Willingness to surrender many of the freedoms you expect in other lines of employment. Specifically, you need a willingness to put your career ahead of nearly anything else in your life, and, at times, to forget the "nearly" part. This is harsh, and this is not always a good personality trait. But rare is the sportscaster who hasn't moved from city to city, who doesn't live far from the place he'd really like to live or even the place he'd really like to work. My road map is a little smaller than others: Since I left college, I've moved from New York to Boston to New York to Los Angeles to Connecticut. Dan's trip was Dayton to Atlanta to New York to Atlanta to Connecticut. They are not only below average in terms of moves, but most of our colleagues envy us for which cities we got to live in. **Your** first five moves may be from Keokuk to Cedar Rapids to Abilene to Wichita to Des Moines to Kansas City.

You also have to forget the forty-hour work week and getting home at six. There are always going to be more sportscasters than jobs, so our employers can always take advantage of us. Kiss your holidays good-bye. Counting college, we are currently in our collective forty-second year in this business. One or both of us will be working on each of the following days this year: New Year's Day, Super Bowl Sunday, Memorial Day, July 4th, Labor Day, Thanksgiving, Christmas Eve, Christmas, New Year's Eve—and our birthdays.

Another part of the attitude adjustment may come as a shock: Do not take sports seriously. Take your **work** seriously: Be dedicated to it, know everything you need to know about it, enjoy it, remember that the viewer or listener may be fanatical about it—but maintain a healthy distance from it. The moment you think that a sports team or league or player is actually important, you become a servant of the "sports media complex" whose only purpose in being is to separate people from their money. **Your** dedication has to be to your viewer or listener, to the truth, and, lastly, and only to the degree that it does not conflict with your ethics, to the success of your employer.

Still not scared off? Give 'em the warnings, Dan.

Make a backup plan. You may not succeed at this. You may succeed at this but find you hate it. What do you do then? Have another line of work available to you.

Do not expect to get rich doing this. There is very little middle ground in terms of what people are paid in this business. Perhaps 90 percent of all sportscasters earn less than $50,000 per year. Perhaps 50 percent of them earn less than $25,000 per year. Remember that at that first job Keith had, his starting salary was $8,870—at a **national radio network.** Keith left radio for CNN in 1982 and his starting salary there was $26,000. I started there a year later for $17,000.

Also, enjoy watching your favorite sportscasters, but you must be very critical of them and stay distant from their styles, manners, and affectations. Be yourself on the air. Do not say you want to be another Bob Costas or another Marv Albert or another Chris Berman or even another Dan or Keith (especially not another Dan or Keith. We don't need the competition. The world doesn't need another one of these books). Bring your own attitude and perspective to what you write and what you say. It's OK to take little elements of other people's styles—there's a little bit of everybody else in every sportscaster in this country—but if you mimic, you will not succeed.

The other part of that is that it can screw up how you approach your career. If you say you want to be another Bob Costas, you might miss opportunities to be someone similar—or maybe someone better. Bob Costas didn't get to "**be** Bob Costas" on a straight line—if he hadn't gone with the flow of the opportunities presented to him he might have wound up doing the local sports on TV, and wasted his many other talents. If Keith had tried to copy Marv Albert, he might have struggled for years as an unsuccessful play-by-play man. And this is very important: If you want to be on the air, **be on the air.** Keith, give Dear Reader your favorite piece of advice, the one you always give to would-bes.

When I was a senior in college, a couple of contacts from an internship I had the year before sent me to see an executive from *Wide World of Sports*—not for a job, just for advice. Ten years before, this guy said, he had been offered two jobs coming out of college: (1) as a weekend sportscaster at a television station in Syracuse, New York, for $10,000 a year; (2) as a gopher ("production assistant") at *Wide World of Sports* in Manhattan for $10,500 a year. Now, he certainly preferred living in New York to living in Syracuse, and while all he wanted to be was an on-the-air sportscaster, he figured the ABC job was better and eventually he could move laterally and get back in front of the camera. Instead, he found, his on-air experience so overqualified him as a production assistant that within a year they had made him **senior** production assistant. A year after that he was a producer. Eight years later he was a vice president making $100,000 a year, and still forlornly hoping he could get back on the air. "Only now," he explained, "I'd have to quit this job and **still** start in Syracuse. Maybe they'd give me $11,000 a year and not $10,000. And I'd have to move my wife and family there." Seventeen years after that conversation, he's the head of a network. His income is now in seven figures. And he'll still never become the sportscaster he wants to become. Moral: Except for an internship, if you want to be on the air, **stay** on the air—never take any other kind of job in this business.

Still with us? Here are the more practical tips:

You cannot start too early. I wanted to do this from the fifth grade on. So I took a lot of writing classes in high school, then majored in communications at Cornell, but that was unnecessary; I could've majored in turf grass management and it wouldn't have made any difference as long as I spent seventy-five hours a week at our college radio station. That led me into an internship at a TV station in New York between my junior and senior years, and connections there got me a chance to have a tape listened to at that radio network. They liked it, they hired me, and then the job advancement happened pretty rapidly to a second network, a TV job at CNN, then spots in Boston and L.A. and then here to ESPN.

I think I knew by the time I was twelve that this was the way it was going to wind up. I was going to do what my father had always wanted to do. Be a sportscaster. So I did anything I could do to stay in broadcasting even though I didn't become a full-time sportscaster until I was twenty-seven years old. Ours is an overnight success story—if you consider 1967 to 1997 overnight. The gist of it is to get the experience before you get paid, whether at a school station or an internship or both.

Beware of one thing about internships, though. I've seen lots of people jump directly from an internship at a station to a full-time job. And not one of them has ever shaken that image of being a rookie, being a kid, being a freebie. Listen to this. In 1983, I was the leading candidate to become the number one sportscaster at WCVB-TV in Boston. I had two full years of work at CNN behind me. I had a great demo tape, I had a great résumé, I had great clippings. The sports director wanted to hire me. The executive news producer wanted to hire me. The news vice president wanted to hire me. Then we go to see the general manager. And he's asking me where I've worked and I tell him. CNN, RKO, UPI, and "all the WNEWs." And he says, "AM, FM, **and** TV?" and like an idiot, I tell him the truth. "You were an intern at WNEW-TV? When? I used to be the general manager there." And like a bigger idiot, I tell him the truth again. And he says, "1978? You were an **intern** for me in 1978? How in the hell do you have enough experience to be the lead sportscaster in a major market five years after you were my goddamned intern?"

Let me guess. You didn't get hired.

Oh, I got hired. A year later. As the reporter. Low man on the totem poll. And the general manager never trusted me. Never.

This is the guy who said it?

Yep. I'll keep his name out of it. When I wound up leaving the station, he told my agent, "He is now our enemy. He will never again work in this business." I can tell you this much: I never used him as a job reference.

Still, other than reminding you that you never know who's going to hire you for your next job, or fire you from it, there aren't too many pitfalls to becoming an intern. But whatever you do, make sure you get on the air as much as you can regardless of the circumstances. There is no broadcasting organization that we know of that has any kind of training program: You have to come in with at least the raw skills and hone them yourself. Brutal, but true.

So start practicing **now**: A lot of it is sheer chance—luck in getting jobs, how's your voice, etc.—but you can control a couple of things. The ability to write—item 1A in the list above—is like gold. The ability to speak well is superficially just as important but can be achieved through exercises, such as taping a radio or TV sportscast, writing it down word for word, reading it aloud several times, taping yourself reading it, and then listening to both tapes to see how you sound compared to the sportscaster. When I was in college, I used to supervise the training program for freshman announcers and had them do this all the time, with good results. It gets rid of accents, teaches you how to read aloud and with confidence, and gives you an idea of how writing-to-be-read differs from writing-to-be-spoken.

My first experience of any kind in front of a camera came because I had a friend who had some primitive video equipment. So I borrowed it, and I wrote a five-minute sports report, and I memorized it, and I sat down in front of the camera and started talking—starting from the beginning each time I'd flub a line. If you're thinking of going into television and you somehow get an interview and the guy asks you have you ever been on TV before and you say no, never, never seen myself "on camera," he'll probably start laughing. Using a home video camera on a tripod is a heck of a way to practice. And you're lucky. We're so old they didn't **have** home video cameras when we needed the practice.

We just practice every night. We'll get it right some day. There's one problem with trying to figure out how to make yourself better. Somebody's going to have to help you. Sometimes you'll get great help. Sometimes you'll get somebody who wants to help but gives you the wrong advice. Sometimes you'll get sandbagged.

Like when you told me at your going-away party that I shouldn't take the New York reporter's job for CNN?

That was sandbagging? No. That was inebriation. And because I wasn't sure I really wanted to leave. You think that threw you? Try this, I'm twenty-one years old and I'm on WNEW Radio in New York. It's six o'clock in the morning, I'm filling in for the regular sportscaster, and Will Spens, one of the most talented, most gifted people I've ever known, is sitting in the booth reading the news. I'm sitting next to him, waiting to do my sportscast. Picture this: I've been listening to and watching Spens since I was in junior high. He's got the toggle switches in front of him to turn both our microphones on or off. This is what happens:

> SPENS: WNEW News Time 6:04. The stocks, and Keith Olbermann's sports report next.
> (Spens turns off both microphones.)
> COMMERCIAL: Here at the Brooklyn Bank for Savings we're interested in you . . .
> SPENS: Olbermann, can you take criticism?
> COMMERCIAL: Loans aren't our business . . .
> ME: Sure, Will. I'd be happy to hear it.

SPENS: Your entire delivery stinks.

COMMERCIAL: People are our business . . .

SPENS: You can go up to Yankee Stadium and interview everybody in the place and edit the tape for ten hours and you
still don't sound good.

ME: Uhhh . . .

COMMERCIAL: When you need help, come see us . . .

SPENS: You have to go back to the start. Me? I can read the phone
book and make it sound like the Bible. You . . .

COMMERCIAL: We're here for you . . .

SPENS: You need to rework it, babe. You can be a star. But not
like this.

COMMERCIAL: Member, FDIC.

(Spens turns both our microphones on.)

SPENS: Now with sports, Good morning Keith Olbermann!

ME (IN MY BRAIN ONLY): What do I do now? Use a falsetto? Do my
Tom Snyder impression? Mommy!

Now, I don't think Will was really trying to sandbag me. He probably thought I was a little further along in my self-confidence than I truly was. But I was stunned for about a day after that. Still, in there was a kernel of truth. I wasn't putting enough energy into the important words I was saying. There wasn't any variety in my delivery. Could he have told me that? I don't know. Would I have found out if he had never done what he did? I don't know. To para-phrase the great philosopher Alanis Morissette: You Live, You Learn. You Get Shredded by Will Spens During a Bank Commercial, You Learn.

Speaking of learning. About college courses and college majors: You can major in communications, but if instead you can minor in it—take a lot of the hands-on courses (radio and TV writing, videotape editing, etc.)—and major in something else (English, history, print journalism, business, whatever interests you) you'll probably be better off. Communi-cations grads are a dime a dozen, but somebody with some communica-tions skills and studies under their belt **and** a "real" education stands out from the crowd of résumés and applications.

The following is the God's honest truth. Communication arts at Cornell was a very small department, graduating no more than forty majors or so a year in the late '70s. Maybe fifteen of them worked at the radio station, WVBR-FM. Maybe another fifteen worked at the newspaper, the *Cornell Daily Sun.* Six or seven had part-time jobs with other media outlets in town. One had an internship at a local advertising agency. But there were a couple who—like Dan said when he got out of Dayton—expected to simply pick up the diploma, say, "OK, where's my job?" and get hired somewhere doing something. One of them was a young woman who shall remain nameless, but whom for purposes of this terrifying story, we'll call Zelda. Eighteen months after I graduated and a week before I started my second job in radio, I went back to Ithaca to visit friends who were still in school. I took an old buddy out to the diner a block from WVBR . . .

You always were a big spender.

Shut up! I was animatedly exaggerating how great his new job was going to be, when the waitress appeared at our table.

It was Zelda.

While you're swallowing hard over that one, consider this about your college major. There is every chance that becoming a sportscaster won't work out for you, or you won't like the business. What do you do with a communications degree then? Become a communications professor? Go see if Zelda's job is open at the diner? It's better to have something to "fall back on."

Most importantly in terms of college: as the former head of the FCC once pointed out, communications departments teach people **how** to say something without ever teaching them **what** to say. Learn things, become well rounded, find out who Marcel Proust was and who Marcel Cerdan was and who Marcel Marceau is, and vistas will open up before you—or at the least you'll have some different way of leading in to a Montreal Canadiens highlight someday.

Additionally on college: We are not encouraging anybody to slack off in class. But neither of us has ever been asked to present our college transcript, nor explain our grade-point averages, nor show our scores on the SATs. Go to college and **learn** rather than simply try to get good grades. Better to get a C in history and actually take something away with you from the class than get an A in communications theory and find it useless. They'll never know about the A and they'll never care about the C. Take the time to learn and go work at the college radio station.

Or take the time and get a college internship—the risks of running into somebody later who'll only think of you as an intern notwithstanding. If you can spend a summer, or part of your school year, working at a local TV or radio station, especially if you're going to get school credit for it, **do it.** You may not think you're learning anything while you do the grunt-and-grind work of which most internships consist. But you will get exposure to how the actual real-life business works and it will either excite you and show you at least the tip of the job-getting process, or it will disgust you, and you'll still have time to go and do something else. And you can get started even **before** college. Would any of the local radio stations—no matter how small—be interested in a free employee? Somebody to help out with the newscasts, or the play-by-play of local games? You might try to call or write them. Failing that, working on your school paper—starting one, if necessary—is a must.

And take those writing classes! At the school Chris Berman and I both attended, once a week from the eighth grade on, we had to come in first thing in the morning, sit down, read a topic written on the blackboard, and write three to five pages on that topic in fifty-five minutes. If you learn how to write well and quickly, not only will that help if you get into sportscasting, it'll also carry you through whatever college you go to, and throughout your life.

OK, you've done everything we've suggested so far (man, you work fast—another great skill to have). How do you actually **get** that friggin' job? We've never encountered one communications department in one university that actually has a course in this. That's probably because no one could ever get into it—there wouldn't be enough seats in the lecture hall. The following will have to suffice for this part of your degree.

If you're in high school, find out the following things about the colleges you are considering: Do they have radio or TV stations? Are these stations restricted to juniors and seniors, or only grad students, or only majors from one department? Do they offer help with finding internships? What is the English and/or writing department like? Are there any practical courses in the communications department? News writing? Videotape editing? What will they let you do and what won't they let you do?

I was on the verge of accepting a very nice merit scholarship from Boston University when I read something in the fine print about how communications majors weren't allowed to take any communications classes until they were juniors, and about how the school radio station was basically the playground of the graduate students. I turned down the scholarship. My father still hasn't gotten over that.

If you're in college looking for an internship: Résumés are nice. Credentials are nicer. Before you send a letter to your favorite sportscaster, find out if he actually chooses the intern or interns. **Call the station up and ask.** "Do you have an internship program? In sports? In news? To whom do I apply? May I submit a tape of my college station sportscast/college newspaper article/whatever with my résumé?" As best you can, find out what they're looking for, or if you can't, presume it's this: At ESPN we have five internships and about five hundred applications a year. Preference is given to the people who have clearly **shown** they want to become professionals in this field: the people who are the sports directors of their college radio or TV stations or sports editors of the college newspaper, etc., or who are at least on the staff.

One more thing about internships—don't be afraid to apply for one in the news department. There are likely to be more of them, and there's nothing you'll learn there that won't help you in sports. I did nothing but news for nearly five years. Keith did it off and on through college and in radio. What do you suppose we are doing when we cover a sports franchise shift, or a player on trial, or a labor negotiation? We're covering news that just **happens** to be about sports.

About getting the job out of college. A résumé won't do it. They don't care. A résumé is what they check to make sure you're not an ax murderer **after** they decide they might want to hire you. They want to see or hear what you've actually done on the air. Gone are the days that you could wander in to a little station somewhere with a good voice and a keen interest in sports and a willingness to work hard, and walk away with a job. Once you get on the air in college, tape everything you do so you can save the best stuff and make your demo or résumé tape. Get *Broadcasting* magazine and look for the ads in the back for sportscasting positions. Flood the market. Send tapes to stations that don't ask for them. What's the worst that can happen? They'll reject you or they won't reply and somebody will take your tape home and record *E.R.* on it. So what? You only need one positive reply to get started—and this isn't the softball toss at the county fair: You're permitted to take as many shots as you like.

Do not take the job rejection process personally. Remember that if the news director of the 1,500-watt radio station in Keokuk decides not to hire you, it may very well be the case that **he's** only working **in** Keokuk because he's not good enough at what **he** does to get a better job. The first guy who ever turned me down for a job not only did that, but he told me my style would never work in this business. He wound up being the traffic reporter flying in a plane over Rochester, New York.

KO, didn't you say something about sending him a present for his tenth anniversary on that job?

No comment. And I should mention here that television and radio management is, well, to give the benefit of the doubt, an **inexact science.** For most of the early 1980s, WCBS-TV in New York went through weekend sportscasters like I go through facial hair styles. Like clockwork, nearly every year, out with the old, and in with the new. Well, listen to this little saga as a further indication that, to paraphrase Mae West: In getting a job as a sportscaster, goodness has nothing to do with it. In 1982, WCBS needed a new weekend sportscaster, so I sent over a demo tape of my work at CNN. A few weeks later it came back with a very courteous note from the news director saying, "Very intriguing but very raw—not enough experience for New York." In 1983, WCBS needed another new weekend sportscaster, so by this time I had an agent so **she** sent over my demo tape. This one comes back with a note from the same news director saying, "His style would conflict with that of our weekday sportscaster, but tell him he's obviously very experienced." In 1984, sure enough they needed another new weekend sportscaster. Out goes one more tape; back it comes like a video boomerang. "Not enough experience; raw, unpolished." Then, in 1985, this news director at WCBS who had rejected my tape three times, moved to Los Angeles to become general manager at KCBS-TV. So my agent sent him a **fourth** tape, and **this** one comes back with a note from him saying, "This style will **never** work in L.A."

Six months later, I've moved to Los Angeles to work for KTLA. In my first four months on the job I won three major awards and the ratings for my part of the newscast had already gone up. So my agent comes to town and she's having lunch with who else but the general manager at KCBS, the guy who has now blown me off four times. And this guy says to her, "Tell me, Jean, who else do you represent in this market?" And Jean tells him, "Well, I've got this guy at Channel 13, and two people over at Channel 7, and of course, Keith Olbermann at Channel 5." And she says he drops his salad fork and blurts out, "Keith Olbermann! You represent Keith Olbermann! He's terrific! When is his contract up? I want to **hire** him."

It's at this point that my agent drops **her** salad fork.

Nothing succeeds like success.

Point being you can knock on a door and while it might be true that you're not good enough to open it yourself, it might also be true that the guy on the other side of the door isn't smart enough to open it—or it might just be true that you're knocking on the right door, but at the wrong time. Tell our dear reader the Wally Pipp rule.

Put yourself in position to be there when fate gives you your one (and possibly only) big break. This is the Wally Pipp rule (if you don't know who Wally Pipp was, forget becoming a sportscaster). Mine came in three parts; you've already suffered through the Ayatollah Khomeini radio newscast part. Part two came when, after four years in radio in Dayton, I made that videotape with my friend's camera. I showed it to all the stations in town and nobody would touch it. Finally, the news director at Channel 2 said, "I don't know why you would want to do this, but I'll let you work as an odd-jobs guy in the sports department." He probably said it just to get me off his back. But I took it. For months, I got no closer to getting on the air than seeing somebody else broadcast the high school football scores I'd taken down over the phone in the office. Then the backup sportscaster, Ken Kettering, had to take the weekend off because his wife was about to give birth to their fourth child. Somebody had to fill in for him. They pointed at me. So I took my one suit, I arrived ten hours before the show, and I filled in—I'd never been on television before. The news director liked what he saw and made me the station's field reporter.

Later that same year I took some vacation to visit friends in Atlanta and, on the last day, on a whim, I took a videocassette of my best TV work and walked into the CNN offices on Techwood Drive. The receptionist told me to just leave the tape at the desk and "we'll get back to you," at which point convention dictated that I just shrug my shoulders and say OK and head back to Dayton. Instead, I explained I was leaving for home the next day, and I just wanted to know what somebody **thought** of the tape. The receptionist actually phoned the sports department to get somebody to come get this guy off her hands, and out came the company's vice president for sports, Bill MacPhail, who just passed away last year. Actual conversation:

> MACPHAIL: We don't look at tapes when people drop them by, young man. Just leave it and we'll get back to you.
> ME: Look, Mr. MacPhail, I may never get back this way again. I'm heading back to Ohio and—
> MACPHAIL: You're from Ohio? I grew up just outside of Columbus. Gee, what do you think State's going to do this year? How do the Buckeyes look? What—well, come on in, let me look at the tape. What was your name again?

They hired me the same day to work at *CNN Headline News.*

Now, if Dan hadn't fibbed about his vast news background and if the Ketterings had quit at **three** kids and if Bill MacPhail had been from Columbus, **Georgia**, Dan might now be the dean of Dayton radio, collecting tapes for his twentieth-anniversary newscast.

My big break also came in three parts. If the Fourth of July hadn't fallen on a Wednesday in 1979, I might still be working on my tan in the side yard of my parents' home in Hastings-On-Hudson, New York. Because the Fourth that year was a Wednesday, it basically wiped out the whole week at most business offices. So, when one of UPI's sportscasters gave two weeks' notice on Monday, July 2, the bosses had no time to look for a veteran guy who'd have to give his own two weeks, or to move. They needed somebody within five or six business days. Guess who?

A year later, I was still working at UPI when a local New York radio station—the fabled WNEW-FM—began running the commentaries I did for the radio network. They ran them at 4:30 A.M. The newscaster, Andy Fisher, and the overnight disc jockey, Tom Morrera, invited me to come in one overnight and do one of the commentaries live. About half an hour after that, I was sitting around the newsroom shared by the AM and FM stations when WNEW-AM's news director, Sam Hall, walked in. Actual conversation:

HALL: Hey, you're, what's your name, you're Oberkfell, right?
ME: Whatever, Mr. Hall. Yep, Nice to meet you.
HALL: You do sports, right?
ME: That's right, Mr. Hall.
HALL: My sports guy, John Kennelly, just called in sick. Would you like to make some per diem and fill in for him this morning?
ME: You bet.
HALL: Can you write fast?
ME: Very.
HALL: Good. Better start writing. You're on in three minutes.

That led to a job filling in for about six weeks a year on one of the biggest radio stations in New York. And that fill-in gig led to one of the biggest TV sports critics in New York, Stan Isaacs of the newspaper *Newsday*, taking an interest in my work. A year later, Isaacs wrote a glowing column about my "funny" radio sportscasts. In those days, one—and only one—of Isaacs's several columns per week was also reprinted in the national edition of the Sunday *Washington Post*, the one delivered only to Displaced Washingtonians in other cities. At his breakfast nook in suburban Atlanta, Rick Davis, Bill MacPhail's number two man at CNN Sports and noted Displaced Washingtonian, was thumbing through his *Post* mumbling to himself about how he needed to find somebody funny to liven up his sportscasts. He stumbled upon Isaacs's column—and the column that had been chosen for the *Post* that week was the one about me.

And of course the whole thing gets even more tenuous. Bill MacPhail, a lovely man who was extraordinarily influential in starting not only each of our careers but also those of an incredible range of great sportscasters running the time line from Jim McKay and Chris Schenkel and Pat Summerall through Gary Miller and Dan Hicks and Hannah Storm, who with Pete Rozelle virtually coinvented the NFL, just happened to be trying to fill out his sports staff for the new CNN venture called *Headline News*. And he just happened to be heading to New York to see his brother, so he just happened to be able to interview me. And even when I was making way too much in radio in New York ($35,000, and when I told him that he nearly exhaled his drink through his nose—he wanted to hire **five** sportscasters for a **total** of $95,000) to consider his offer, he just happened to need somebody to fill in for his New York bureau sports reporter, who was taking two weeks' vacation. That's a lot of "just happeneds."

No Wednesday Fourth of July means no visit to the WNEW newsroom at 4:30 in the morning means no Isaacs column means nobody at the *Post* choosing the one about me means Davis keeps turning his pages and I never get into TV.

It's frightening if you look back at it, isn't it? Kind of like being on a tightrope for fifteen years but only just realizing it **is** a tightrope! Anyway, if you get as far as a fairly good local television job, you'll probably need an agent to get a better one. Ask your colleagues or even successful people you don't know to suggest possibilities. Don't necessarily go with the big agency or the big name: Odds are you'll never be able to get through on the phone to that big name. You'll do better with somebody who actually cares about you, your work, and your success.

There are lots of other things you can do. Read up. As kids, we each got a tremendous feel for what we might be encountering by reading books on sportscasting. Red Barber wrote a marvelous one called *The Broadcasters*, and Maury Allen edited another called *Voices of Sport* (both long since out of print—but you have been maybe to this quiet place they call a "library"?). Though Barber talked a lot about the preparations he would make for an individual broadcast, these weren't **how-to** books, per se. But they told stories of what sportscasters did, what they said, how they reacted. Histories of broadcasting companies are useful—sometimes chilling. Ever read *Monday Night Mayhem* by Marc Gunther and Bill Carter? The one about the history of "Monday Night Football"?

Lindsey Nelson wrote an autobiography. The great Bob Wolff did, just last year. Terry O'Neil, a sports executive at three networks, wrote *The Game Behind the Game*. Maybe you thought Howard Cosell was a little tough to swallow. We know that without Howard Cosell, we couldn't say one one-thousandth of the things we say every night. He invented critical sports journalism. He also wrote two books about himself, and if nothing else they'll teach you about when you should stand up for a principle.

Find a book about Edward R. Murrow or the decline of CBS News. Even the official history of CNN has **something** in it.

Though not a mention of either of us—maybe in the second edition. There are nuggets to be mined in all of these books; nuggets that you may find sitting in your pocket twenty years from now just at the very moment you need them.

Lastly, there is The Covenant. A lot of people helped us before we got started (and afterwards, too) and we pass on to you the one demand they made of us. If what we've said helps you get to be a sportscaster, remember that when somebody writes *you* a letter and asks for your advice and help—give it to them!

Dan and Keith's Top Ten Free Pieces of Advice to Other Sportscasters:

1. Stop saying "Hi, everybody!" Most people still listen to radio or watch TV by themselves. Subconsciously, when you say "Hi, everybody" to one guy sitting in a room alone, he thinks you're talking to everybody **else**. You're just underlining your own ego.

2. Never do an infomercial. Your career is over. You are done. Toast. Fried. We don't care if you're selling salad dressing that gives eternal life—you will never be taken seriously again.

3. Don't say "welcome back." The viewer didn't go anywhere: **You** did.

4. A game where the score is 21 to 21 is a tie game, or tied at 21, but saying it's a 21–21 tie is redundant and annoying.

5. Remember that the term "Super Bowl" is a **brand name,** not an adjectival phrase.

6. If a player has a slipped, bulging, or herniated disk and you've had an alcoholic beverage anytime in the preceding ninety-six hours, just say he has a "back injury."

7. Never read the name of a sponsor of an event or a stadium unless there's a gun pointed at your head. Just because **they** call it the Your-Name-Here Open doesn't mean **you** have to.

8. Don't say "grand slam homer." The only kind of grand slam in baseball is a homer. You might as well say "a run-scoring RBI."

Who knows how
Keith's life would
have turned out if
not for ESPN?
*(photo by
Scott Clarke)*

9. Avoid the overly specific synonym for "beat." Better to say "defeated" ten times while you read a bunch of scores than get caught the way one sportscaster once did. Several years after the tragic campus shootings at Kent State (now Kent) University, he announced that "Colorado buffaloed Colorado State, Harvard outsmarted Yale, and the Air Force shot down Kent State."

10. As Warner Wolf long ago pointed out, whatever **they** call it, since a ball hitting it is a **fair** ball, that thing sticking up in either corner of a baseball outfield logically **has** to be "the fair pole."

PETE ROSE AND THE HALL OF FAME

OK, KO, let's talk about Pete Rose.

Here we go again. He may be a dishonored baseball great, but he's **your** dishonored baseball great, right?

I view Pete Rose like I do a graduate student who gets caught cheating.

No, that was Ted Kennedy. Sorry. I'm interrupting. Climb as far out on that limb as you care to. I've got the saw all ready.

Keith, Pete Rose was accused of betting on baseball while he was managing the Cincinnati Reds. That cannot delete what he did as a player.

Hold on there, Bunky. Sure, when Pete was kicked out of the game in 1989 he was a retired player and **just** the manager of the Reds. But he became the manager in August of 1984 and continued as a player the rest of that year, and for all of 1985, and for all of 1986. The betting slips don't just start the day he took himself off the active roster. We know Pete was in financial trouble dating back to the '70s and there's ample evidence that this baseball betting stuff began long before he was just the skipper. Apart from which, trying to separate Pete's days as a player and his days as a manager is like saying Richard Nixon was one of our greatest internationalist presidents and we shouldn't hold this Watergate thing against him. The Hall of Fame is for great baseball **people**, not great baseball players who later damaged the game when they became management.

Let's talk about what the Hall of Fame is for. I find it hypocritical that the Hall of Fame charges admission for people to see the nineteen artifacts that belong or relate to Pete Rose. They can put the **artifacts** on display, but Pete is not worthy of inclusion.

Hey, I'm all for putting Pete Rose on display in Cooperstown. As an artifact. In a big glass case.

This argument is sophistry, too. The Hall of Fame has a copy of a book I wrote when I was fourteen listing all the first and third base coaches for teams from 1921 through 1973. It's right there in the library. That doesn't mean **I'm** worthy of inclusion.

I bet there's a waiting list to borrow **that** book.

Hush. And anyway, the Hall of Fame is screwed up from top to bottom and if they had a big display featuring the bat Juan Marichal used to beat John Roseboro over the head with in 1965, I wouldn't be the least surprised. None of this has anything to do with Petey. You're just a Reds fan looking for something—anything—to obliterate the fact that Pete Rose was banned from baseball and until and unless he's reinstated, you **can't** put him in the Hall of Fame.

I admit I'm biased when it comes to Pete Rose. But I've also been a very harsh critic of Pete Rose. Growing up in Cincinnati in the '60s, I was like every other kid in the area at the time. I was a Pete Rose fan, right down to wearing number fourteen, to sliding headfirst, to running to first base after being walked—to wearing that God-awful Pete Rose haircut.

Pictures?

Mysteriously disappeared. In 1966, I attended my first baseball game. I went to Crosley Field with my father, Reds were playing the Phillies, and after the game, I told my Dad I wanted to get Pete Rose's autograph. We made our way down into the bowels of Crosley Field and waited fifteen minutes outside the Reds locker room and Pete Rose emerged and I shoved my program in his face. I didn't even say anything, I was so awestruck. He signed his name, and my dad said, ''Do you want to stay and get more autographs?'' and I said, no, he was the only guy I wanted to get. Of course, I didn't realize that thirty years later that auto-graph would probably cost me fifteen dollars if I wanted to get it from Pete.

Uh, it's up to twenty-five now. Thirty if you want a baseball. Jeez.

It's funny you should mention the autograph stuff, though. You know where the first inkling of Pete's problems came out, right? In the memorabilia business. At the card shows in the early '80s, you couldn't find a Frank Robinson uniform, you couldn't get a Jim Maloney autographed ball, you couldn't locate a game-used bat from Chico Ruiz, for crying out loud. But if you wanted some-thing from Pete, they had it at every table. The old joke about him was you could go up to a dealer and ask for a Pete Rose game-worn uniform and the dealer would say, "Cincinnati, Philadelphia, or Montreal?" and you'd choose and then the dealer would say, "Home or away?" and you'd choose and then the dealer would say, "What size?" All of us collectors knew he was strapped for money—he was selling off anything he could get his hands on.

Every year during the Hall of Fame induction ceremonies, I think of the fact that if Pete Rose had not managed in the majors, he would be in the Hall of Fame. Because the allegations, the accusations, the finger-pointing, the documentation, about Pete betting on baseball, all surfaced while he was managing the Reds. Lord knows he wasn't really **managing** the Reds—he had to have something else to do.

But part of what made Pete Rose such a great player was his ability to win, to want to win, to make sure you **didn't** win, to never admit defeat. Maybe you got the better of him that day, but you never got the better of him that year, or in his career. Nobody played on more winning baseball teams than Pete Rose. He took part in more victories than any other player in baseball history. That's why it's hard for me to swallow the fact that Pete Rose is looked upon as a loser. A guy who refuses to admit he made a mistake—and I believe that if Pete would have said that, would have said, "I had a problem, I want to rectify it, I made a big mistake, I did what I was not supposed to do, I bet on the sport that made me a millionaire, I bet on the sport that defines who I am as a person"—I believe he would've been elected to Cooperstown as soon as he was eligible.

We're back to Nixon again. If he had said, "I screwed this up" he probably never would have resigned. But your point about his mentality is right on the money. Pete's still sliding into third and refusing to give up when all he had to do was shut up and apologize—but that would be defeat for him, wouldn't it?

What about Paul Hornung? He bet on games, bet on NFL games, and he's in the football Hall of Fame.

Yeah, but he admitted it, made a big public statement about it. "I made a terrible mistake. I am truly sorry," the whole deal. They suspended him for a year—and he was probably just the tip of the iceberg on gambling in the NFL—he and Alex Karras took the heat for a lot of guys. Read Dan Moldea's book *Interference* and your blood'll run cold. What Pete doesn't understand is that unless you kill somebody, an apology is usually enough. I'm a bitter, cynical guy when it comes to a lot of things in this country. But, jeez, people will forgive and forget almost anything—Hornung's a perfect example of that. And I think Pete could **still** get himself into the Hall if he's say something like that. You tried to give him that opportunity, remember?

Oh, do I remember. Four years ago I went to his home in Florida to do the Sunday Conversation with him. And I didn't want to do the interview, because I had mixed feelings about him. Here was a guy that I idolized, here was a guy who was from my hometown, here was a guy who I considered one of the ten greatest players of all time. And I had to interrogate him about betting on baseball. And I admitted to him, right to his face, that I felt he embarrassed the city of Cincinnati with having to be kicked out of baseball over the gambling. So the emotions ran the gamut that day: thrilled to meet him, thoroughly enjoyed talking baseball with him, but I knew I was just postponing the inevitable. I had to ask him about gambling on baseball. I knew he wasn't going to tell me that he **did**—but there was a **possibility** that he could have told me, or some wild scenario that it was just a bad dream.

Sorry, Toto, we're not in Kansas anymore.

I know. Pete Rose bet on baseball.

Growing up in Cincinnati, I know. If you want to find out about people, particularly about athletes, you can. It's a small town; that's part of the charm of it. So a guy who lived in my neighborhood, growing up, was a guy who worked with one of the bookies that Pete bet through, and this guy told me that Pete was a big bettor. Everybody knew that—

and everybody also knew that Pete was not a very **good** bettor. So they loved taking Pete's action. So this guy, who wants to get on with his life and has no vendetta against Pete Rose, he told me specific **games** that Pete bet on: He told me the 1986 play-off series between the Astros and the Mets. I didn't want to believe it. Still don't want to.

But you do. And I do. And it's a fact, and from what I know of it, when Bart Giamatti threw him out in 1989, he didn't reveal **half** the stuff they had on him. They used only enough to win by one run. Only enough to make sure he was out of the game. Just enough punishment.

But it still comes back to Pete Rose the ballplayer. He's **been** punished. His image has been stained. But it would be nice to let him restore a little dignity. Put him in the Hall of Fame, and you'll probably never hear from him again. But until you do, he'll continue to display the same determination, the same never-say-die attitude as a ballplayer. Pete Rose will get into the Hall of Fame one day, some way. Let's just hope it's not posthumously.

But you're saying give him the honor he doesn't currently deserve, and then he'll be a good boy and not rock the boat and then it'll look like he deserves the honor. This isn't Shoeless Joe Jackson who confessed that he took money as part of a scheme to lose the 1919 World Series—ironically enough to your Reds—and said it was wrong and tried to repent and not only hasn't gotten into the Hall of Fame, but was thrown out in the middle of his career! He was thirty years old, he had hit .356, he had nearly 1,800 hits in only nine full seasons—he had his life taken from him.

But Joe Jackson fixed games.

Did he?

He sure took the money. No way of telling if he really tried to lose. But it makes no difference.

I'll give you that. But I think you just hanged Pete Rose on the same point. He fixed games.

No evidence he tried to fix games! None! Betting, yes. Betting on the Reds, maybe—but only to win. Fixing? No!

What do you call it when the same guy who decides whether or not to bring in his best reliever or his worst one, has **already** decided whether or not to bet that his team is going to win that game? That's fixing. That's passive-aggressive fixing. I'll save so-

and-so for tomorrow. And lay an extra five large on our team. Only the nature of the result differs: Trying harder to win when you have a bet favoring your team is the same damn thing as not trying to win at all when you have a bet against your team.

We'll never agree on this, will we?

Bet we don't.

I suppose you want to move on to your annual Hall of Fame complaints.

May I?

I can stop you somehow?

No.

Go ahead. Just don't mention the 1899 Cleveland Spiders.

Rule One. It should be remembered at all times when dealing with the Baseball Hall of Fame that no matter who has picked the members, the honor or pressure of making the choices has made morons of them all. We should consider ourselves lucky that Babe Ruth is **in** the hall and Ruth Buzzi **isn't**.

They simply don't know what the frig they're doing.

Tell the "Courtesy Votes" story.

With relish. Rick Ferrell was a pretty good catcher from 1929 through 1947, a pretty good farm system director and general manager for Detroit, and, by all accounts, a pretty good guy. Rick played eighteen years (admittedly in eight of these he didn't catch 100 games in a season). He hit .281 lifetime, with twenty-eight career homers. His brother Wes had hit .280 lifetime, with thirty-eight homers. Of course, Wes was a **pitcher.** While he was still eligible in the writers' balloting, Rick got one vote in 1956, another in 1958, and a third in 1960. For years, reporters covering the Committee on Veterans would tell tales of how its members, old sportswriters, players, and executives, would cast "courtesy votes" for old buddies, knowing full well that these guys would never actually get elected. It was a nice, folksy touch. You know: Hey, Smiley, you didn't get in, but look, I voted for you, old pal, old sport. Everybody was happy but nobody got hurt. Then in 1984, it happened. Apparently **everybody** cast a courtesy vote for Rick Ferrell. Bingo—he's a Hall of Famer.

I suppose that that's how Pete will eventually get in. The Veterans

Committee will each vote for him in protest. It's certain the writers aren't goint to put him in.

I'm not sure. They might put in **Don** Rose, the other pitcher the Mets gave up in the Nolan Ryan trade. Listen to this. In 1966, the Baseball Writers Association of America actually cast two votes for Morrie Martin. Left-handed pitcher from the 1950s, made exactly forty-two starts in his life, garnered exactly fifteen saves, and had a lifetime won-lost record of 38 and 34. Orval Grove, a pitcher during World War II: 63-and-73 lifetime, got five votes in '58 and seven in '60. In 1980, somebody voted for Sonny Jackson, an Astros and Braves shortstop who in five full seasons hit less than .240. For crying out loud, Sonny Jackson?

I love Sonny Jackson.

For crying out loud, Sonny Jackson! Yeah, well, I'm a Dan Patrick fan but that doesn't mean I'm voting for you for the Hall.

You're not?

Stop it. Let me get back to Pete for a moment. I think there's a pretty obvious argument that **precedes** all that we've been talking about: If a guy's been banned from baseball for what the game considers its most heinous offense—gambling on games—you can't put him in the flipping Hall of Fame! If he gets rehabbed, if he gets exonerated, if he gets reinstated, splendid. Consider him all you want. Vote him in if you want. For chrissakes one of you voted for Sonny Jackson—who the heck are we to tell you who's a Hall of Famer? Obviously, you know your stuff.

Every year the writers come a little closer to fomenting a revolution among baseball fans and historians. I mean, there's a guy **with** a Hall of Fame ballot, whose baseball writing career is now unraveled to such a degree that he does a weekly column for a memorabilia hype magazine called *Sports Collectors Digest*, who wrote last year that Kirby Puckett's not a Hall of Famer ("not on my ballot. At least not the first time around").

Give me his name. Give me his address.

Why bother? The guy's argument included the fact that Puckett only hit 207 homers and had fewer hits than Dave Concepcion, so he didn't belong. What kind of stuff is going to impress a moron like this? You have to compare a guy—especially a guy with an injury-shortened career—to the other players of his own era. So here's Kirby, who had more hits than anybody else between 1984 and 1995, was first in his own time in total bases and slugging, third in batting average (behind Gwynn and Boggs), third in RBI and fifth in runs scored, and led two otherwise mediocre teams to World's Championships and he's not a Hall of Famer. These guys just don't get it. This guy and his out-of-touch colleagues have screwed it up so badly that what we should do now is just scrap the Hall of Fame and start all over again. But we can't. Our only option is to admit every player who was better than the worst guy already **in** Cooperstown.

So anyway, I've got this list here of guys who should be considered for the Hall long before we have to start letting in the unrehabilitated, whether it's Rose, Jackson, or Buck Weaver. I'm leaving out the lead-pipe cinches like Brett and Ryan and Puckett and all the active guys, too.

How long is this list?

Exactly one hundred guys.

Uh-oh. I think I have to go read my kids a bedtime story. I'll be back when you're done. I know I always say you're the most knowledgeable baseball guy I've ever known but don't push it, OK? A hundred guys.

I had to **drop** some! Lou Criger was the last guy dropped from the list. Cy Young's personal catcher. Read and learn. I'm not saying they are all DiMaggios, Ruths, and Gehrigs—but did you ever see the film with Alan Arkin and Graham Greene? *Cooperstown?* A very poignant film about what it means to be on that cusp between immortality and mere history. As the film suggested, it's not like there's a housing shortage there. I always used to be real prissy about the Hall. Select group and all that. Now I say if you can reasonably argue that a guy's a Hall of Famer, they why not? Put them all in.

And have a separate tier for the true immortals. The top twenty or so. Ruth, Aaron, Cy Young, Pete Rose . . .

Go read the kids the book. Alphabetically, the Olbermann 100:

1. **Dick Allen:** During the years of his career (1964 through 1977), only four guys hit more homers, and they're all in the Hall of Fame. Only six guys drove in more runs, and **they're** all in the Hall of Fame. Only four guys with as many at bats had a higher average. This guy is, at worst, the seventh best hitter of his time.

Sometimes he was a great leader, sometimes he was a cancer in the clubhouse. We don't seem to hold that against Barry Bonds. This guy should be in.

2. **Sparky Anderson:** Pennant in his first year as a big league manager? Pennant in his third year? Back to back World Championships in his sixth and seventh years? They should've put him in right then; 1984 in Detroit was gravy. Walking out on the Tigers rather than stand for the replacement players in '95 should be a badge of honor, not a black mark. They should name a stadium after him.

No-brainer.

I thought you were reading the kids a book?

Yeah, "The Bid Red Machine Story."

Then you'll like the next one, too.

3. **Frank Bancroft:** Field manager of six different teams in the 1880s. Won the first World Series with the National League Champion Providence Grays in 1884. And then, about thirty years as the first general manager in the game's history—with the Reds. Organized tours of Cuba, rebuilt the tradition of baseball in Cincinnati, helped get them two new stadiums built, including your beloved Crosley Field.

4. **Charlie Bennett:** Another nineteenth-century great. Lasted fifteen years as a catcher in the days when they didn't have chest protectors, helmets, masks, or gloves. Backstop on three World Champs, the last two when he was thirty-seven and thirty-eight years old. Hit .256, slugged .387, in a pitcher's era. His career only ended when he was run over by a train and lost both legs. The place now known as Tiger Stadium? It was Bennett Field.

5. **Vida Blue:** With everything he screwed up, from the holdout of 1972 to the drug disaster of 1984, Vida Blue still ranks eighth in wins between his first full year, 1971, and his last season, 1986. He's seventh in strikeouts. He's seventh in ERA. He won in double figures eleven out of his fifteen full seasons—this even though he pitched for some very bad ball clubs after 1976. Lifetime, batters hit .237 off him. Their on-base percentage against him was only .300.

And he spent a year in the pen on drug charges.

I'm not forgetting that. But let me ask you this: How many Hall of Famers drank, possessed, and/or distributed alcohol between

1920 and 1933? That was just as illegal then. Was Grover Cleveland Alexander really hungover the day he came in in relief to strike out Tony Lazzeri with the bases loaded, to more or less clinch the 1926 World Series? If so, he had broken a federal law the night before. I'm not equating drinking and drugs. I'm just pointing out that the moral line moves around a lot. And in the '70s there was a sizable part of the population that viewed the illegality of marijuana as just as much of an informality as their grandfathers viewed the illegality of alcohol during Prohibition, and that same kind of stupid, blasé attitude even extended to some degree to cocaine, especially in the early '80s, especially in sports—until it started killing people like Len Bias. I'll use your Rose argument. This guy really **was** punished for his crimes. Were Ruth? Cobb? Alexander? A dozen others?

   6. **Bert Blyleven:** Third all-time in strikeouts and not likely to be passed. He won 287 games and the way pitchers blow themselves out early, we're never likely to see anybody win even that many again. There are ten guys who've struck out 3,000 or more men and of them, only Fergie Jenkins had a better strikeout-to-walk ratio. Blyleven's second. Nolan Ryan is **ninth.** There are forty-four guys who've struck out **2,000** or more: Blyleven's tenth in ratio. Ryan's **twenty-ninth.** One of the greatest curveballs of all time. One of the greatest control/power pitchers of all time.

   7. **Bobby Bonds:** Fifth in his own era in homers. Fifth in his own era in stolen bases. Yeah, he should have been better. Yeah, he played on only one division winner in his life. But this guy is the prototype of the player we admire today: speed and power and defense; 332 homers, 461 steals, three Gold Gloves. His son will probably top him in homers but I doubt he'll top him in steals and his son is going to Cooperstown.

   8. **Ken Boyer:** Should have been in years ago: 282 homers, .287 batting average as a third baseman. Won the first four National League Gold Gloves at the position and added a fifth later. Talk about consistency: He hit twenty-four homers in 1961, twenty-four in 1962, twenty-four in 1963, and twenty-four in 1964.

   9. **Pete Browning:** Another pile of bones from the charnel house that is our memory of nineteenth-century baseball . . .

   You said you weren't going to get carried away. How can you judge these guys you never saw? You always do that! How do I know how good these players were? How do you? And leave out the "charnel house" stuff.

OK, that's a little florid. But he won four batting championships in leagues that were considered "major" while he was playing in them. Batted .341. On-base: .403. Slugging: .467. The whole Hillerich & Bradsby "Louisville Slugger" stuff started with him. Played most of his career battling inner-ear problems that eventually cost him his sanity. For crying out loud, he hit .300 or better in nine of his ten full seasons—I don't care if he was playing in the League of Women Voters.

10. **Bill Buckner:** Do you know what the dividing line is at Cooperstown for base hits? 2,763. Every eligible player who ever got 2,763 hits is already in there. All the as-yet ineligibles will be . . .

Except Pete?

Till we hear otherwise, he's permanently ineligible. My point here is that the line exists. You're one of the thirty-seven guys who got 2,763 hits, you're in, or you will be. After that it's catch-as-catch-can. But Bill Buckner retired just forty-eight hits short of that magic number—and considering the fact that he screwed up his ankle in 1975, I think he did pretty damn good. He played eighteen full seasons between 1971 and 1988 and during them, only Rose got more base hits than Billy Buck. Considering what he's remembered for—and that was John McNamara's mistake, not his—he was not just a fine first baseman, he was an **influential** first baseman. I was in Boston when he came over from the Cubs in 1984 and he made Wade Boggs and Marty Barrett into quality big-league infielders. He was the glue that put them all in the World Series two years later.

11. **Lew Burdette:** Dan and I had this mind-bending discussion after Greg Maddux went 19-and-2 in 1995. Remember?

Oh, I remember. I asked you if you thought that if the Greg Maddux of the year 2025 came back in time and told the Greg Maddux of 1995 that he'd done all he was going to do, that he would never win another Cy Young Award and maybe he'd be hurt and maybe he'd be a .500 pitcher the rest of his life, should the Greg Maddux of 1995 simply retire and get into the Hall of Fame based only on what he'd just done.

And my answer was . . . ?

You said "Lew Burdette."

Thank you. At the end of the 1961 season, Lew Burdette was almost as good a bet for the Hall of Fame as Greg Maddux was at the end of the 1995 season. In his era to that point, only four pitchers had better ERAs. He was 163–106 lifetime (winning percentage .606) and he'd won at least seventeen games for each of the preceding six seasons. He won three games in the 1957 World Series against the vaunted Yankees, had led the league in wins, winning percentage, and ERA one time each. Oh, and he'd managed to accumulate twenty-one saves as well. Problem was, for the remaining six years of his career he was a journeyman .500 pitcher. He ended up with 203 wins and only 144 losses, but it wasn't the same.

Still, you know something about those three wins in the '57 World Series? The Yankees won the first game, then Burdette won game two to tie the series. Then the Yankees won the third and fourth games and they were up three to one and needed one more to take it. And Burdette beat Whitey Ford 1–0 in game five. Then the Braves tied it by winning game six. And then Burdette beat Don Larsen 5–0—on the **road**, on **two days' rest**—in game seven. He won two do-or-die games in about seventy-five hours. That's worth something.

Yeah, but he threw a spitter.

And Burdette has never seriously been considered because of it. But think about this. Burleigh Grimes and Red Faber and Ed Walsh are in the Hall of Fame and they threw spitballs—they were just lucky enough to be pitching when it was **legal** to throw a spitball.

12. **Gary Carter:** What's the one standard rule the voters seem to follow? Were you the best at your position for a long time? Did you last? Gary Carter caught, every day, for fourteen years. He won three straight Gold Gloves. He hit 324 homers. Sure, he sullied his stats a bit by hanging on with the Dodgers and Giants. But he drove in 100 runs four times—which is only two years less than Bench.

I was in the other room. Did you say something about Johnny Bench?

I said he was a notch below Bench offensively. With you back here I'm not going to get into any of the stats that suggest he might have been just as good as Bench defensively.

13. **Bob Caruthers:** Short career, amazing results. Full-time

pitcher for the St. Louis Browns and Brooklyn Bridegrooms from 1884 through 1891. Won 218, lost 99. Twice won forty—**forty**—games and had three more over twenty-nine. He pitched in four World Series and beat Hall of Famer John Clarkson in the decisive game in 1886—the first time the National League ever lost the World Series to its then-rival, the American Association. Oh, and he played the outfield when he wasn't pitching. Batted .282, slugged .400, and **stole** 152 bases.

14. **Norm Cash:** Ninth in his era in homers. Eighteenth in RBI (even though he had only one season with more than ninety-three). Five times he hit thirty or more homers, to a total of 377. Had one of the greatest offensive seasons of all time, leading the league in hitting (.361), on-base percentage (.488), and hits (193). Threw in 41 homers, 132 RBI, 124 walks, 119 runs, and a .662 slugging percentage. Unfortunately the season was 1961—the year of Maris and Mantle—and Stormin' Norman couldn't get the time of day. And this was the story of his life—overshadowed by the Yankee sluggers that year, by the elegant Al Kaline in his own town, even on the day he drowned in 1986, which just happened to be the same day the Angels blew the pennant to the Red Sox in the Dave Henderson/Donnie Moore game.

The writers cast six votes for him in 1980 and he dropped off the ballot.

15. **Orlando Cepeda:** The Veterans Committee will probably forgive him what the writers wouldn't. Can't be carrying more pounds of marijuana than your highest single-season RBI total. But he not only hit .297 lifetime, with 379 homers, 1,365 RBI, and nine seasons over .300 including his MVP year with the World Champion Cardinals of '67, but he **actively** tried to repent his wrongs by working with inner-city youths—none of this ''chairing a committee'' stuff: hands-on work.

16. **Cupid Childs:** Great second baseman for the Cleveland Spiders in the 1890s . . .

You said you wouldn't mention them. You promised.

I said I wouldn't mention the **1899** Cleveland Spiders. He was in St. Louis that year. Look, this guy's lifetime on-base percentage was .414. This was nineteenth all-time. This was better than Jackie

Robinson. This was better than Rickey Henderson. This was better than Joe DiMaggio, Joe Sewell, and Joe Morgan.

17. **Rocky Colavito:** The Rock is the batters' answer to that question about Greg Maddux and early retirement. If he had quit—let's say arthritis in the back or something—at the end of the 1966 season, he'd be in Cooperstown. He'd **averaged** thirty-four homers a year for eleven seasons. During his glory years he was outhomered by only Aaron, Mays, Mantle, and Frank Robinson, and only Aaron, Mays, Robinson, and Ernie Banks had driven in more runs. Between 1956 and 1966 Colavito drove in 130 more runs than Mantle! He was even eighth in his era in runs scored. He'd hit four homers in a game, was as popular a player in his home city as anybody in the big leagues, he had an amazing throwing arm, and he had just turned thirty-three years old. Retire then and you're a star cut off in your prime, a guy who with just four more average (for him) seasons would've ended up with five hundred homers. Instead, he collapsed completely—sixteen homers in two pointless seasons split among the Indians, White Sox, Dodgers, and Yankees—and he was washed up in 1968, stuck among a bunch of guys who seem to have similar numbers.

But Colavito did most of his slugging in the pitching-dominated '60s. And if you take all the guys who've ever had as many hits as he did in the majors (1,730), there are only ten players, ever, who drove in more runs **per** hit than Rocky did (so we know what kind of clutch company we're talking about here, those ten are, in order, Ruth, Killebrew, Gehrig, Foxx, Schmidt, McCovey, DiMaggio, Williams, Stargell, and Bench).

18. **Dave Concepcion:** This guy . . .

Now you're talking. Davey C. The Big Red Machine. Five Gold Gloves—the most anybody had before there was an Ozzie Smith. Nineteen years with the Reds—in the lineup every day for the first sixteen of them. Four pennants and two World Series. Davey!

I'll give you something else. You've gathered my favorite barometer is what these guys did against the competition during the exact years of their career. Do you realize that of all the guys between 1970 and 1988 who had as many at bats as Concepcion, only Rose, Garvey, Buckner, and Buddy Bell outhit him? .267 doesn't seem like much. But he managed to drive in sixty-four or more runs seven times, usually batting low in the order. And for a guy who really wasn't that fast, 321 stolen bases was pretty damn good. Nineteenth best in an era when twenty-five guys stole 300 or more.

19. **Wilbur Cooper:** Completely forgotten star pitcher of the Pirates from 1912 through 1924; 216–178 lifetime, which doesn't sound great. But in his span in the majors, only Walter Johnson and Grover Cleveland Alexander won more games. And check out the ERAs in his span in the majors:

1. Walter Johnson (2.20) HOF
2. Grover Cleveland Alexander (2.37) HOF
3. Stan Coveleski (2.81) HOF
4. Red Faber (2.82) HOF
5. Wilbur Cooper (2.82) Forgotten

There's a guy **behind** him on this list (Eppa Rixey) who's in Cooperstown. And Cooper did all this while his Pirate teams finished second once, third twice, fourth five times, and fifth or worse four times. This wasn't a legendary pitcher on a bad team (Walter Johnson) that everybody could feel sorry for. This was a great pitcher on an eminently mediocre team that nobody noticed.

20. **Jim Creighton:** Don't go looking him up anywhere. Never played an inning of pro ball. But he was the first superstar—an unbeatable pitcher in the fast amateur game in the 1860s—and as a hitter, he once went a season without making an out. Oh, and remember the story of the guy hitting the homer, feeling something snap as he connected, rounding the bases, and then collapsing at the plate, dead with a busted spleen or something? That's more or less what happened to Jim—when he was twenty-one years old.

21. **Lave Cross:** With the dearth of third basemen, we have to consider somebody who played just about every day from 1887 through 1906, and drove in 108 runs at the age of 35 in a season in which he didn't hit even one home run. Played for Philadelphia teams in four different big leagues. Clearly a victim of the squash-like quality of the baseball in his era: He had more hits (2,644) and more doubles (411) than say, Ernie Banks, Mike Schmidt, and Mickey Mantle. We're talking a slugger in a later era. Oh, and guess what, Dan?

I couldn't possibly. What?

He had exactly as many triples as Pete Rose (135).

22. **Mike Cuellar:** Let's use our Maddux analogy again. At the end of '74, after nine full seasons as a big-league starter, Cuellar had a winning percentage of .616 (through 1995, Maddux's was .617). He'd won twenty or more in four of the previous six years (eighteen each in the other two). Unfortunately, Mike was (at least) thirty-seven years old the day the '74 season ended. He didn't have much left. He only ended up with 185 lifetime victories.

23. **Bill Dahlen:** This was an extraordinary shortstop sometimes credited with a forty-two-game hitting streak for the 1894 Chicago Colts, although this has been questioned. What is for sure is that he was a royal pain in the ass who was fourth in his own era in RBI, with 547 stolen bases and a .272 lifetime average even though he never cleared .242 for the last seven years of his career. Considered brilliant defensively.

24. **George Stacey Davis:** One of the top five guys not in Cooperstown. Brilliant, switch-hitting shortstop from 1890 through 1908 who led his era in at-bats and RBI, was third in hits, eighth in homers, slugged .405 lifetime, and of all the guys with at least 7,000 at bats (he had 9,031) he was outbatted by only five guys—and they're all in the Hall. Working against Davis apparently was a bad taste in the mouths of the early electors, all very gung-ho and establishment types who evidently held it against him that he bristled at being the last part of the peace agreement when the American and National Leagues settled their war in 1903. Davis had just jumped back from the White Sox to the Giants, for whom he had starred from 1893 through 1901. Part of the leagues' deal was that he return to Chicago. He didn't want to. He played exactly four games for the Giants in 1903, got hit with a lawsuit, and eventually slinked back to Chicago in time for the 1904 season. Why this should matter to us now, I don't know. Oh yeah, he was a switch-hitter.

25. **Willie Davis:** You know who was sixth in stolen bases between 1961 and 1976? You know who was third in batting average for anybody who came up at least 9,000 times during the same span? You know who was seventh in runs scored in that era? Eighth in doubles? Fifth in hits? First in triples? Fourth in NL outfielders' Gold Gloves? Yep, Willie Davis. Good grief, he was even sixteenth in

RBI. He was the center fielder on three National League champs and cleared .400 in slugging percentage twelve times. Today, he'd be negotiating a contract for five million a year.

His candidacy had been hurt, don't you think, by the story that came out that he allegedly threatened to beat up his folks?

I'll give you that one, Dan. If he apologizes and Pete Rose apologizes I'll vote for both of them.

26. **Dom DiMaggio:** Had everything his brother had except power. Missed three seasons due to the war, had to quit due to injuries at age thirty-six, and still was third in his era in runs scored, sixth in doubles, and second to Musial in batting average for anybody who came up at least 5,637 times during that span (admittedly Musial outhit him by forty-eight points, but Musial was Musial). This is the classic guy who should go in on the very politically correct "career shortened by circumstance" theory. He got 1,680 hits in ten full seasons. Give him an eighteen-year career and he's got 3,000 hits. Johnny Pesky told me in spring training in 1996 that his old teammate would be in the Hall if his name had been Dom Smith.

In spring training in 1996, Johnny Pesky also gave you a soul handshake.

27. **Larry Doby:** Probably lost five seasons between the war and the color line and was still tenth in his time in homers. Twice led the American League in homers and five times drove in more than a hundred runs. And he fought the same battles Jackie Robinson fought—broke in with Cleveland just three months after Robinson started with Brooklyn—without the positive support and attention of the progressive elements of the time that helped Robinson to some degree. The guy had a lifetime slugging percentage of .490 and managed the White Sox in 1978, back when Al Campanis's view of black skippers was probably still held by 75 percent of the baseball hierarchy. Criminal that he's not in there.

28. **Larry Doyle:** The top three hitters who got 6,500 at bats between 1907 and 1920 are Ty Cobb, Tris Speaker, and Eddie Collins—three of the all-time greats. Number four is Laughing Larry Doyle, the second baseman who coined the phrase "It's Great to be Young and a Giant!" For **everybody** in that span, he's fourth in total bases, fifth in hits, fifth in doubles, sixth in homers, sixth in

runs, tenth in triples, tenth in RBI, fourteenth in stolen bases, and he hit .300 five times in the pitchers' era before the First World War. Completely forgotten because he wasn't spectacular at one offensive element and good at all the rest; he was just excellent all around with the bat.

29. **Darrell Evans:** The guy hit 414 homers lifetime—topped 40 twice. He was a solid third baseman, he got a lot of walks (nearly 200 more walks than strikeouts), scored 1,344 runs (Mike Schmidt scored 1,506. Take away the 134 more homers Schmidt hit and he leads Evans by only 28 runs scored), and was still an everyday player when he was forty-one years old. But he hit .248 lifetime, and .248 doesn't sound like a Hall of Fame batting average. Yet Schmidt only hit .267 and Eddie Mathews only hit .271 and Graig Nettles only hit—gosh—.248. If there is any position where some leeway needs to be given on the subject of batting average, it's third base. I'm not saying Darrell Evans is a lock for Cooperstown. But the year he and Schmidt came on the ballot the writers gave Schmidt 444 votes and Evans 10. Ten votes? Schmidt was **forty-four and a half times the player Evans was?**

30. **Dwight Evans:** Once again, a guy who was a pillar of his own era but just never excelled in what Bill James so aptly called the "black type" category, so called because it refers to the number of times in the encyclopedia his stats are in black type to indicate league leadership. Seventh among his time peers in homers. Seventh in RBI. Third in runs scored; 2,446 base hits and 1,391 walks and played every day for eighteen years. And defensively? Eight Gold Gloves, and a master in the trickiest corner extant in the game: right field at Fenway. Dan can tell his anecdotes, I can tell mine. Sitting high behind third base at Fenway for a Yankees–Red Sox game in 1974, I saw him throw a ball from the deepest part of his corner that **accelerated** past Elliott Maddox, who was trying to go from first to third. And don't blame him for what the Red Sox did to their fans in '75 and '86—he hit three Series homers in fifty at-bats and got on base 39 percent of the time.

31. **Roy Face:** Before the era of the closer, **this** was **the** relief pitcher—not Hoyt Wilhelm or Lindy McDaniel or anybody else. From the time the Pirates started using him almost exclusively out of the bull pen in 1956 till the day they sold him to the Tigers in

September of 1968, he saved 183 games—20 more than anybody else. He also won 100 games. In those seasons in Pittsburgh the Bucs won exactly 1,050 games—and he saved or won 283 of them.

32. **Charles O. Finley:** Irascible, pushy, arrogant, disgusting at times. So was Ty Cobb. And though his peers assert he got his information by wheedling other execs and scouts for it, he did manage to scout and/or draft the likes of Reggie Jackson, Catfish Hunter, Vida Blue, Rollie Fingers, San Bando, Joe Rudi, Bert Campaneris and—forgot about this guy, didn't you? Rickey Henderson. Bought a franchise in Kansas City that by 1960 was nothing better than a Yankees farm club and managed to turn it into the last true dynasty in the game. Tried to innovate (some ideas good, some ideas horrific). Only owner to suggest that when players won free agency, the owners should give **every** player free agency **every** year, thus creating a sellers' market only for the top echelon of stars, and preserving the buyers' market for the 90 percent that remained. Read Marvin Miller's book about this. He knew the one thing that could screw up free agency for the players was **complete** free agency, and he was praying that Finley or maybe Steinbrenner would bring it up and everybody would laugh them out of the room. So, **when** they laughed Finley out of that room, he went home and decided to sell off the stars he couldn't keep and reseed his farm system (at least that's what he **said** he wanted to do with the money; Bowie Kuhn told me last year that Charlie wanted to keep the cash and then sell the franchise). They stopped him from doing that.

Twenty years later, the owners tried to force down the players' throat the same kind of buyers' market Finley wanted (and got the strike of 1994). And the process of dumping your impending free agents is now considered **wisdom** and not heresy.

My favorite Finley fact is that if you look up the front office of the A's in 1975, the year after they won their third straight world title, you'll find it consisted of ten people—including the two team doctors and the ticket manager.

33. **Curt Flood:** Who is more deserving? First guy I'd vote for. The first.

You like those iconoclasts, huh? How about an "Iconoclasts Wing" in Cooperstown?

How about a wing for guys who sacrificed? A few months before his thirty-second birthday, with twelve wonderful seasons behind him as the brilliant center fielder of the St. Louis Cardinals, Curt Flood was traded to the doormats of the National League, the Phillies. And he said no. He said you don't have the right to ship my butt anywhere you please—not after I've given you a dozen years of my life. And he stood up against the establishment—and whatever you think the players have done to the game in the last twenty-five years, what the **owners** had done to the players for the 100 years previous was a million times worse. And Curt Flood refused to go, and he sued, and it cost him his career. This wasn't some fringe guy; through 1969 he had 1,854 hits—all he needed was seven more average seasons to get to 3,000—he'd batted .293 (only six guys outdid him and five of them are in the Hall), he'd slugged .390 (that was ninth best in the era), he'd had six .300 seasons, two seasons with 200 or more hits, he'd won seven straight Gold Gloves, and he'd been on three pennant winners and two World Champs. And he gave it all up. The man got exactly thirty-five more at-bats in his life. No million-dollar contract, no free agency, not even a job as a first-base coach somewhere. He even lost the lawsuit—but he paved the way for the freedoms and salaries and rewards that those who followed enjoy to this day. He was thirty-two—and he gave it all up for a principle. The **least** he deserves is a plaque in Cooperstown.

34. **Bud Fowler:** The way a lot of modern African American players forgot Jackie Robinson and Don Newcombe and Larry Doby, even the old-timers forgot Bud Fowler. He was the first black man to play pro baseball, and he did it for ten years before the color line clamped down in 1895. By all accounts, and all surviving minor-league records, he was a fine second baseman and a great hitter—he hit .306 for Topeka when it won the Western League title in 1886 and was hitting .350 for Binghamton in the International League in 1887 when his "teammates" suddenly decided he wasn't white enough for them. And when the racists finally eased him out completely, he helped organize one of the first touring all-black teams, the Page Fence Giants. He tried to put together the "National Colored League" in 1904—the embryonic stage of organized ball for African Americans that we so readily celebrate today. A pioneer.

35. **Nellie Fox:** Possibly still the cause célèbre among the non–

Hall of Famers and deserving of most of his reputation: 175 hits, 76 runs, a .285 average—or better—every year from 1951 through 1960. Six seasons above .300. 9,232 at bats, and only 216 career strikeouts? The son of a gun even shows up twenty-seventh on the RBI list for his time. And though they didn't start giving out Gold Gloves until he was thirty years old, he still won three of the first four awarded to American League second basemen.

36. **Jack Glasscock:** We simply diss this guy . . .

Wait a minute. Jack Glasscock? Any relation to Dick Trickle?

The name alone would increase attendance at Cooperstown. Seventeen-year shortstop star whose career ended in 1895; defensively brilliant before gloves were standard; .290 hitter when you were lucky to hit .260 (fourth in his era, also third in base hits and ninth in runs scored). Made 2,040 hits even though he broke in when the National League was still playing an eighty-five-game schedule. That means he averaged 1.18 hits per game (your pal Petey averaged 1.20 hits per game).

37. **Joe Gordon:** When Ryne Sandberg "retired" in 1994 I said on the show that he shouldn't get into the Hall before Joe Gordon did. At the time of his departure, Ryno had 245 homers to Gordon's 253, 905 RBI to Gordon's 975. But Sandberg's figures were only eighteenth best among his contemporaries. Gordon's were fourth (homers) and seventh (RBI). He was even seventeenth in his time in stolen bases (Sandberg was twelfth in his). Oh, and Gordon played on six pennant winners and five World Champions.

38. **George Gore:** Great center fielder and leadoff hitter from 1879 to 1892 and lost in the history books. Once again, the four guys ahead of him in batting average in his own era are all in Cooperstown—he's not. Started in Chicago—they won five pennants with him on the team. Went to the Giants in 1887, they won two more. And I know how tiresome it gets to throw these endless numbers out there, but the guy **led** his era in runs scored. Number one. Lifetime average of .301 and cleared .300 in eight of his fourteen seasons. Hit .360 in 1880 when the National League average was .245. He got 102 walks in 1886, which sounds OK but not impressive, until you realize that in 1886 it took **seven balls** to get a walk!

KO, calm down, you're burning a hole in the paper. What is this fascination with nineteenth-century players? It was a different game then. Who knows if George Gore could do anything like this today?

I'll give you that. But just remember, within your son's lifetime people will be saying exactly the same thing about **twentieth**-century ballplayers. Could Paul Molitor really get 3,000 hits against the great pitchers of 2029? All we know is what these guys—Gore, or Molitor for that matter—did **in context;** what they did against the best players who were playing at the time. And George Gore hit .301 in an era in which the total big-league average was .252. That's got to count for something!

39. **Frank Grant:** Another African American pioneer who is as deserving of being there as Buck O'Neil or Satchel Paige. Spent three years with Buffalo of the International League, hit .344 in 1886, .353 in 1887, and .346 in 1888 and survived beanballs and spikes-high slides at second base. For a black man to play six seasons in the unimaginable world of the white minors of the nineteenth century, and not earn himself a place of honor in baseball history, is criminal.

40. **Ron Guidry:** Even if a guy doesn't break into a big-league rotation until he's twenty-seven, before we consider him for the Hall we still expect him to win 200 games? 300? The most wins by any big league pitcher between 1977 and 1987 is Guidry's 168. The second best ERA is Guidry's 3.25. The fourth most strikeouts is Guidry's 1,719, and of all the guys in the era with at least 1,000 Ks, Guidry had the best ratio to walks of anybody except Dennis Eckersley (nearly three to one). Eleven full seasons: only lost in double figures three times. Only **didn't** win in double figures twice. Eight years in which his winning percentage was .630 or better. I'm thinking we need three categories for the Hall: the Immortal Tier, the Greatness Tier, and the Shortened Career Tier. And Guidry goes into the latter.

41. **Stan Hack:** Because we think all third basemen should be sluggers, he's not in Cooperstown. But here's a left-handed-hitting third sacker who could hit. 301, run up an on-base average of .394, and slug .397. That he only hit fifty-seven homers is held against him, instead of being offered to his credit. Despite the lack of dingers, he was still ninth in total bases in his time, was second in batting average, first in runs scored, fourth in doubles, fifth in stolen

bases. He hit .300 six times. He was a great nonslugging ballplayer in an era populated by great sluggers, and he deserves better.

42. **Keith Hernandez:** Ever seen anybody play first base better than Keith Hernandez? Ever seen anybody with a greater **impact** on a game because of his defensive skills at first base than Keith Hernandez?

I'll say no to both questions. He was amazing—and you used the right word about his defense. It had impact on the game. He wasn't just fancy.

How do we translate that statistically? We don't. We don't have sophisticated enough defensive stats. We say, "He won eleven straight Gold Gloves" and somebody says, "Yeah, but I saw Don Mattingly make a great catch once. So what?" So Keith Hernandez and his .296 batting average and 162 homers get thrown in there with first basemen like Jack Clark and Eddie Murphy and Steve Garvey and some future voters says, "This guy wasn't even as good as Cecil Cooper." But he was still third in his own time in average, seventh in hits, eighth in runs, and even twelfth in slugging and eighteenth in RBI. Offensively, like Stan Hack, he's a victim of position prejudice. First basemen are supposed to hit homers. Instead, seven times he was over .400 in on-base percentage, and even though he didn't hit homers, he was above .413 in slugging percentage every year but one from 1976 through 1988.

43. **Paul Hines:** This guy had more hits per game than Joe DiMaggio or Lou Gehrig or Tris Speaker. He just had the misfortune to play the bulk of his career when they didn't even play 100 games per season. So give him his four years in the National Association and sixteen more in the National League and he still ends up with just 2,135 hits and people look him up and mistake him for Jose Cruz or somebody. But in his era only Cap Anson had a higher batting average, and only six guys hit more homers, and only two guys drove in more runs. He won the first Triple Crown, he was a fine center fielder, and he's been retired since 1892 so there's not exactly a group of us holding bonfire rallies to get him into Cooperstown. But he belongs there.

44. **Gil Hodges:** What percentage of fans who know anything about the Brooklyn Dodgers just presume Hodges **is** in Cooperstown? Here's the first baseman on six National League pennant

winners, a guy who drives in 100 or more runs seven years in a row, hits twenty-seven or more homers eight years in a row, a guy who on the day he hit his last home run was *second* on the all-time list for right-handed hitters, then manages the "Miracle Mets" to the 1969 World Championship, then dies young in the prime of his managerial life of a heart attack the Saturday before opening day 1972, and there's every reason **to** presume. I mean, gee whiz, he was even ninth in **batting average** for the length of his career.

45. **Tommy John:** This, to me, is one of the great no-brainers of all-time. Wins 288 games (fourth best all-time for southpaws), pitches on four pennant winners and two more division winners, comes back from the kind of arm injury that ended the career of every pitcher before him to sustain it, wins twenty games three times **after** the surgery, goes 13-and-6 at the age of forty-four, ends up with a better ERA than Fergie Jenkins—and he's **not** in the Hall?

46. **Bob Johnson:** A's, Senators, and Red Sox outfielder from 1933 through 1945. Didn't get to the big leagues until he was twenty-six and **still** hit 288 homers (third in his era), drove in 1,283 runs (second in his era), hit .296 (sixth in his era). Scored 100 runs in six seasons. Drove in 100 runs in eight (seven in a row). Johnson is discredited because he played in a sluggers' era, but his lifetime slugging average of .506 is twentieth best for anybody with his number of at bats—better than Jim Bottomley, Ernie Banks, Reggie Jackson, Billy Williams, Roger Connor, and a bunch of other guys who are in there primarily because of their heavy bats. We credit guys like Addie Joss or Sandy Koufax whose careers were shortened by injuries. Why don't we credit guys who were stuck in the minors for years back when there were only sixteen teams? What would Bob Johnson have done over a twenty-year career?

47. **Jim Kaat:** In the Blyleven/John/Kaat/Sutton What-Are-You-Kidding Me? Department. We're just not going to see any more 283 game winners! As Bill James has pointed out, Jim Kaat and Robin Roberts basically ended up with the same numbers:

	WON	LOST	INN.	K'S	W'S	ERA
Roberts	286	245	4,689	2,357	902	3.41
Kaat	283	237	4,529	2,461	1083	3.45

But Roberts was spectacular for six years, a mediocre pitcher the rest of his career. Kitty won twenty-five in '66 and then twenty-one and twenty games eight and nine years later. He was in double figures in wins every season from 1962 through 1976 and **then** had a respectable second career as a middle reliever. And Jim was a left-hander, pitching most of his career in a park noted for favoring right-handed bats. As Bill James pointed out, if Kaat had bunched his talent into six years and then stunk up the place the rest of the time, he'd be in Cooperstown just like Roberts.

Oh, and there's that small matter of the sixteen consecutive Gold Gloves.

And fifth place all-time in wins by left-handers.

48. **Bowie Kuhn:** I know, I know. As recently as 1982 I referred to him, on the air, as "Alleged Commissioner Kuhn." But context does wonders for him. Are we ever likely to see another commissioner open the spring training camps after the owners lock the players out—and survive? (Eh, Mr. Vincent?) Has anybody said a word about the "best interests of baseball" since they squeezed Bowie out? Had the temerity to oppose the sales of players because they might upset competitive balance? If Bart Giamatti had lived, we might have seen him do enough to exceed Kuhn's record as a commissioner who actually gave a damn about the game and occasionally snuck in some neutrality even though he was the hired hand of the owners. But Giamatti didn't, and the facts are that if you rank all the commissioners in terms of what they did **for the game,** Kuhn comes out no worse than third behind Judge Landis and Happy Chandler. And if you don't like the Judge's shoot-first, ask-questions-later attitude or Chandler's part-timing of the job, maybe Bowie's the best we've ever had. Besides which, this is a good guy. Still says his fondest memory in baseball was working the old manual scoreboard at Griffith Stadium in Washington when he was a kid. And he's volunteered at AIDS hospices and gives motivational speeches encouraging businessmen to do the same thing.

49. **Sam Leever:** Never heard of him? Join the club. Throw out his first two seasons in the majors and he was 158 and 65 lifetime (that's a **.710** winning percentage) for the Pirates from 1901 through 1910. The full record, warts and all, is 194 and 100 (.656 winning percentage) with a 2.47 ERA (that's tenth best, all time, for

his number of innings). The Pirates won four pennants in his time, he won twenty games four times, all this despite the fact that he injured his shoulder in his fifth full season in the bigs—and still hung on to throw more innings than our short-term Hall of Fame guys Joss and Koufax.

50. **Herman Long:** Fascinating, power-hitting shortstop of the great Boston National League teams of the 1890s (five pennant winners) who was tenth all-time in homers the day he retired in 1904. But more fascinating than any of his on-the-field work was how the voters treated him. The first balloting was done by two committees: the writers for more recent guys (Ty Cobb, Christy Mathewson), and the veterans for turn-of-the-century and earlier folk. In that first election, in 1936, the veterans gave nobody more than 39.5 votes. Herman Long got 15.5 votes—more than eventual HOF electees King Kelly and Amos Rusie. Long never got more than one vote in any ballot again. Must have pissed a lot of people off in the winter of 1936–37, which was a neat trick considering he had been dead since 1909.

51. **Bizz Mackey:** Buck O'Neil says he should be in there. Roy Campanella said Mackey taught him everything he knew. That should be enough. A switch-hitting catcher in the Negro Leagues from 1919 through 1950 (there's no typo there), and with such a defensive reputation that at the age of thirty-six he was the East's All-Star catcher in the first Negro All-Star Game in 1933—beating out Josh Gibson.

52. **Sherry Magee:** Forgotten outfield star of some dreadful Phillies teams, and others, from 1904 through 1919. Over the span of his fifteen full seasons, he was second in RBI, fourth in homers, third in runs, fourth in hits, third in total bases, fourth in slugging, fifth in stolen bases, fifth in batting average. He hit .300 five times— he's the man who snapped Honus Wagner's run of four batting titles in a row in 1910—and only once hit less than the league average. He was also a phenomenally aggressive base runner. On July 12, 1906, he stole second, third, and home—in the ninth inning. Stole home **twice** in one game in 1912. Stole home twenty-three times in his career. Why exactly has he **been** forgotten? Today we'd call him Rickey Henderson.

53. **Roger Maris:** Did you realize that when 1996 ended and

he still had the record for most homers in a season, that meant he'd held it longer than Babe Ruth did? We're still holding it against him just like the commissioner who stuck the asterisk on the record did. And it wasn't like that's **all** he did in his life. He was the MVP two years running, and even though he was only healthy enough to get even 500 at bats four times in his life, he still finished tenth in his time in homers and thirteenth in RBI. Hypotheticals are always annoying and risky, but at the rate at which Maris went yard, if you gave him Hank Aaron's number of at bats, he'd have hit 667 home runs.

54. **Mike Marshall:** The odd reliever, not the even odder outfielder. We've recognized the closer as a legitimate Cooperstown candidate, so where's Mike? Still being voted out because he didn't like: (a) sportswriters, (b) baseball owners, and (c) autograph collectors. When he was nudged out of the game in 1981, his 188 saves were the fifth best of all time. Pitched in 90 or more games three times—106 in 1974 when he became the first reliever ever to win a Cy Young Award (forgotten: He was **third** in the MVP balloting that year). And in most of his years as a closer he doubled as a setup man. What closer today would have seasons in which he pitched 179, 208, and 143 innings?

55. **Billy Martin:** Put the drinking on the plaque. Put the obscenities spat venomously at women reporters on the plaque. Put the brawl with Reggie on the plaque. Only once in nine complete seasons as a manager did Billy Martin's team not win the division or finish second. He took five divisional titles, two pennants, and a World Championship. At least twice, with the Rangers in '74, and the A's in '80, he pulled pennant-contending teams out of his own ass. And lost in our image of this demonized, even demonic manager, is a player who contributed vitally to six Yankee pennant winners.

56. **Bobby Mathews:** The greatest example of time passing somebody by in baseball history. When he retired in 1887 at the age of thirty-five, he had more wins than anybody else in history. The number was 298—right next to the standard by which we judge greatness, even for nineteenth-century pitchers. But 132 of those wins came in a league that some of the historians have decided wasn't "really" a big league—the National Association—and his

three straight thirty-win seasons from 1883 through 1885 have been dismissed because they were in the American Association, which, from our clear and perfect perch here eleven decades later, wasn't "quite" a big league. Hogwash. Some baseball historian in the year 2100 could look back at the American League West from 1982 through 1990 and make the same kind of observation. Mathews was the first prominent curveball pitcher and may have invented the spitter (legal throughout his career), and in his ten seasons in the NL and AA, he pitched 2,734 innings but walked only 336 men.

57. **Carl Mays:** Only seven pitchers won 200 or more games between 1915 and 1929 and they're all in the hall—except Carl Mays.

Wait a minute. This name I know. This is the guy who killed a batter with a pitch. Ray Chapman. 1920. You want **this** guy in the Hall? Killing a man is a lesser offense than betting on baseball games?

If it was unintentional it sure is. Mays was a submarine pitcher, and part of Chapman's success was that he crowded the plate and frequently got hit by pitches. Some witnesses swore that if the ball hadn't hit Chapman, it could have been called a strike. The tragedy of Ray Chapman was magnified by the fact that he was one of the most popular players in the game, and his wife was pregnant with their first child. Mays, in turn, was often gruff, had been involved in the near-strike during the 1918 World Series and a huge controversy over his sale by the Red Sox to the Yankees a year later. It was classic bad guy/good guy. But it has nothing to do with whether or not Mays should be in Cooperstown. He was a 208–126 pitcher and a five-time twenty-game winner who pitched on six pennant winners in fifteen years. In 1921 he led the American League in games, innings pitched, wins, winning percentage, **and saves.** In a hitter's era his career ERA was 2.91—fourth best for his time and three of his contemporaries, all in the Hall, are well behind him.

58. **Bill Mazeroski:** The calculations are too complicated to explain here, but in *Total Baseball* Pete Palmer and John Thorn have tried to synthesize fielding statistics that can give us an idea of a guy's **overall** abilities. The first stat is fielding runs—the number of runs a fielder has prevented from scoring, with 0 being the league

average. The second stat is fielding wins, based on the statistical conclusion that over the course of a season, each additional ten runs **scored** above the league average produces a win, and each additional ten runs **not allowed** produces a win.

Bill Mazeroski is the all-time leader in fielding runs **and** fielding wins. The *Total Baseball* stats suggest he saved the Pirates 351 runs by how he played second base for them from 1956 through 1972, and that his defensive play **alone** was worth thirty-six and a half victories to the Bucs. His fielding runs total was 9 percent better than the runner-up, Nap Lajoie (this difference is as amazing as it would be if Hank Aaron were the all-time leader with 755 homers, and the all-time runner-up only had 687). Not surprisingly you will find him having led the league in fielding runs for eight of the nine seasons starting in 1960, and having won eight of the first ten National League Gold Gloves at second. In brief, he was the Babe Ruth of infielders.

The defensive brilliance, of course, blinds us to the fact that Mazeroski was a pretty good hitter (twentieth in RBI during his ten years as an everyday player, 1956–68), and that he ended up with 2,016 hits (eleventh in his own time and more than Hall of Famers Johnny Mize, Dave Bancroft, Jimmy Collins, Bill Dickey, and many of the nineteenth-century guys), so it's not like he was an offensive embarrassment or anything.

Oh, and there is that little matter of that bottom-of-the-ninth, World Series–winning homer in game seven in 1960.

59. **Bid McPhee:** The first great Cincinnati Red, probably the greatest second baseman they ever had . . .

Huh? What? Reds? Second baseman? Little Joe's already in the Hall of Fame, isn't he?

Never mind him. Remember that "fielding runs" stat? Bid Mc-Phee piled up 271 of them in eighteen years at second for Cincinnati—and he didn't wear a glove until the last four seasons of his career. He hit .271 lifetime with 303 doubles, 188 triples, and 53 homers, all of them before 1900 when you couldn't have knocked a ball out of a stadium with a howitzer. Easily the finest second baseman of the nineteenth-century. You're a Reds fan, Dan, you should be pushing harder on this.

I'll get right on it.

60. **John McSherry:** For all the umpires who sweated and grunted under a weary life, who better to go to Cooperstown than the man who died on the field on opening day, 1996? There are no stats for umps—other than service (Mac was starting his twenty-sixth year)—but reputation is everything. Every National Leaguer I ever talked to said McSherry was **never** out of position for a call, **never** held a grudge against a manager or player who beefed, and **never** was afraid to admit he might have missed one. Pitchers said his strike zone never varied, not from game to game, not from inning to inning. There weren't many better, and there weren't any better loved.

61. **Fred Merkle:** I've said and written a lot of things about Fred Merkle . . .

Here we go. I'm going to read the kids another story. *War and Peace* maybe.

In fact, every year on September 23 I do some kind of report on the danger of scapegoating and the saga of Fred Merkle. As an eighteen-year old with the New York Giants, starting for the first time in a big-league game, Merkle got a critical two-out single in the bottom of the ninth of a 1–1 tie against the Cubs, the Giants' chief rival for the pennant in that season of 1908. Merkle's hit into the rightfield corner at the Polo Grounds sent the winning run, Moose McCormick, to third. Al Bridwell followed with the apparent game-winning hit, and the Giants had a victory vital to the pennant race.

Then, as now, there was a rule that said that a run couldn't score on the third out of an inning if that third out came on a force play. But in situations like the one in which young Fred found himself that unforgettable Wednesday afternoon, the rule was never enforced. The moment the winning run scored, the game was over—it **had** to be, because the moment the winning run scored, the fans customarily ran to the exits: They ran **across the field** to the exits. So, for their own safety, the players were encouraged to get to the clubhouse as quickly as possible.

The clubhouses in the Polo Grounds in New York were in dead center. So, as soon as McCormick crossed the plate, Merkle—and all his teammates—took off on a dead run for center field. Unfortunately, Fred, breaking from first with Bridwell's hit, apparently took off long before he advanced to second base. Somehow in the chaos that ensued the Cubs made a force play on him at second, the umpires declared him out and nullified the run. They then called the game a tie because of unplayable conditions (ten thousand fans on the field) and National League President Harry Pulliam ordered the game replayed if and only if the Cubs and Giants wound up tied for the pennant.

Which, of course, they did.

And when the Cubs won the replay, poor Merkle, victim of a rule that had never previously been enforced, was blamed. They called him "Bonehead" for the rest of his career—and he managed to last another fourteen seasons in the big leagues, playing on six pennant winners and finishing up as a fine ballplayer. But to this **day** people talk about Merkle as if he "cost the Giants the pennant." His daughter once told me of going to church in her native Florida thirty years after the game, only to hear the visiting minister apologize for being from Toledo, Ohio, "hometown of the infamous Bonehead Merkle."

I think Merkle's perseverance in staying in the game—imagine if the Mookie Wilson ball had bounced past Bill Buckner in Buck's second year in the majors instead of his eighteenth—by itself merits his inclusion in Cooperstown. But it turns out Fred's stats do some further arguing still. In his years as an everyday player (1910–20) he's fifth in doubles, sixth in slugging, eighth in average, tenth in homers, tenth in total bases, twelfth in hits, twelfth in stolen bases (mind you, this is a guy who used to bat cleanup), thirteenth in RBI, sixteenth in runs scored—and he was on five of the eleven National League pennant winners. All this **after** the 1908 incident.

Two footnotes about this. When I was in Los Angeles, Fred's granddaughter and her husband visited my home to see some of my Merkle memorabilia. They brought with them their son, then still a toddler. I swear this is true. Fred Merkle's great-grandson spied an ornamental piece of wood on a mirrored wall, crawled over to it, propped himself up, pried the piece of wood off the mirror, and swung it around his head.

The other footnote is this. The team that got the previously un-enforced rule enforced on him, the Cubs, went on to win the World Series. And the bastards haven't won one since.

62. **Marvin Miller:** He freed the slaves. Abraham Lincoln

wasn't universally popular until he was dead. Whenever you think of how Marvin Miller and the union "ruined" baseball, think about this. If, after free agency began in 1977, the owners could suddenly afford to pay guys millions whom they claimed ten years before they couldn't pay thousands, **how much money were the owners keeping for themselves all that time?**

How about putting Miller, Bowie Kuhn, Curt Flood, and Charlie Finley in all in the same year? Sure would liven up the induction weekend.

63. **Minnie Minoso:** The fans of 1965 and since see him as that kindly old guy who wants to suit up every time the decade changes. In fact, this was a damn good ballplayer. His last three comebacks with the White Sox cost him a lifetime average of .300 (he finished at .298). He outhit everybody between 1951 and 1963 but Musial, Mays, Mantle, Ashburn, and Kuenn. His slugging average was the fifth best of the era. Fifth in runs. Fifth in hits. Fourth in steals. Ninth in RBI. And even though he hit only 184 homers during the era, he was eighth in total bases. The punch line, of course, is this: He was kept out of the majors by the color line until he was twenty-eight years old—a fact that seems to be conveniently forgotten whenever it comes time to pass judgment on him for Cooperstown.

64. **Tony Mullane:** He pitched seven seasons in the wrong league—that blasted old American Association—so again we just kind of ignore the fact that he won 285 games in thirteen seasons. Should've been 300 or more, but he sat out a year and a half in contract disputes (there's a nineteenth-century pitcher **in** the Hall named Amos Rusie who won 245 games, sat out three years in contract disputes, but has been given "credit" of some kind for his independence). Oh, and although he was primarily a right-hander, every once in a while, when a left-handed batter came up, Mullane would **pitch** left-handed. Won thirty games five times. Twenty games thrice more. Led the league in **saves** five times. What else does he have to do to get to Cooperstown? Come back to life and join us for the Sunday Conversation?

65. **Thurman Munson:** I grew up watching the Yankees, loving the Yankees. I bet I saw, in person, Thurman Munson catch 400 games for the Yankees. Even after I became a reporter in college and became aware how disagreeable he was in person, I still thought he

was better than Carlton Fisk and just one notch below Johnny Bench. Yet, the day he died, and all the years since, I thought Thurman Munson wasn't a Hall of Famer. Didn't play long enough (admittedly, this wasn't his idea), and didn't play well enough while he did.

And then I saw one of the "Baseball's Greatest Games" series on TV. Deciding game of the '78 World Series. And I saw it again—what I'd seen 400 times but had forgotten. Thurman Munson **owned** a game defensively. Ran the ballclub. He pulled great games out of his pitchers. He lined Nettles up at third. He fought every battle and yelled every argument. And the Yankees won three pennants and two World Series in the last three full years of his life—and they've won two pennants since. He caught four twenty-game winners, three nineteen-game winners, three seventeen-game winners, and six sixteen-game winners in nine seasons. Sixteen pitchers with sixteen or more wins in his nine seasons. The Yankees have only had a dozen guys get as many as sixteen since. He won three Gold Gloves (Fisk won one—Fisk played twenty-two years).

And offensively, he holds up. Sixth in batting average in his era—five .300 seasons in nine full years. Rookie of the year in '70, MVP in '76, and he drove in 100 or more three years running while averaging only sixteen homers. And perhaps most impressive of all, he was a fiend in the postseason. Hit .339 in the three play-offs. Hit .373 in the three World Series. The man scored nineteen runs and drove in twenty-two in those fateful Octobers—the Yankees only **scored** 133 runs in the thirty-one games—so he was responsible for 31 percent of them. That, simply, is a Hall of Famer.

66. **Dale Murphy**: Once again we're too close to the forest to see the individual tree. Dale Murphy fizzled out, big-time, and fell right through the floor of the Hall of Fame lock box. But from the day he broke into the Braves' lineup in '78 through the end of the '91 season, Dale Murphy hit more homers than anybody else. He drove in more runs than everybody except Eddie Murray, Dave Winfield, and Andre Dawson. He cleared a hundred RBI five times, hit thirty-three or more homers six times, and drew ninety or more walks four times. He went from being a catcher who couldn't hit the broad side of Darrel Chaney with a throw to second base, to becoming a four-time Gold Glove outfielder. This guy won an MVP

award in 1982, wasn't satisfied, went to the fall Instructional League, and came back and won another MVP award in 1983. We don't put him in Cooperstown because he hit 398 homers and not 400?

67. **Jim Mutrie:** The inventor of the World Series is **not** in the Hall of Fame. The man who brought major-league baseball back to New York is **not** in the Hall of Fame. It was Jim Mutrie, four years after the National League expelled its franchise in Gotham, who organized an amateur team called the Metropolitans, who finally gained acceptance to the NL's rival, the American Association, in 1883. And it was Jim Mutrie, as manager of the 1884 American Association champ New York Mets, who challenged the Providence Grays of the National League to a "World's Championship"—the first ever played to a conclusion by pro baseball champs from different leagues, and the progenitors of the Series that continued through 1890 and resumed in 1903. And in eight years as manager of the Mets and then the crosstown Giants, Mutrie won three pennants and two Series—and had a **runner-up** in 1885 that finished 85-and-27 for a .759 winning percentage. Mutrie's career winning percentage was .611—second all-time only to Joe McCarthy's .614.

Oh yeah, he's also the guy who named the New York team "the Giants."

68. **Graig Nettles:** Fifth in homers in his time, ninth in RBI. First among third basemen, defensively—but that's still a subjective evaluation and the memory, even if it's of what he did to the Dodgers in the 1978 World Series, is forever fading. But he scores on the same kind of longevity meter we applied to Darrell Evans: eleven seasons of twenty or more homers, the first as far back as 1970, the last as recently as 1984. And mysteriously we're now shortchanging the players who stay in the game rather than exit early. Nettles hit .248 lifetime—and you know where that ranks him for players of his era with as many at bats as he had? Seventh. Seventh best. Because there were **only** seven players who came up that many times between 1967 and 1988. Through the 1996 season, Graig Nettles ranked fifty-third in baseball history—in times at bat. Does it count for anything that the guy risked his stats by continuing to play four years **after** his fortieth birthday?

69. **Don Newcombe:** 165–87 lifetime sounds smart, but not

Cooperstownish. Does a pitcher get into the Hall because of numbers like that? No. Not until you hear details: 165–87 isn't Don Newcombe's lifetime record, it's Sandy Koufax's.

Don Newcombe was 149–90 lifetime. Now the details.

1. Major league debut delayed by the color line. Still led the National League in shutouts as a rookie.
2. Had won fifty-six games in his first three years with the Dodgers when, at age twenty-five, he was drafted. Missed two and a half prime years in the service.
3. First two full seasons back in Brooklyn he goes 20–5 and then 27–7, winning the MVP **and** the first Cy Young Award in the latter year.
4. Succumbs to alcoholism. Beats it for a time, goes 13–8 for the '59 Reds, walking just twenty-seven guys in 222 innings.
5. Falls off the wagon and is out of the majors a year later.
6. Recovers from alcoholism, becomes a prominent figure in awareness and treatment of chemical dependency inside baseball and out of it, and at age seventy is still one of the game's great ambassadors.

I've done a lot of theorizing and extrapolating and manipulating numbers here. Let me try something different.

Uh-oh. KO's got the chemistry set out again. It's gonna blow! Run for your lives!

Relax, relax. Put on your goggles, but relax. Let's reorder Newk's career. Let's take his alcohol years (1957, 1958, 1960) and his just-back-from-the-army year (1954) and make them the **first** four years of his career. Make the good years (1959, 1949–1951, 1955–56) the **last** six years of his career. This way, Newcombe **starts** as a mediocre pitcher (33 wins, 42 losses) and finishes as an immortal (116 wins, 48 losses, winning percentage .707).

You know who he is then? He becomes the '50s version of Sandy Koufax. Koufax started off with six mediocre years (36 wins, 40 losses), and finished with six immortal ones (129 wins, 47 losses, winning percentage .791). Give Newcombe those two years in the service and maybe the numbers are even closer.

We don't blame Koufax for his bad start, or for bowing out

because his body wouldn't work anymore. Are we blaming New-combe because of his bad finish, or because his body wouldn't work because it was addicted to alcohol?

70. **Tony Olivia:** He won batting championships his first two years in the majors, stuck it out through terrible knee injuries, and still managed to hit .304 lifetime—second only to Pete Rose in his era. We think of him as a pure hitter (why not—six times over .300, five times leading the AL in hits) but he was also eleventh in total bases in his time and even sixteenth in RBI. Do we blame him because he was the first hobbled star to extend his career via the designated hitter rule?

71. **Al Oliver:** Never did much for me while he was playing. Pretty good left-handed hitter. Pretty good left-handed hitter from the year I was in the sixth grade through the year I won my first Golden Mike as the best sportscaster in Los Angeles. Eleven seasons over .300. Gee. Eight in a row—four in the American, four in the National. He hit .303 lifetime in 9,049 at bats. You know how many people have done that? Hit that well for that long? Nineteen. And all the others, save for Paul Molitor and George Brett, are already in Cooperstown. He slugged .451—only twenty-three other guys have done **that** for so long. He hit 529 doubles—that's the twentieth most all time. And our longevity rules don't really apply here. Scoop had sixteen full seasons in which he did all this—"this" being a bona fide Hall of Famer.

72. **Steve Palermo:** From the day Steve Palermo broke in as an American League umpire in 1977, he was considered the best balls-and-strikes guy in the game. Like McSherry, his reputation for being in the right place to make the right call was impeccable. Players and umpires alike glowed about him. And what more can be said about a man than that he was willing to sacrifice his safety, indeed, his livelihood, to protect strangers. That's the only reason he's not umpiring still—he intervened in a mugging outside a Texas bar and got himself shot. Great umpire, great man. Where's the plaque?

73. **Milt Pappas:** In his bible on the subject of Cooperstown, *The Politics of Glory*, Bill James points out . . .

Oh, no, you're not putting **him** in. Don't you remember the trade? When I was nine years old the Reds sent Frank Robinson to Baltimore for

him. Robby won the Triple Crown and the Orioles swept the World Series and all we got was a pitcher who once announced he was a candidate to become commissioner.

Hey, Dan, blame Bill DeWitt for that trade. He made it—not old Milt. Besides which, the Reds also got Jack Baldschun in that deal. And stellar outfield prospect Dick Simpson. I'm sure he'll be cracking that Red lineup any day now. He's still only fifty-three. He just needs some more time down at Indianapolis.

Anyway. Bill James said it this way: Look at the careers of two pitchers:

Pitcher "A": 209 wins, 166 losses; 465 starts; 167 complete games; 49 shutouts; 3,432 innings pitched; 2,486 strikeouts; 858 walks. Lifetime ERA 2.95 (about 21 percent better than the average for his time and league).

Pitcher "B": 209 wins, 165 losses; 465 starts; 129 complete games; 43 shutouts; 3,046 innings pitched; 1,728 strikeouts; 855 walks. Lifetime ERA 3.40 (about 11 percent better than the average for his time and league).

Pitcher "B" is Milt Pappas. Pitcher "A" is Don Drysdale. Could any two contemporary guys generate career stats that match any more closely? Other than the strikeouts and the ERA they're twins. So why is Drysdale in Cooperstown and Pappas simply the second half of the Frank Robinson trade story? Are we crediting Drysdale with making the Dodgers so successful during his years with them, or are we blaming Pappas because the O's, Reds, and Cubs never won anything, or both? Because Drysdale had two and a half fewer years in the majors than Pappas, does he deserve the Hall?

Perhaps the most remarkable stat Bill James ever generated was about Drysdale's impact during the seven pennant races in which he actually pitched. From August 10 to the end of the seasons in 1956, 1959, 1961, 1962, 1963, 1965, and 1966, against the Dodgers' key opponent in each of those seasons, Drysdale made a total of twelve starts and went 0-and-6. Against other contending teams in that span he went 6-and-7. In the clutch, in the heat of the pennant race, he was a net 6-and-13 against the teams the Dodgers had to beat to win the flag.

This, of course, doesn't mean a thing about Milt Pappas's wor-thiness. It just means that those few differences between his numbers and Drysdale's are even smaller than they appear in print. In his full seasons, 1958–73, he was third in wins behind only Juan Marichal and Bob Gibson. He was fourth in ERA behind them and Jim Bunning. He's as much of a Hall of Famer as Drysdale is.

74. **Dickey Pearce:** Apart from Merkle, perhaps my favorite obscure candidate. Look him up in *The Baseball Encyclopedia* and you'll see he played thirty-three games for St. Louis in the National League in 1876 and 1877 and hit a career .198.

And?

And he happened to be forty and forty-one at the time, looking back on a twenty-one-year career as one of America's greatest baseball players, already a legend in the game as the man who invented the shortstop position. And he completely vanishes from our horizon because he was an old man when they founded the first pro league we "recognize." Pearce signed on with the Atlantics of Brooklyn, the most famous team in the nation, in 1855, and between then and the team's folding in 1870, he changed the shortstop's role from the guy who just stood there between second and third, to the player who could make any play in the diamond cornered by second, third, short left field, and the pitcher's rubber.

We don't have any stats on him. So he doesn't go to Cooperstown. Phooey.

75. **Tony Perez:** Another absolute no-brainer. Nine times over twenty homers. Seven times over 100 RBI. His span as an everyday player is 1965 through 1981, during which he not only had more RBI than anybody else—he had **93** more RBI than anybody else: a **season's worth** more than Carl Yastrzemski (1,500 to 1,407). Slugging percentage? Number one there, too, for anybody with his number of at-bats (just edges Yaz). He was even fifth in batting average during the time. The argument against him most commonly heard from sportswriters is, if he was so good, how come he was never the Most Valuable Player? Maybe because the sportswriters vote for the Most Valuable Player?

76. **Billy Pierce:** One of my favorite books when I was a kid was a thing *The Sporting News* put out called *Daguerreotypes of Great Stars of Baseball.* It contained the career stats for all the guys in the Hall, plus all the other reasonable candidates. Any pitcher who reached any of the following three criteria was in the book: 175

wins, 4,000 innings pitched, 2,000 strikeouts. Billy Pierce is in there—211 lifetime victories, 1,999 strikeouts. In his years as a starter for the White Sox and Giants (1949–63) only Warren Spahn, Robin Roberts, and Early Wynn won more or struck out more. Of all the pitchers in the era with more than 3,000 innings, only Spahn had a better ERA. And of all the left-handers, ever, only sixteen had more victories.

77. **Vada Pinson:** You're going to get us in trouble again, aren't you? Remember? When Robin Yount was about to get his 3,000th hit you had us do a breakdown on how Yount compared to Pinson and a couple of other guys and I had to say the tough stuff and I got four billion letters from Wisconsin saying we had some nerve saying Robin Yount wasn't a Hall of Famer. I love Vada Pinson—but you're on your own here.

I never said Robin Yount **wasn't** a Hall of Famer. I said the only difference between Robin Yount and Vada Pinson was that Yount was going to cross a magic number that everybody knew about—3,000 hits—and Pinson hadn't, and that that was a damned shame. And Vada's since passed away and now it's even more of a shame.

That old dog-eared *Daguerreotypes* book of my youth listed four credentials for hitters: hit .300 for at least ten years, play in 2,000 games, get 2,000 hits, or hit 200 homers. Vada did 'em all except the .300 part. But between 1959 and 1975, only four guys managed to come to the plate even 6,000 times and hit .300. In that context, Vada's .286 over 9,645 at-bats looks pretty damn good. He's second in hits for his era, fourth in total bases, sixth in runs, eighth in stolen bases, twelfth in RBI. And, sorry Dan, here's the line-by-line with old first-ballot Robin:

	AB	H	HR	RBI	R	SB	SLG	AVG
Robin	11,008	3,142	251	1,406	1,632	271	.430	.285
Vada	9,645	2,757	256	1,170	1,366	305	.442	.286

Yount also had three more full seasons than Pinson. Vada nonetheless outdid him in four categories. The argument isn't that Yount **isn't** deserving of a spot in Cooperstown. It's that he and Pinson **both are.**

78. **Boog Powell:** The Boogster suffers because of the veritable horde of slugging first basemen who moved stiffly but imposingly

through his era. But even with McCovey and Stargell and Banks and Cash and the lesser lights like Hawk Harrelson, Deron Johnson, and Dick Stuart, Powell finished eighth in slugging between 1962 and 1975, ninth in RBI, and tenth in homers—he even shows up seventeenth in average. He had nine years with 20 or more dingers, and more importantly, he played on as many pennant winners (four) during his time as did the other seven first basemen listed above—combined. We get awfully selective about deciding who helped to create the dynasties and who just went along for the ride. The Orioles won the pennant in 1966, 1969, 1970, and 1971, and also took the division in 1973 and 1974, and finished lower than third only twice in his thirteen years with the club. Why do we presume that the Robinsons or the pitchers always carried Powell and not the other way around?

79. **Ed Reulbach:** Another amazing short-term guy from the twentieth century. Do we not pay attention to a pitcher who went 60 and 15 over three seasons? I mean, if he screws up the rest of his career, maybe we don't. But Reulbach was 122–91—31 games over .500—for the rest of his career. For any pitchers who've thrown 2,500 innings in this century, there are only five with better ERA's—and they're all long since in Cooperstown. Ed's was 2.28—and this wasn't a trick of the time. Three days after the Merkle incident, in the heat of the amazing 1908 pennant race, Reulbach shutout Brooklyn in the first game of a doubleheader—and then shut them out again in the second game.

80. **Allie Reynolds:** The problem with voting in Sandy Koufax was that the writers opened up a can of worms about careers shortened by injuries. If doctors tell Koufax when he's thirty-one that his arthritis could cripple him, and he retires, does that excuse him of the burden of longevity? If the Yankees' team bus stops short and Allie Reynolds, who didn't make the majors until he was twenty-eight, falls and screws up his back and has to quit at age forty, does that excuse him the same burden? Considering Reynolds was 63–27 **after** his thirty-sixth birthday, maybe it does. The Superchief spent nine years in the Yankee rotation and only once lost more than eight times in one season. Only twice did he **win** fewer than 16—and in those years he was 13–7 and 13–4. And consider his World Series record:

1949: Wins Game 1, 1–0 over Newcombe. Saves Game 4.

1950: Wins Game 2, 2–1 over Roberts. Saves the decisive Game 4.

1951: Loses Game 1. Wins Game 4.

1952: Loses Game 1. Wins Game 4, 2–0. Saves Game 6. Wins decisive Game 7 in relief.

1953: No decision in Game 1. Saves Game 6. Wins decisive Game 7 in relief.

So, he was the winning pitcher in the decisive World Series games three times. And in the '52 and '53 Series, in four games in which the Yankees are facing elimination, he wins two and saves the other two. Lifetime record 182–107, thirty-six shutouts, forty-nine saves (tied for sixteenth best ever at the time of his retirement).

81. **Jim Rice:** Lots of writers had lots of problems with him. They must have, because that's the only excuse they could possibly give for keeping him out. There are only eighteen guys who've come up 8,000 times and slugged .500 or better—he's the only one not in Cooperstown. There are only thirty-seven guys who've come up 8,000 times and hit .298 or better—he and Al Oliver are the only ones eligible who are not in Cooperstown. Leader in total bases for his era. Leader in RBI. Second in homers. Second in average (to Brett, who had 500 fewer at-bats in that span). Sixth in runs. Eight seasons with 100 RBI. Four with thirty-nine or more homers.

And on the other subject. I was working in Boston the day Ralph Houk retired as manager of the Red Sox, and I dashed out to the park to get player reaction. First guy I saw was Rice. "No, no, man, I can't talk. I just heard about it ten minutes ago. I'm sorry." Twenty minutes later there was a very heavy tap on my shoulder. "You still need me? I just needed some time to get my thoughts together." Rice proceeded to give an eloquent, emotional testimonial to Houk's goodness as a man.

And here's a last thought about old Jim Ed. Lots of crazy reasons have been put forth to explain why the Red Sox haven't won a World Series since 1918. How about this: The Red Sox came within a run of knocking off the vaunted Reds in 1975. Think they might've gotten it if Rice hadn't broken his arm on September 21? Think the team of the mid '70s might just as easily have been the Big Red **Sox** Machine?

82. **Jimmy Ryan:** Great eighteen-season outfield star, primarily for Chicago's National League teams, from 1885 through 1903. As William McMahon pointed out so succinctly in a marvelous SABR publication about the nineteenth century, the day Ryan quit, he was third all time in career games played, third in at-bats, fourth in doubles, homers, and runs, fifth in hits, and, despite being principally a leadoff man, eleventh in RBI. The numbers look great in any context: .306 average, 2,502 hits in 2,012 games, a .444 slugging percentage.

83. **Ron Santo:** Bill James considers him probably the greatest player not in the Hall. In just fifteen years, he hit 342 homers (most for anybody in his era who wasn't a first baseman or an outfielder) and drove in 1,331 runs (fifth for anybody in his era, first among the "nons"). Even if he'd **been** a first baseman, he would probably be a serious Cooperstown candidate. But he was a third baseman, good enough to win five straight Gold Gloves in the '60s with Ken Boyer as his chief rival at the beginning and Clete Boyer as his chief rival at the end. This was a remarkable, consistent, ballplayer whose absence from the Hall is enough by itself to make us question whether or not the writers should continue to do the voting.

84. **Frank Selee:** The Veterans Committee took a huge step in 1996 by electing Ned Hanlon, manager of the turn-of-the-century Orioles. Selee should be next. His Boston teams won five pennants in the nine seasons starting in 1891. He switched to the Cubs in 1902 and was still managing them in 1905 when tuberculosis forced him to turn the job over to Frank Chance. The Cubs he assembled went on to win the next three pennants. In Selee's days, the manager was responsible not merely for strategy and running a team but also for scouring the minors and amateurs for talents. He dug up Hall of Famers Kid Nichols, Jimmy Collins, and Vic Willis for Boston, and uncovered three more—Johnny Evers, Joe Tinker, Three-Finger Brown—for Chicago.

85. **Ted Simmons:** Remember those crazy ads that suggested Eddie Murray was the greatest switch-hitter of all-time? Ted Simmons would've been a better guess. Seventh best batting average among switchers, third highest slugging percentage, fourth most RBI, fifth most homers, sixth most hits. And he was a **catcher** and a damn good one—and he lasted twenty-one seasons. He also hit

.300 seven times (Berra did it three times. Bench did it once—in a season in which he got 178 at-bats). Topping it all off, he was a promising executive with the Cardinals and Pirates when a near heart attack convinced him to get out of the crucible.

86. **Reggie Smith:** Speaking of switch-hitters, here's the guy behind Mantle and Murray for homers. Second only to Reggie Jackson in slugging percentage in the 1967–82 era, ninth in his time in RBI, eleventh in homers, and a veteran of four World Series (13 RBI in his nineteen games as a Series starter).

87. **Joe Start:** One of the game's first base greats from his debut with Enterprise of Brooklyn in 1860 through his retirement from the Washington Nationals in 1886. Another victim of our ignorance of the great era of amateur baseball, and of the National Association. Start was already thirty-four when the National League was founded—yet he still played ten more years and batted an even .300, pounding out 1,031 hits in just 798 NL games. By all accounts and statistics, he was a flawless fielder, especially adept at catching infielders' throws. So? He played much of his career before **gloves.**

88. **Harry Stovey:** Voted by the SABR nineteenth-century committee as the most qualified candidate from the 1800s, Stovey is another victim of the prejudice against the old American Association. His seven most fearsome seasons were played in the AA, but he showed equal punch in seven years in the National League. Five times a homer champ, four times a runs scored champ, three times a slugging champ, and twice a stolen-base champ, he ended up with 1,769 hits and an extraordinary 1,492 runs in just 1,486 games.

89. **Bruce Sutter:** Rollie Fingers is in the Hall. Dennis Eckersley is going to be. Lee Smith more or less has to be. Rich Gossage and Jeff Reardon could be. And Bruce Sutter led his league in saves more often than any of them. Five times in the six seasons between 1979 and 1984 he was **the** National League closer. Fingers and Gossage only did it three times each, Eck and Lee Arthur just once each. And again we have to invoke the shortened-career theory. Bruce Sutter was wiped out by a bad arm that exploded on him at the age of thirty-three—Gossage was still pitching at age forty-two, and finished with only ten saves more than Sutter.

90. **Don Sutton:** Which young pitcher in the game today is

going to win 324 games? Which one is going to pitch on five pennant winners? Which one is going to win in double figures in each of his first seventeen seasons—and **four more times later**? Which one of them isn't going to miss a start for the next twenty-three years? The answer to each question is "none of the above," and the sooner the writers figure that out, and put the man who did all that, Don Sutton, into the Hall, the better.

91. **Ezra Sutton:** It's obvious by now that there simply aren't enough third basemen in the Hall of Fame. Santo and Boyer are obvious candidates from recent history, and Ezra Sutton is the obvious candidate from the distant past. Played the position every day from 1871 through 1888 and batted .300 or better eight times. All of our defensive evaluations from the time are subjective, but he had a throwing arm that contemporary accounts called "remarkable for its swiftness and accuracy."

92. **Luis Tiant:** Give Bill James the nod on this one, too. Luis Tiant is Catfish Hunter with poorer marketing:

	GS	IP	W	L	ERA	SO	BB	20 WINS
FISH	476	3,449	224	166	3.26	2,012	954	5
LOOIE	484	3,486	229	172	3.30	2,416	1,104	4

The five more wins and six more losses Luis Tiant had is keeping him out of the Hall of Fame?

Catfish's teams did better. Three straight World Series with the A's, two more with the Yankees; we think of Tiant and we see Cesar Geronimo chasing him in the eighth inning of game six in '75.

It is amazing, isn't it, that Hunter pitched in six out of seven World Series between '72 and '78? But we can look at a clear, complicated stat called "wins above team" that calculates a pitcher's won–lost record compared to his exact teams' performance without him. Any average schmoe should have been able to win 204 games for the teams for which the Cat pitched. Any average schmoe should have been able to win 208 games for the teams for which Looie pitched. Hunter's WAT is 20.2, Tiant's 20.6.

This means that when all the stats are adjusted and readjusted for the strength of the teams behind them, Luis Tiant was four-tenths of a win better than Jim Hunter.

93. **Mike Tiernan:** When you look at Mike Tiernan, right-

fielder of the New York Giants from 1887 through 1899, and you see he hit 105 homers and stole 449 bases and batted .311 and slugged .462, he looks pretty good. And then you think: He only played twelve and a half years; he only came up 5,906 times. He was out of baseball at age thirty-two. But the fact is, nineteenth-century players just didn't have long careers. The Hall's voters have never adjusted to that. Before 1900, only twenty-four guys even got 5,000 at-bats in the National League. These days, a guy like Scotty Fletcher can last long enough to get 5,000 at bats.

94. **Joe Torre:** As time passes, it becomes more and more clear to me that the two most remarkable individual seasons I've ever seen as a baseball fan are Ron Guidry's 25-and-3 for the Yankees in 1978, and Joe Torre's 230-hit, .363 season for the Cardinals in 1971. How did he do this? This man was very slow. This man started his career as a very slow catcher and then became a very slow third baseman. This man played his home games on old-fashioned AstroTurf. This was the seventh highest single-season batting average **ever** for a right-handed hitter with at least 600 at bats— **the** best since 1937. And it's not like that's all he did. Torre hit .297 lifetime (behind only Rose and Aaron in his own era), slammed 252 homers, slugged .452, and was an excellent receiver and adequate third baseman. And he's already managed fifteen years in the majors with a world championship and other above-average results with some really awful clubs (did the Braves really win the NL West in 1982—or did I dream it?).

95. **Cecil Travis:** On the morning of December 7, 1941, Cecil Travis was a twenty-eight-year old shortstop who had just hit .359 and led the American League with 218 hits in the same year of DiMaggio's streak and Williams' .406. Through the first eight full years of his career with the Senators, he'd batted .327 and slugged .436—only once had his average dipped below .317 for a full season. Then came the war. Cecil Travis not only didn't play another baseball game until he was thirty-three years old, but by that time he had lost some feeling in his feet owing to frostbite suffered during his service time. He managed to play all of 1946 and part of 1947, but it wasn't the same. Now, in evaluating Joe DiMaggio or Bob Feller or Hank Greenberg or any of the other greats who lost time to military service, we give them at least philosophical "credit"

for the interruptions of their careers. Why haven't we done this for Cecil Travis? Because he couldn't pick up where he left off? The war injury doesn't count for him? It's macabre to say this, but if Cecil Travis had been **killed** during the war, wouldn't he have immediately gone to Cooperstown?

96. **George Van Haltren:** How many lifetime .316 hitters aren't in the Hall of Fame? Throw out the short-term guys, limit it to lifers—5,000 or more at bats. You know how many? One. This guy. Twelve-time .300 hitter, pitcher-turned-outfielder of the Chicago White Stockings and then the New York Giants. He averaged 1.27 hits per game and scored 1,639 runs in his 1,984 appearances and we've forgotten him. Shame on us.

97. **Willie Wells:** When I spoke with him for about an hour in spring training in 1996, Buck O'Neil insisted this was the number one guy missing from Cooperstown. A brilliant shortstop, what exists of the records of the various Negro Leagues credit him with a lifetime average of .334, plus a .392 mark in exhibitions against big-leaguers, and a .320 lifetime mark in the Cuban Winter League, whose numbers were meticulously well kept. His career spanned thirty-one seasons and as late as 1942, when he was thirty-seven years old, he was considered one of the top three prospects to star in the big leagues if and when integration ever came.

98. **Bill White:** Between his eleven years as a topflight National League slugger (four 100-RBI seasons, .286 average, .455 slugging, seven consecutive Gold Gloves) and his distinguished tenure as president of the league, he seems like a Hall of Fame lock—so, when already?

99. **Deacon White:** Another nineteenth-century mistake no one's taken the time to rectify. He was principally a catcher and third baseman—the two positions taking the greatest toll on offensive production then as now—and he only played from 1868 through 1890—from the last great days of amateur teams like the Forest Citys of Cleveland to the first players' strike. Oh, and he only made 2,075 hits in his 1,558 big-league games. And he only batted .312 lifetime and only crossed the .300 mark a dozen times. **Does anybody besides me read the history books?** Also probably the first victim of the kind of neglect only known to the guys on this list. He died in July of 1939, just as the Hall was opened, and the

obituary in *The Sporting News* said he spent his last few months terribly depressed that he hadn't been invited to the ceremonies, let alone elected.

100. **Sol White:** Another nineteenth-century African American who survived five seasons of prejudice and hate in the white minors to play a solid second base and hit .360 in 152 career games. But White was much more than just a player; as early as 1887 he got an all-black National League off the ground, only to see it fold due to lack of financial support. He cofounded and managed the Philadelphia Giants, one of the early great black franchises, and was manager of the Newark Browns as late as 1926. This work, and his efforts to chronicle the early history of the segregated game, have earned him admittance in the pioneer category.

Are you finished?

Yes. But I have the distinct feeling I've left twenty or twenty-five guys out.

There aren't twenty or twenty-five guys **left!**

KEITH'S COMPLAINT:
IF YOU BUILD IT FOR ME, I WON'T LEAVE

Barely seven months after Art Modell became the Walter O'Malley of the 1990s, after he pulled the beloved Browns out of Cleveland for no reason other than personal financial goofiness and greed, after he erased the last tenuous moral thread that bound sports franchises to the cities that supported them, the city of Cleveland thought it had figured out what to do with the vast cavernous bowl of Municipal Stadium that Modell had rendered obsolete. They were going to push it into Lake Erie. To create the world's largest artificial freshwater reef. And the unspoken hope was simple: When they dropped it in the drink, maybe Modell might just happen to be inside it.

As I have suggested many times in my weekly column on the ESPNET *SportsZone* and in an article in this year's edition of *The Information Please Sports Almanac* from which much of this chapter is taken, the whole issue of building sports stadiums at public expense, or having them sponsored so that every time a sportscaster has to refer to one he gives that sponsor a free and very insidious commercial, is the thing in sports that most quickly and most severely frosts my editorial beer stein.

However, in an irony as painful and hinting of divine intervention as the infamous bathroom accident that befell Modell not long after he moved the Browns ("I scraped my scrotum," was how he phrased it to *Sports Illustrated*), Art's midnight run may have precipitated the greatest outbreak of sanity in sports of the second half of the century. In large part because Modell yanked the lid of Pandora's Luxury Box, as far as stadium construction goes, the free lunch may be over. In fact, the free lunch may soon become a **crime.**

After Modell got his shameful deal in Baltimore, and after Maryland found it had enough largesse left over to give Jack Kent Cooke **his** own new ballpark, and after the Mariners got their deal, and Pittsburgh its, and a dozen other cities rang with the sound of none-too-subtle threats, even the government began to sit up and take notice. Senator Daniel Patrick Moynihan (D–NY) married his outrage over the stadium construction to one of his pet projects. For years Moynihan's buns have been broiling over the fact that private universities have a credit limit. Through the states in which they are located, tax-free bonds can be floated on their behalf for construction of new research facilities, new classroom buildings, new laboratories. But once the debt limit of $150,000,000 has been reached, the spigot gets turned off and no new tax-free bonds can be issued until the old ones are paid off. No new tax-free bonds means no new construction.

Why, it suddenly occurred to the white-tufted New Yorker, was spending on behalf of universities limited when such spending on behalf of sports franchises not? The state of Maryland was to sink $177,000,000 into Modell's new park in Baltimore alone—never mind the state's commitment to Irascible Stadium, or My Three Sons Park, or whatever it was Cooke wanted to call his new home for the Redskins—and a large percentage of that figure was to come through tax-free issues. Conceivably, Moynihan argued, Maryland could float enough tax-free bonds to build a new stadium for every club in the state, up to and including the Baltimore Colts Band, ringing up billions of dollars of such issues and on top of everything else, denying the federal government huge amounts of taxes (that's what a tax-free bond **means**). But if John Hopkins University was at its $150 million tax-free limit, the state couldn't build its students, well, new **johns.**

Moynihan proposed, simply, to change the rules. Remove the cap on tax-free bonds for facilities of higher learning, and so the world isn't then saturated with vast armies of tax-free bond issues absolutely leveling the economy, make it **illegal** for a state to float a tax-free bond to build a sports stadium. Oh, you could grandfather in the projects already under way so that Senators DeWine and Glenn of Ohio wouldn't have to choose between what's right (new microscopes for Oberlin) and what's politically expedient (new stadiums for Mike Brown and Marge Schott).

Even while political pundits predicted doom for the legislation, even while Bob Dole considered opining that building new sports stadiums was not addictive, the chilling effect was immediate. If state governments had to actually **raise** the money to build new stadiums, which one of them would, or even could? And if no government could build a new stadium, with what could they lure a new franchise or keep an old one? And if there suddenly were no more out-of-town ballparks to move **to**, what kind of blackmail gun could an owner hold at the head of his current city or its fans?

Why, the entire fabric of Franchise Free Agency would be rent asunder!

The long-term implications were astounding. Never mind the elimination of the Modell shuffle. Never mind the neutering of such macho games of relocation chicken as those played by the Seattle Mariners and Seahawks. Even a team with no real intention of moving (say, the New Jersey Devils) could no longer wrangle concessions out of their incumbent states and cities. And if you couldn't threaten to move out, how could you raise ticket prices year after year? And if you couldn't raise ticket prices year after year, how could you run your business with the acumen of your kid's front-yard lemonade stand, knowing that no longer would some government, somewhere, bail you out of that $15 million deal you just gave this year's Matt Young? Even short term, would-be ballpark builders in Florida and Arizona confessed that while they could still issue their tax-free bonds, they believed that merely the introduction of the Moynihan bill would make it more difficult to sell them. They would have to scramble.

Of course, some owners were already scrambling. As his tenure in office now neared exceeding that of yet a fourth of his eight full-time predecessors, baseball's Acting Commissioner for Life Bud Selig proved to be far better at the out-of-the-pocket dash than he was of maintaining the fiction that he didn't want to be the boss. First Selig managed to get the state of Wisconsin to agree to a new Brewers stadium worth $250 million. In the liberal, quality-of-life-minded Badger State, nobody gets a completely free ballpark: The Brewers' obligation to the new palace was $90 million. But on the eve of the consummation of the deal, Selig suddenly announced he couldn't come up with the $40 million loan he needed to secure the team's part of the price tag. He'd have to consider moving, he said as he wandered through his nearly empty stadium, wringing his hands like some stricken poet, listening to the support of the literally hundreds of fans to whom it made a difference. Selig hinted he might move to Charlotte, North Carolina. Nobody commented on the coincidence that the bank from which he tried to get his loan was **based** in Charlotte, North Carolina. As usual, Selig got his way; local businesses and foundations anted up more than half of the Brewers' commitment. And Selig added irony to "financial synergy." The new stadium of which he dreamt was not only to be built in the first city to lure a modern baseball franchise away from its ancestral home, but moreover it would be reminiscent of Ebbets Field in Brooklyn, gone these forty seasons precisely **because** cities were willing to pay taxpayers' money to lure modern baseball franchises away from their ancestral homes.

When Seattle got its second publicly funded stadium in less than a quarter of a century, it turned up the heat in New York. George Steinbrenner figured that since the Yankees hadn't gotten a new ballpark out of the taxpayers of the Big Apple since 1976, it was time. He talked about a new facility in Manhattan and another one in the Bronx and another one in New Jersey (to which the Yankees had been threatening to move more or less since the day Mickey Mantle retired). He talked about the bad neighborhood and the bad access. He talked about walling off the area around the park to make a "Yankee Village." He talked about attendance so mediocre that he'd have to fire the seventy-six-year-old guy who opened and closed the clubhouse door for the players. He did **not** talk about the fact that the price of the best box seats in the house had gone from $4 each the day he took the team over to $35 each in 1997.

He did **not** talk about the fact that the owner of one set of four season box seats who wanted to buy all the play-off and World Series tickets offered to him had to fork over $4,770 within eight business days—and no personal checks, please. He did **not** talk about what he and the city of Tampa might have been thinking when he built the Yankees a Roman Temple of a ballpark just for spring training, costing only $31,000,000 and specially designed with the right-field fence ten yards from the main drag of a city about to get a big-league team so that it could never be expanded from its current capacity of barely nine thousand souls.

While Senator Moynihan conceded late last summer that his bill was dead for the year, several neutral public policy magazines and newsletters said it stood an excellent chance of being passed in 1997. And as cities scrambled to get their deals in place just in case the Moynihan bill became law, good taste was thrown to the wayside. The Pirates' new ownership and the mayor of Pittsburgh revealed plans for a new thirty-seven-thousand-seat "old-fashioned" ballpark with extensive foot access and a beatific environment visible over the outfield wall. They even pursued the facility under the nickname "Forbes Field II," apparently oblivious to the irony that **previous** Pirates' ownership and the **past** mayor of Pittsburgh had destroyed a beautiful thirty-eight-thousand-seat "old-fashioned" ballpark **called** Forbes Field with extensive foot access and a beatific environment visible over the outfield wall in 1970—because it was too "small"—and replaced it with one of those mail-order, cookie-cutter, paint-by-numbers giant irradiated multiuse ashtrays called Three Rivers Stadium.

The unthinkable was thought throughout the land. While anti-ballpark forces continued to fight heroically in Detroit, the future of Tiger Stadium was, at best, in doubt. In the virtually soundproof press box of the spring training complex built for them by the city of Fort Myers, Florida, two Red Sox officials blithely mentioned—in front of several reporters—that Fenway Park had become "inadequate" and would eventually "have to come down," and the columnists of that city prepared its denizens for the holocaust. In Baltimore, the Orioles, celebrating just their fifth season in Camden Yards, reacted with annoyance to the gelt being thrown at football teams and suggested that, at the least, they deserved some more tax breaks. In Chicago, the White Sox had the good manners not to say that six-year-old Comiskey Park was nothing more than a gaudier Three Rivers, but owner Jerry Reinsdorf had begun to Seligize—to publicly and loudly ruminate about the park's future. The Minneapolis Metrodome, not even fifteen years old, was declared "economically infeasible" by the Twins. Oakland had to play its first homestand in Las Vegas because workers were remodeling the Coliseum as part of Al Davis's Plan Nine from Outer Space for the Raiders. Wayne Huizenga got himself a new arena for Miami's hockey and basketball teams and whispered about one for baseball. The Astros, for whom Houston had built the largest indoor arena since the sailors from Ostia Harbor used to stretch out a tarp to keep the rain off the patrons at the Colosseum in Rome, threatened to move to northern Virginia or Monterrey, Mexico, or Katmandu, Nepal. North Carolina, which had only supported even triple-A minorleague baseball for four seasons, had no less than two separate groups hoping to get a major-league team, one for the so-called "Triad" around Greensboro, the other for Charlotte, which was incidentally hindered in its pursuit of the Brewers or an expansion club because the owner of its six-year-old NBA team wanted another new building there.

Eons ago—as sports time is measured—the late, great San Francisco sportswriter Wells Twombly observed that the first law of sports was "larceny abhors a vacuum." Even teams that neither moved nor got themselves a new arena managed to develop more virulent strains of ethics-resistant stadium folderol. In Hartford, NHL Whalers owner Peter Karmanos managed to enlist the local government to join him in a full-fledged attack on his own customers. Though the Whalers still had two years to go in a firm commitment to stay in Connecticut (an annoying leftover from the team's **last** shakedown of the state), Karmanos threatened to move the team out. He managed to hoodwink the state to name its own lieutenant governor to head a "Save the Whalers" campaign and establish a high-pressure, short-term deadline to boost season ticket sales from 6,500 to 11,000. In a market consisting of less than a million souls, 11,000 season tickets meant one for every ninety residents; in metropolitan New York, with three teams selling (optimistically) 40,000 season tickets, the ratio was one ticket for every 360 residents—in other words, there had to be four times as many ticket buyers per capita in Hartford than in New York.

The real beauty of the deal, of course, was that if the fans failed to fulfill this herculean task, the blame would not fall on the Whalers, nor the NHL, nor even politicians who refused to pony up for the sake of the fans. The villains would be the fans themselves. Connecticut governor John Rowland said as much: "This decision will not be made by the Whalers, nor by the state. It will be made by the fans." Owner Karmanos and the politicos could have escaped untouched, but in the middle of the six-week-long marketing blitz, it was revealed that the Whalers had a deal, ready to sign, to move to Nashville. And the same day Karmanos was denying **that** story, he was quoted in the *New York Times* as saying that what he really wanted to do was move the team to his native Michigan.

As it was, the "Save the Whale" campaign fell roundly short. Eight thousand season tickets were sold, not eleven thousand. Karmanos angrily announced that the politicians had refused to be reasonable about a buyout of his agreement to stay for two more years, and the Hartford Whalers were now lame ducks and would have to trim salaries. Nobody mentioned that Karmanos had upped the average ticket price by $9, so that the 6,500 renewals would be paying an **additional** $2,340,000 for a lame-duck team in 1996–97, and that the 1,500 new customers would be coughing up around $2,100,000.

Got it? Last year, the fine folks of Connecticut gave Karmanos four and a half million fish to let him break their hearts no later than 1998.

Against this kind of blinding, mind-numbing relocation not seen since the movie *Doctor Zhivago*, the Moynihan bill loomed as a measure of titanic importance. Moreover, economists were finally beginning to speak out about the lunacy of public construction of new ballparks and arenas. As Roger Noll of Stanford wrote in the *New York Times*, if new stadiums actually made money—for **anybody**—the owners would build them themselves and keep all the profit themselves. As for building the Yankees a new park as part of an "investment" in the city, Noll suggested that New York was better off putting its billion dollars in a savings account at the corner bank. Even the old bromide about the construction process being good for creating jobs was savaged by the Congressional Research Service. It pointed out that Maryland's own estimate was that 1,394 new jobs would spring up as a result of the state's $177 million investment in the Ravens' stadium. Fine, said the number crunchers from Congressional Research. That's 1,394 new jobs at $127,000 per job. But Maryland already has a job-seeding investment process called the Sunny Day Fund, which can put a man or woman to work at a state cost of $6,250. See the math yet? If the state puts $177 million in the Sunny Day Fund, it generates 28,320 jobs. If it puts $177 million in Baltimore's Modell Greedatorium, it generates 1,394 jobs. That means building this new ballpark will **prevent** 26,926 new jobs from being created.

But, Dear Reader, even if you're just a sports fan and the thought of tens of thousands of unemployed Marylanders doesn't touch your heart, think about it from a selfish viewpoint. If somebody doesn't stop this franchise roulette, within ten years not one of us will be able to correctly name the city in which each major sports franchise plays. Football has already taken the first steps over the precipice in Los Angeles, Cleveland, and Houston and the "N" in NFL might as well stand for "Nomadic." The only baseball teams happy with stadiums more than six years old appear to be the Cubs, Royals, and Dodgers. New NBA and NHL facilities were seeming to pop up before the carpeting needed to be replaced in the old ones. Temples of sport ranging from the Montreal Forum to Boston Garden to Cleveland Stadium to even Durham Athletic Park fell and generic "facilities" replaced them. And a bill sat on a senator's desk which, if forgotten, could turn all the gravity off and send franchises ricocheting around the country like billiard balls after a break; a bill that, if passed, could change the concept of "complete refurbishment" of a sports stadium from millions of dollars out of the public coffers to the appropriation of $32.50 for a new can of Sherwin-Williams Rust-Proof Magenta.

This whole dirty ballgame gets more sullied still when one considers the process of "naming rights," wherein a team can take a stadium it didn't even pay for and charge some corporation several million fish a year to stick its name on it. Some franchises can even count the anticipated revenue from "naming rights" toward their contribution to an as-yet unbuilt stadium! Lord, this is better than owning your own toll road! And talk about bad taste: Candlestick Park, whose name was just about the only thing **nice** about the place, became "3-Com Park," invoking images of Marx, Lenin, and Stalin. USAir spent a couple of million to slap its logo on the Capital Centre in Landover at just about the same time it was laying off a few dozen ground employees in New York—two of whom had dived into icy waters to pull survivors out of a USAir wreck at La Guardia Airport. Time it was that such crass, invasive commercialism was actually frowned upon. When August Busch took over the founding St. Louis Cardinals in 1953, he announced he was changing his stadium's name, "Sportsman's Park"—which had been used for St. Louis baseball fields since **1875**—and rechristening it "Budweiser Stadium." The hell you are, said the other National League owners, whereupon Gussie announced he would name it after himself ("Busch Stadium"). Thereupon, goes the story, he rushed back to the brewery and instructed his marketing nabobs to immediately introduce a new brand called Busch Beer.

Any semblance of manners was lost to the process during the debacle over Joe Robbie Stadium in Miami. While the late Dolphins' owners descendants had sold the park and the rights to rename it to Wayne Huizenga, they were outraged when he made a deal with an underwear company to call it "Pro Player Park" after one of their brands. A few weeks later, the stadium was **again** renamed in some kind of bizarre compromise: "Pro Player Stadium." It makes you feel almost **grateful** that Ted Turner bought the rights to rename the Olympic facility in Atlanta and christened it after himself. Geez, he could've called it "TNT Monstervision Park at Cartoon Network Yards."

Of course it **can** get worse. Inspired by the Miami mess, last September I did a "Breakdown" segment on *SportsCenter* suggesting the worst possible stadium sponsorship names:

BASEBALL:

Anaheim—by the National Safety Council: "Anaheimlich Maneuver Stadium."
Atlanta—for the new ballpark: "Olympic Stain-dium."
Baltimore—if the West Coast supermarket chain wants to go national: "Ralph's" Camden Yards.

Houston—by the TV cartoon producers Hanna-Barbera: "The George Jetson Memorial R-astrodome."

Kansas City—"Hall's Mentholyptus" Kauffman Stadium.

Mesa—by the Dodger pitcher, for the venerable spring training facility there: "Park Chan Ho" Ho Ho Kam Park.

Milwaukee—by the publishers of the megabook: "The Bridges of Madison" County Stadium.

Minnesota—a no-brainer: "The Hefty Bag" Metrodome.

San Diego—by the tire and automotive chain: "Pep Boys' Manny, Moe, and Jack" Murphy Stadium.

Seattle—to keep those paintings-on-velvet of him selling: "The Elvis Presley" KingDome.

Toronto—considering the unfortunate history of open windows at its residence suites: "The NoTel Motel" SkyDome.

BASKETBALL AND HOCKEY:

Calgary—to keep those rental videos moving: "Mel Brooks' Blazing Saddledome."

Chicago—to relaunch their singing career: "The Peaches and Herb Re" United Center.

Dallas—by TV syndicators, also to help the dissension-ridden Mavericks: "The Walton Family" Reunion Arena ("G'night Sam. G'night Jimmy Jack.")

Detroit—to boost her hotels: "Leona Helmsley's" Palace.

Hartford—considering who moved and who didn't, by the cable outfit: "The Nashville Network" Hartford Civic Center.

Houston—by the new Women's NBA to honor the great women's hoops coach at Tennessee: "The Pat" Summit.

Los Angeles—by Guccione Publishing: "The Penthouse" Forum.

Portland—by owner and computer billionaire Paul Allen: "I Beg Your Pardon, Microsoft Promised Me A" Rose Garden.

Sacramento—a part buy-in to the current sponsorship from the Padres' utilityman: "Arco Cianfrocco Arena."

San Jose—to keep the popularity of the craze going: "The San Jose Macarena."

Seattle—by the security people: "The Yale Locks" Key Arena.

Tampa—by street vendors everywhere: "The Italian" Ice Palace.

Syracuse—by the Centers for Disease Control: "The Typhoid Mary" Carrier Dome.

FOOTBALL:

Atlanta—by the Hair Club for Men: "The I'm Sy Sperling and I Can Cover Up Your" Georgia Dome.

Baltimore—why not? "Art Modell" Memorial Stadium.

Denver—a natural: "Zig Zag Rolling Papers" Mile High Stadium.

Green Bay—to boost lagging sales of his "I Didn't Do It" tapes: "O. J.'s On The" Lambeau Field.

New York—for the sake of truth, and construction integrity: "The Quick-Dry Concrete Jimmy Hoffa Memorial and **We Mean That**" Giants Stadium.

Oakland—let an owner sell the renaming rights to **himself**: "Al Davis Always Wants a New" Oakland Coliseum.

Tampa—gotta sell those *M*A*S*H* tapes: "Hot Lips" Houlihan's Stadium.

Are you laughing? Good. Will you still be laughing when **your** team moves somewhere, to a facility in another city financed by a tax on out-of-towners like you who use the city's hotels or rental cars, into a ballpark with a sponsored name even more tasteless than, say, "The General George A. Custer Arrowhead Stadium"?

Dan and Keith's Top Ten Most Troubling Sports Team Names:

1. Chicago Fire, World Football League, 1974–75. How much fun do you suppose the **real** Chicago Fire was?

2. Miami Hurricanes, NCAA. Nothing like honoring death and destruction. And the football program there has even given real hurricanes a bad name.

3. Washington Redskins, NFL. We can do this ''politically correct'' stuff to death, but truthfully, how long do you think this would've lasted if it had been the ''Washington Brownskins''?

4. Los Angeles Lakers, NBA. The classic meaningless vestigial nick-

name, just a notch worse than the Utah (ex–New Orleans) Jazz. The lakes the Lakers were named for are in Minnesota, where the team began. What lakes are being honored in Los Angeles? To-luca Lake? Arrowhead? Rikki?

5. Colorado Avalanche, NHL. See Number 2.

6. San Jose Earthquake, North American Soccer League; Rancho Cucamonga Quakes, California League (Baseball). See Number 5. Ever **been** through an earthquake? You can't stand up, you ex-pect to see your friends under piles of rubble, and the lights go out. Perfect imagery for a sports team. Makes you want to race out to the ballpark, huh?

7. Kissimmee Astros, Florida State League (Baseball). Yes, it's pro-nounced ''Kuh-SIMMY'' and yes, they changed it to ''Osceola County Astros.'' It's still pretty strange. One of your authors once had a rotisserie baseball team called the ''Keith Myaths.'' Say it aloud and you'll figure it out.

8. Montreal Manic, North American Soccer League. Pronounced ''Manique'' but still a very unhappy image. Were losing streaks Manic depression?

9. Kansas City Wiz, Major League Soccer. As has been pointed out, a game between the Wiz and the San Jose Burn is a urologist's de-light. It's just a dumb, dumb name. What did Kansas City do to deserve it? Is there more wizzing going on in Kansas City than any-where else in the country? The change to ''Wizards'' doesn't make up for it. They admitted they were only doing it to avoid a lawsuit.

10. Cleveland Indians, MLB. Would be number one except that when originally chosen, it was done so to honor tragic Cleveland out-fielder Louis Sockalexis, a member of the Penobscot. But times change. How about finding a good, noble word from the Penob-scot language and renaming the team after it?

DAN'S COMPLAINT:
WE BLAME ATHLETES FOR
THE WRONG THINGS

I'm probably in the minority, but I don't care what an athlete makes. I don't want to **know** what an athlete makes. People come up to me all the time and ask, "Is such-and-such worth *x* number of dollars?" Well, If somebody's willing to pay, then you're worth it. If you're not worth it, they don't pay—plain and simple. You get what the market bears.

People say, "Oh, is Michael Jordan worth $25 million?" No! He's worth twice that, at least to the Chicago Bulls, to the city of Chicago, to the NBA, to the **global empire** of the NBA. Is Juwann Howard worth $100 million? It's hard to put that in perspective. What does "$100 million" mean to you or me? It's a lot of money, but how do the Bullets recoup that? I don't know, but I do know that they're not going to pay that money if they're not making money off of that player, which the Bullets are; which the Bulls are from Michael Jordan.

Oftentimes on *SportsCenter* we'll announce the terms of somebody's contract. I once asked Tom Glavine if it bothered him that people knew exactly how much he made: They know how much his salary is, they know the incentives, they know how much he gets for an appearance. And he said, "Yes. Because I don't go and ask my neighbor what he makes. Why are people obsessed with knowing what I make?" And he's right, I feel like it's an intrusion in a lot of ways. I don't want people to know what **I** make—I don't think it's anybody's business. But we're obsessed with that.

There are, however, some secondary reasons that I believe suggest that salaries should be revealed. Among them: If it effects what your team can do under a salary cap—if you've signed Deion Sanders for *x* number of dollars and you therefore can't afford to go out and get defensive linemen, well, you as a fan would probably want to know that. So, I understand those things. I understand that for your team's success, and your role as a fan, you need to know where they stand moneywise under that great invention, the salary cap.

Sometimes I wonder if the salary cap will be the end of all sports as we know it. It's going to be the end of the world one day. **ESPN** will probably have a salary cap—well, they **do** have a salary cap, I think. But one day, every corporation, never mind every **team,** is going to have a salary cap. I'm sorry, we can only offer you $72. We're over the salary cap here at ESPN. We went out and re-signed Berman, and that's all we have left. Or we're over the salary cap here at Happy's Wholesome Bakery. We re-signed the Swedish Chef. You get $239.27 a week. That's all we have left.

The analogy I like to use when people point out how much an athlete makes is: Bruce Springsteen can make $40 million on the "Born in the USA" Tour. Madonna can make $20 million on her tour. Now what is the difference between those entertainers and Magic Johnson, Hakeem Olajuwon, or Michael Jordan? They're **all** entertainers. Michael **performs** one hundred nights out of the year. Springsteen and Madonna do the same. So for some reason Michael can't make $40 million but Springsteen can? Well, you say, Michael's just one player. He has a team behind him. Springsteen doesn't? Ever heard of Clarence Clemons?

And I know what the average fan's argument is. Well, **we** would play for nothing. We all want to play sports, and we all played sports for nothing. But we also all sing in the shower for free, too. And would you really want to go through all that a professional athlete has to go through—for free? For much, much less than the team is making from you? Play a rain-delayed game in Montreal one night, leave at 3:00 A.M. for Chicago, and play a day game at Wrigley the next afternoon? Week after week? Month after month? Year after year? With your job perfor- mance judged by millions? Booed? Reported on TV? With sportswriters?

Stalkers? The chance you could turn a corner, rip a hamstring, and get fired because you run 10 percent slower than you did last year? With your career lasting an average of four or five years—**after** you put in ten or fifteen years of preparing for it, sacrificing the rest of your life for it? For free? For less?

Would you have traded places with Donnie Moore? Remember? The Angels, a strike away from going to the World Series in 1986 and Donnie Moore gives up a two-run homer to Dave Henderson of the Red Sox. The Angels lose the game, lose the Series, and Donnie Moore spends the rest of his life dwelling on it, reliving it. He's booed—not viciously, not even more than average. But something slowly snaps and not even three years later he takes a shot at his wife—misses, thank God—then kills himself. No matter how bad your job is, can you conceive of anything at it going so bad that you wind up killing yourself over it? And it's not like there was only one Donnie Moore in sports history.

I think when you begin to look at the price tag affixed to an athlete, you begin to expect certain things you never expected before. Once an athlete starts making a lot of money, the fans' perspective of him changes, because it's almost as if his salary automatically goes into the same sentence as his name. It's going to be ''Juwann Howard, making $100 million . . .'' ''Michael Jordan, making $25 million this year . . .'' I think we—reporters **and** fans—have to be careful with that. Because instead of just sitting back and enjoying athletes, and watching the games, and being a fan, we become highly critical because **our** player is not performing like a $100 million player should.

Don't blame the player. Blame management for signing him, for spending that kind of money! I look at my friend Jeff Blauser of the Atlanta Braves—a marginal player, a little better than average—but starting for a great team. And he wasn't breaking the bank: He was making a good salary. All of a sudden he hits arbitration, he's making three million dollars a year! Well, he started to really **press,** and I don't know if he's recovered from that. I think he's tried too hard to **live up** to making three million a year. Whereas before that, nobody expected anything out of him. Jeff Blauser? You know, the guy who just does the little things. He's tried to help this team. He has a clutch hit occasionally. He's a role player. But when you start to make big money, the **game** is over. Now it is big business. You've entered the fan's head as a bank statement instead of as an athlete. Oh, how can a three-million-dollar player make **that** play?

That kind of error? What a bonehead play! Well, the greatest players still make mistakes.

Where I think today's players **deserve** criticism is in how they've responded to their own success and their own celebrity. We want athletes to be entertainers, and there's a fine line between show **biz,** and showing **up** another player. When I see Henry Rodriguez stand at the plate and admire his home run, I say "Who's Henry Rodriguez to do that?" It's a great story that Henry Rodriguez had a career year for the Expos last year. But you would think that a guy who has been through all the hardships, the troubles, the problems with injuries, that he would be a little more humble. Maybe that he would be thankful that he's **playing,** that he's starting every day, that he emerged from the Dodgers organization when so many others didn't, and got his chance with the Expos. But it's usually the guys who are not worthy who wind up doing most of the show-boating.

Now, Pete Maravich was as good as it got when it came to entertaining. But I think Maravich was not all about showing you up, as much as he was about knowing that **he** had to put on a show. That's what he was all about in college. He came into the NBA labeled as flashy, flamboyant—I mean, he was an entire off-Broadway musical rolled into one basketball player. And he knew that he was being paid to perform and be an entertainer: the long hair, the floppy socks, the great passes, the wild shots. But it's not like he got in your face and taunted you. He loved the game, and he loved being a showboat, but he drew the line at showing the other guy up.

Some people, even players, suggest this all started with Julius Erving. But any athlete who feels this way saw only Dr. J's sizzle, not his steak. Anything you have to do to beat the other guy—twisting in midair, changing hands at the hoop, slam-dunking—is fair game. If it looks flashy, if it looks amazing, that's fine. That's part of the game. Julius Erving didn't land from a slam dunk and bump chests with his teammates or shoot imaginary six-guns at his opponents. His imitators, who didn't have his athleticism, could only duplicate the flash. Don't blame Dr. J—he was just playing ball at a different level, figuratively **and** literally.

Now you see athletes who act almost as if it's scripted: This is how I'm going to dance after I do this. Barry Sanders, who has been a friend of mine since he left Oklahoma State, doesn't spike the football, and he has told me, "I don't know what I'd do if I tried to. I'd look silly if I did a touchdown dance.'' What he **won't** tell you is that he wants to act like he's been there before. He doesn't need to show somebody up. He's one of the greatest running backs of all time, and he doesn't **need** to do that. He is so flashy when he runs that he might show you up, he might embarrass you, but that's only with his God-given ability while trying to avoid tackles. To the degree that he's showing you up, it's only during a play—he doesn't take his helmet off in the end zone, thump his chest, point to himself. And that's admirable; consider the ''other'' Sanders.

Deion Sanders knows that what he does **sells,** just like Dennis Rodman. They are businessmen. I think both of their histrionics are overbearing at times. But people—you, the fan—pay to see them. I think you've got to be careful when you get into this ''I'm the star, I'm the show, I want center stage'' stuff. If people saw Deion Sanders as just the person, and not the player, they wouldn't even know him. A concerned father, a guy who loves to go fishing, a self-admitted bore. Look at Dennis Rodman when he was with the Pistons: good player on a great team—but he wasn't a star. All of a sudden, Dennis started piercing every part of his body that he could, tattoos all over his body, changing his hair color— and then he became this superstar. I mean, he's *La Cage au Folles* on a basketball floor.

I know that the media is sometimes accused of being out of touch with today's athlete. It's not like I don't enjoy honest celebration. When you see the enthusiasm, and joy, and sense of accomplishment, it's thrilling—and genuine. I've seen Steve Young spike the ball, being very demonstrative. Well, if you do it at the right time, I'm all for that. But when you do it because you think that you're expected to do it—''Let's do a touchdown dance''—I think it cheapens what you've just done. If you've just scored on a great touchdown run, do you need any more showboating? Haven't you **just** entertained? Haven't you **just** had the stage all to yourself? Sometimes you'll see somebody score on a one-yard touchdown run and then spike the ball and taunt and point in a guy's face, and yell and scream, and you think, ''**I** could've done that. **I** could have fallen forward three feet and scored a touchdown.''

And ESPN and every other television outfit in this country deserves part of the blame that goes around on this. We show those athletes. They **see** those highlights. They think, ''If I'm going to be on the show, I've got to do that as well.'' So, I take part of the blame, just by proxy. I am media. I just like to see the genuine enthusiasm of players who accomplish something, not the Rockettes out there. Remember when Mark Gastineau used to do his "Sack Dance"? I begin to think it's a cry for help. Look at me! I just did something! Aren't I great? I don't know how today's athlete would've been twenty years ago, or how Willie Mays, Gale Sayers, or Jim Brown would've reacted nowadays. So I try to be fair in making those observations about showboating, because it is a different world today for the athlete. But it is kind of sad when I isolate an athlete like Barry Sanders because he simply hands the football back to the official after he scores a touchdown. It's the period at the end of a sentence—I've done my job. I've scored. Here's the football, ref. I plan on being back.

So as fans, reporters, and athletes, let's make a contract. We'll stop harping on how much money players make when their employers always make more **from** them. But you athletes have to stop showing people up. The money should be enough. So should the touchdown you just scored or the home run you just hit.

Dan and Keith's Top Ten Favorite Types of Sports Figures to Interview

1. **Hockey players.** They rarely get angry at you, they don't blame you for their problems, they don't hide in the trainers' room, and they seem to genuinely appreciate their own good fortune. Plus, if you meet them in a social setting they'll not only invite you over, they'll probably also buy you a beer.

2. **Rookies.** Grateful for the attention. Also still young enough to actually listen to your question and not have a prepared answer to it. Still young enough to think the two of us **count** somehow.

3. **Guys with senses of humor.** Make a joke about yourself, make a joke about your teammate, make a joke about us.

4. **Golfers.** Usually big fans of other sports, and not too life-or-death about their own game.

5. **Baseball players—other than stars.** Your average to above-average guys usually are comfortable with the media, can have a real conversation with you, and don't mind that you sit in their dugout.

6. **Women basketball players.** This entry was submitted over Dan's protest.

7. **NFL, NBA, NCAA players.** Generally way too full of themselves. Use the third person a lot. Make you wait.

8. **Hockey executives.** Nothing wrong with them really. It's just that 90 percent of them use that damn Ontario pronunciation of "organ-i-zation" and it just drives you nuts after a while.

9. **Union leaders.** Whether it's Marvin Miller's sighs or Gene Orza's labyrinthine sentences, we'll pass. They also never have good news. Never.

10. **Team owners.** There are exceptions. But, generally speaking, if they were all on fire and we had a real pressing need to go to the bathroom, we'd wait till we got to the next gas station.

OUR TWENTY-ONE
TOP TEN ATHLETES

We wanted to take some space to pay tribute to the people who our jobs are all about: the athletes. We wanted to include one list of "Top Ten" admired, favorite sports figures. But, as you know by now, Dan and I rarely agree on anything, so rather than present one list full of disclaimers and "Keith doesn't really like #7 and Dan doesn't really like #4," we set the format thusly: Dan got to pick his Top Ten, and I got the chance to rebut. He left out a couple of people he figured I'd include; I left out a couple of people I knew he'd include. So, first you'll read his choice, then my answer, then my choice, then his answer.

However, we did agree immediately on someone who should be at the top of every list like this so we're not only putting him first, we're considering this Top Ten list as a list of Top Ten guys **besides** him.

As Howard Cosell always used to call him: Jack Roosevelt Robinson.

For all the problems that still exist in this country, for all the racism—in both directions—for all the bigotry and the idiocy, imagine what everything would be like if a half a century ago Jackie Robinson hadn't done what he did and hadn't done it the **way** he did. It's amazing that so many athletes, especially baseball players, don't know his story, don't know his sacrifice.

But I wonder sometimes if it isn't a sign of progress that they don't. Don't get me wrong: I feel there's not just racial pride but moreover great human warmth in the fact that Mo Vaughn chooses to wear number 42 because Robinson did, or that there's this surge in interest in the segregated leagues, or in the fact that I could sit down with David Cone last year and he could go on and on in amazement at what Jackie had to survive and what an impact he had. But the ultimate goal is supposed to be a time when nobody can really believe that only white men played major-league baseball for the sixty-odd years before Jackie Robinson broke in with the Dodgers in 1947, just as the ultimate goal is supposed to be that nobody can really believe there were ever whites-only drinking fountains, just as the ultimate goal is supposed to be that nobody gives a damn what color you are or what personal beliefs you have—only whether or not you're **worth** a damn as a human being.

My mom always said that the goal of being a parent is to make yourself obsolete. Maybe, long term, Jackie Robinson's goal was to make himself, in the social sense, obsolete.

And when we reach that goal, he'll still be on the top of the list. For paving the way for everybody on this list—black and white. For personal courage. For being a revolutionary **ballplayer.** And then he'll still be on our lists.

Amen. So let's go to our Top Ten—of everybody else. The first selection belongs to Dan Patrick:

1. **Kirby Puckett:** A man of his word. When he signed his contract, he lived up to it, even though he knew he was vastly underpaid. Played with enthusiasm; you never heard a negative word about Kirby Puckett. He was a winner, a Hall of Famer, and when he knew he couldn't play anymore, he bowed out with such dignity. He stayed with the same team—he stayed with the Twins his entire career. I knew I always got my money's worth when I watched Kirby Puckett play. And he made me smile when I watched him play. And he tried. He always looked like he was trying—but he always looked like he was having fun.

The saddest part about Puck is that when he had to quit last year, he still had it. Believe it or not, I was **in uniform** for his last two homers in a Twins game. This was when we did the stunt where I coached first base for Edison Community College of Fort Myers, Florida. In his first competitive at-bat since Dennis Martinez had hit him, he took one of "our" pitchers over the wall in right. A rocket. The second time up he got fooled on a pitch, then hit the next one twice as far as the first. Then the cloudiness began in his eye and it was over.

And remember how he insisted that the eye problems had nothing to do with Martinez hitting him? Last fall Kirby was a guest commentator when the network did the Orioles-Indians series. And Dave Campbell mentioned how Kevin Seitzer wore a face guard attached to his helmet because he'd had his cheekbone shattered? I think Kirby let the truth slip. He said of Seitzer, "I wish he'd have told me about that. I'd still be playing." I think he just **told** everybody that the Martinez pitch had nothing to do with his retiring. I don't think it was true. I think he just said it to alleviate Martinez's guilt. Not a tragedy on the Lou Gehrig level, but at least as sad an occurrence as Sandy Koufax having to give it up at thirty-one.

And that's baseball's loss. There are not enough Kirby Pucketts to go around—and they could certainly use a lot more.

That having been said, the guy on the top of my list is still:

1. **Jim Thorpe:** There has never been a greater athlete, there's never been a more influential athlete, there's never been a more tragic athlete. He's first on all the lists. Summarize his career in a few sentences and it seems like it has to be fiction. A kid off the native reservations in Oklahoma becomes the greatest college football player of his day, running, kicking, punting, playing defense. Then he concentrates on his hobby, track and field, and he goes and wins the decathlon **and** the heptathlon at the 1912 Olympics. Wins every speed event, wins every durability event. Then they find out he made $60 a month one summer three years before playing baseball in the lowest of the minor leagues, and they strip the medals from him. He's hurt, he's devastated, so he goes pro. In baseball **and** football, at the same time. For ten years. Now, he was only an average outfielder; just six years in the bigs (he kept playing in the minors). But what he did in college football for Carlisle he repeated in the years in which the NFL was being formed. In fact, in the first year of the NFL he was **the** star player, coach of his team, **and the league's president.**

Can anybody be compared to him? As late as 1950 he was voted:

1. The greatest college football player of all time.
2. The greatest pro football player of all time.
3. The greatest Olympian of all time.
4. The greatest track-and-field athlete of all time.
5. The greatest athlete of the first half of the twentieth century.

We thought Michael Jordan was doing something phenomenal when he spent a year trying to be a baseball player. This man was four Michael Jordans wrapped up into one. He was four Babe Ruths. And mix in the prejudice because he was a Native American, and the loss of the Olympic medals—which hurt him to his dying day—and he's got to be the greatest. The worst part is, there had been under-the-table money for "amateur" athletes for as long as there had been amateurs. But Thorpe hadn't taken any of **that** money—he had tried his hand at pro baseball for seventy-three games for Rocky Mount of the flippin' Eastern Carolina League in 1909 and 1910, made a solid $300, $400 for his two summers—in a game that wasn't even an Olympic sport—and they took his medals away for that. Today we take athletes who make $40 million a year and put them in the Olympics and we don't think twice about it.

Jim Thorpe was, all by himself, The Dream Team.

But none of us ever **saw** Jim Thorpe do any of this. How can you evaluate guys you never saw? We don't even have film of this. I'm not belittling his accomplishments, but how do we **know?**

A fair argument. A wrong argument, but a fair one. I'll tell you how I know. In 1982, when I was with CNN, Fred Lebow of the New York Marathon held a ninetieth birthday party for Abel Kiviat, who was one of the great distance runners before the First World War and still had shiny eyes and a wiseass attitude and ran up Fifth Avenue as a stunt and still went so fast he shot right past our cameraman.

And Abel had been Jim Thorpe's roommate at the Stockholm Olympics. And what he said was that Thorpe was **greater** than any of the records suggested. He said that all Thorpe had to do was watch **you** do something, practice it once, and he'd be better than you were. Swimming. Playing pool. Card games. Crossword puzzles. The javelin. He told me Thorpe could've watched me do the interview we were doing, then taken the mike out of my hand and done my job better than I did.

No big effort there.

I saw that cab coming down Broadway with its doors open. Anyway, Kiviat insisted that the only reason they didn't enter Thorpe in **all** the track-and-field events was simply to give the other Americans a chance at a medal or two. And he told one great story. After the Stockholm Olympics of 1912, the American team took a victory tour of sorts through Europe, because all the heads of state wanted to meet Thorpe. And in Paris there was this great party for the entire U.S. and French Olympic teams. And Kiviat said that in the huge, high-ceilinged dining room there was a chandelier, so after the meal and after the brandy and after the cigars, all the athletes decided to put a little money down and see how many of them could leap and touch this chandelier. All these great high-jumpers and distance jumpers took shot after shot at it, and Thorpe just stood there in the corner, leaning against the wall with his arms folded. And after the guys who had just won the Olympic gold medals in the high jump and the pole vault tried and missed, Thorpe smiled, took his jacket off, stood a few feet from the chandelier, took three quick steps and leaped up and **grabbed** the bottom piece of the chandelier and released it just before he would have pulled the whole thing down from the ceiling.

You're right. The record books distort. I don't think Abel Kiviat was distorting.

Pick up your list.

2. **Michael Jordan:** I don't know him as a person, but I have great respect for him as an athlete. He is **the man** every single night out. Not only knows that he has to win—he also knows that he has to be a **star,** that he has to entertain. When he comes to town, people come out to **see** Michael Jordan. And he never disappoints. He continues to amaze. He may be the greatest basketball player we've seen. Money wasn't the issue with Michael Jordan—he wanted to win. Criticized the Bulls the first couple of years in the league because he wanted to be surrounded by better players. He was willing to reduce his salary so other players could be brought in. But he wants to win more than any other athlete I've ever seen, and will do whatever it takes. And that kind of fire, and that kind

of passion in today's athlete—where the average athlete generally puts money first, winning second or third—is almost gone. But to Michael Jordan, who has more money than he knows what to do with, he knows you still can't **buy** one of those NBA Championships, and he savors every last one of them.

But to know that you're going to be the villain every single night when you go into the opposing arena, and to love to be that guy, to savor it, to put the dagger into the other team's heart, **that's** sports.

When he won the title in Phoenix in 1993, he came in after winning the title, had a cigar in his hand, had one shoe on, one shoe off, a bottle of champagne, did an interview with me, and then he said, "Do you care if I just sit here? I just want to savor this—it's crazy outside." And he sat there, almost childlike, and just let it seep in, what he had just accomplished.

I'd put Mike somewhere on the list. But I can't rate him ahead of my second choice:

2. **Muhammad Ali:** Forget what he did in the ring. It's very possible that Marciano might have floored him, or Tyson, or whoever. You can even forget the fact that perhaps he lost the four prime years of his career because he stood up for some very unpopular principles of a very unpopular religion for a very unpopular race of people. You can even forget that **after** that persecution he came back and won his championship all over again—twice. I put him here simply because of the indescribable magic he could, and still can, use on everyday people. He was part of a boxing news conference I covered in 1983 and by that time his speech was already beginning to go, so he didn't say much. But he'd been doodling on the tablecloth at the dais throughout the thing, and the moment it all ended, I saw this mad dash to the front of the room. It was the bus boys. They all had scissors in their hands and they were there to cut up the tablecloth Ali had been doodling on. Technically, they were risking their jobs—not to get Ali's autograph or shake his hand or get a picture with him—but just to get a meaningless little scribble on a piece of cloth he had touched.

And this happened to him nearly every day. My agent Jean Sage once had to bring Ali from a news conference to a meeting, and they were riding in a limo when they got stuck at a traffic light. And Muhammad looked out the window and saw some guy selling watches or newspapers or something. He pointed at him and said, "Scuse me, Miss Jean, I want to get out and say hello to that man," and before she could stop him, out he went. And she says that within a minute, he was surrounded by a thousand people. They came out of the office buildings. Drivers jumped out of their cabs. A mounted policeman got off his horse. Just to be near Ali, just to see him. And when he spoke, they all became silent, and when he said he had to go, nobody protested, nobody asked for one more autograph. They just spontaneously started chanting his name and waving. What we're really talking about here is the impact of a religious figure. Or a mythical one. And Ali knew that he could make people smile just by being out there with them, just saying hello, just **being there.**

I have a problem with his making millions in this country and then refusing to do what Elvis Presley did by serving in the military, or what a million other guys did by serving in the military, or what the dead in Vietnam did, making the ultimate sacrifice. I don't know if I'm comfortable with that.

Fair enough. But you know damn well it was no coincidence that the draft board called him at what, the age of twenty-seven, just after he converted to the Muslim religion. This larger-than-life athlete, suddenly becoming a black activist, biggest mouth on the planet and the ability to back it up, and he just **happens** to be drafted when he's eight years older than the standard age? There's all kinds of crap in the FBI files suggesting this was a deliberate, racist act—and if Elvis Presley had been a Quaker and refused induction, do you think the government would have prosecuted **him?**

Anyway, throw in the Olympic gold medal, and what he meant to his race, and the fact that he might be the greatest boxer of all time (or, at worst, in the top five), and the fact that he continues to try to make people happy even though he can barely speak, and you've got yourself one of the great **people** of all time.

3. **Cal Ripken:** You and I go back and forth on Cal's value, Cal's streak, but it's hard to criticize somebody for **wanting** to play. He was criticized because he wanted to **play.** Athletes sit down for a variety of reasons. They get hurt lifting their wife's suitcase. They hurt their eyelids. Cal Ripken wanted to play—was he selfish? Maybe he was selfish because he wanted to play, and there were times when a rest probably would

have done him good. But as he rationalizes it, "Who was better than me in the lineup at that position? Even if I am tired, who is better than me?" I found him to be sincere, genuine, and a person who loved to compete, loved to beat you—no matter what. Three days before he broke Lou Gehrig's streak, I went up to do a Sunday Conversation with him, and when I got there, he apologized because he was twenty minutes late—he'd just done something for *Redbook* magazine, and they kept him a little bit later than he thought. But he walked in, and the first thing he said was, "I apologize for being late." Everybody wanted a piece of Cal that week, but he did the interview, and when we got done, I figured he was going to politely get up and get out. But he wanted to talk to me about football rotisserie—he wanted to tell me about the team he had just drafted! And he was so excited, because he didn't know if he had a good team or not, and he was new to it. And he also talked about playing golf. And I think being in the position that we're in, we get to see glimpses of athletes when their guards are down, when they do just want to talk.

I just think it's rare nowadays when you see somebody who wants to play every day, who wants to know that their name is in the lineup, and it's not to say that I don't appreciate what Lou Gehrig did—and you've updated me, clued me in, on what Gehrig was going through at the time. And I don't know if it's harder to set a record, or more difficult to chase a record. But you look at the purgatory Hank Aaron was put through while he was chasing Babe Ruth, by the fans, the media, and you sometimes wonder if these guys wonder if it's worth doing it. But Cal Ripken did his interviews, he still showed up, he stayed after and signed autographs—he didn't **have** to do it, and he doesn't only do it when a camera's on him. But he knows he has to give back; he should give back; he **wants** to give back—and I have great admiration for that.

I criticize Cal Ripken only for his lack of knowledge of who Lou Gehrig was. So I **have** to take Gehrig over him at number three. The whole purpose of this big storm I stirred up in '95 by suggesting Cal should consider tying Gehrig's streak and then intentionally sitting out game 2,131 was because I thought if Cal only knew about Lou Gehrig, he would've wanted to see Gehrig stay in the record book. And Cal was the only man on earth who had the power to make that happen.

And you're right. He admitted it. He said he didn't know much about Gehrig other than that he was a great player.

What he said was, he was going to wait until after he **retired** and then he might read up on him. I said this then, and I say this now. I think if and when Rip does that, he's going to have at least a passing regret that he didn't just tie the record. A record is a record, but to deliberately **choose** to stop something to preserve somebody else's piece of history would be a far greater accomplishment. I have extraordinary respect for Orel Hershiser. When he was chasing Don Drysdale's shutout innings streak in 1988, he said he wanted to tie it, then, if the Dodgers were comfortably ahead, give up a homer or walk the bases loaded and force in a run so he wouldn't break it. Only Drysdale was able to talk him out of it.

But why should Orel have done that? Why should Cal have done that? What's the old saying? Records are made to be broken?

The point is that Gehrig's streak didn't end the way Ripken's will end. It didn't end because the Yankees found somebody better, or because Gehrig got hurt, or because Gehrig simply didn't have it anymore. It ended because Gehrig was dying of a terrible, debilitating disease. Gehrig was two months short of his thirty-sixth birthday when he came out of the Yankee lineup. Cal was a month **past** his thirty-sixth birthday when he broke the streak. A healthy Gehrig could've played another six hundred consecutive games.

But the point is he **didn't.**

Do you know what got me started on Gehrig? In 1989, on the fiftieth anniversary of the day his streak ended, I interviewed the man who replaced him, Babe Dahlgren. Babe was a wonderful man who just passed away last year at the age of eighty-four and if this list was twenty or twenty-five guys long instead of ten, I'd put him on it. Anyway, Babe said the Yankees beat the Tigers 22-to-2 that day, and after each inning he'd go to the bench and sit next to Lou and plead with him to come in for an inning or pinch-hit or do something to keep the streak alive and Gehrig just kept shaking his head and saying, "It's over. I can't do it anymore," and Babe said he got chills because he knew something was very, very, wrong.

On a rainy day in 1935, Babe told me, he was playing first for the Red Sox and Gehrig got a single against their pitcher, rounded the bag, and slipped and fell on a muddy patch. And couldn't get up. Just couldn't pull himself off the ground, for a minute or maybe longer. Babe said that in thinking about it, it was obvious the disease that would kill Gehrig six years later had already taken hold of his body. And of course, that **has** to have been true! People with amyotrophic lateral sclerosis don't die quickly—that's the horror of the disease. We saw Bob Waters, the college football coach, go slowly and terribly over the course of a decade.

Lou Gehrig didn't suddenly get ALS in 1939 and die two years later. He must've had it in 1935. Or 1933. Or 1929 for all we know. **Lou Gehrig was dying while he played the last five hundred or thousand games of his streak.** Can you imagine that? You talk about players coming out of the lineup for silly injuries—this man didn't come out of the lineup while his bones were disintegrating and his muscular coordination was dissolving. There has been nothing comparable to that, and there will never be anything comparable to that.

Still, that shouldn't detract from what Ripken did.

I never said it should. I just said he missed a chance to do something far more noble, far more impressive, than just breaking a record.

But since we're on this subject, I've got to say it. I don't think the streaks are comparable, I don't think what they did during the streaks is comparable. Gehrig hit .340 lifetime and **averaged** 147 RBI per year. If the ALS started in 1935, he hit .332 with 145 homers in the four years **after** he began to die. There was a stretch from 1987 through 1990 in which Cal hit .252, .264, .257, and .250—if Gehrig had done that he wouldn't have just been benched, he would have been sent to the minors. The Yankees had at least four guys who went on to become starting first basemen for other big-league clubs because Gehrig fended them off. Did the Orioles ever have anybody to push Cal? Of all the middle infielders they had in the '80s and '90s only one of them even briefly earned a starting short-stop's job somewhere else.

What I'm saying is, Ripken's performance shouldn't detract from **Gehrig's**, and I think in a real sense it has. Gehrig goes back into the history books and Ripken is lionized. I think it would have been better if there'd been one pedestal upon which they could stand, **together.**

4. **Barry Sanders:** I find him to be naive at times, but also one of the great practical jokers. He loves to kid, he loves to act like he doesn't

know what you're talking about. The first time I met him, he had just won the Heisman Trophy, and the first thing he did was look at what I was wearing and say, "Do you think I'll be able to afford suits like that?" And I didn't realize he was being serious. He had come from modest means; his car had broken down on the day he went to announce he was going pro! And still, money has never been an issue to him.

But I remember him telling me that he wanted to go out and get another car, and he wanted to know what I thought of a Honda Accord. I told him he could afford any car he wanted. But he was so concerned about how he would be perceived that he went and got a Honda Accord. His house is modest—not much in there except for a few TVs and video games. During his rookie year with the Lions, I went to do a story on him, and I said, "Barry we'd like to film you walking into practice," and he begged me not to—because he did not want to be singled out.

A great athlete, and a humble guy. That part about "singled out" reminds me of a lot of ballplayers, though. My pal Joe Magrane didn't want me to do a story on him trying to come back with the White Sox last year and he said exactly the same thing. "I'm just trying to be a middle reliever here," he said. "Don't want anybody to think I think I'm a big deal." It's a very endearing personality trait.

One neither of us has.

Correct. No time for false modesty. Back to the list:

4. **Martina Navratilova:** I always refer to her on the air as "my hero" and I mean it. How many athletes have been in the public eye so long under such trying circumstances, done so well in their sport, and maintained not only their dignity but also their sense of humor? One of the funniest people I've ever known, forever making jokes at her own expense, and not only admitting to a lifestyle that probably dozens of pros in all sports have kept secret, but becoming politically active about it. All those years when she wore the black hat to Chris Evert's good-little-girl routine, sometimes seemingly jobbed by the refs for that very reason, and only once did she ever lose her composure or blame anybody. She threw a **towel** at a cameraman in 1982. With the provocation and the name-calling and everything else, she probably had the right to throw a **cameraman.**

5. **Wayne Gretzky:** In 1978 I went to Indianapolis on a job inter-

view, and I remember reading in the papers about this eighteen-year-old kid playing in the WHA and I was thinking, "How do you pronounce that name," and somebody said, "They just call him the Great One." So, I'm in Indianapolis and the job interview doesn't go very well, but I decided to go see the Indianapolis Racers, and I remember seeing this frail kid coming out and I said, "My goodness, **that's** the Great Gretzky?" But he never seemed to get hit, he always seemed to have the puck, he always seemed to get it to the right person. Wasn't fast, wasn't big, wasn't strong, which made it even more of a marvel to watch him, and then realize, fifteen, sixteen years later, that I got a rare chance to see the greatest hockey player of all time in the embryonic stage of his career. Not too long after that, he was sold to Edmonton, and the rest, as they say, is history.

Whoa. Hold on. Stop right there. The greatest player of all time? The greatest **scorer** of all time. Gordie Howe was a greater **player** against tough competition. Bobby Orr was a greater player. Probably Bobby Hull. Possibly even Mark Messier. And this reign in which he owned the league was over by the time he got to Los Angeles. He's been slowing down ever since.

Of course he's slowed down! He's been carrying the league for over a decade! What he did as a player will never be matched. He dominated. Everybody knew what he was going to do, and they couldn't stop him. He's another athlete who would stay there until the last question was asked, and he tried to be interesting, because he knew he had to be interesting because the league **needed** him to be interesting: say something quotable! One of the few things that he ever said that **was** quotable was when he called the New Jersey Devils "a Mickey Mouse franchise." He was being honest, and he was saying what he thought was good for the league: Improve that franchise! You're in the shadow of the Rangers. And as to his goal scoring, it's not like there was the era of the "juiced puck."

Yes there was. My number five: Gordie Howe. Think about this. Gordie Howe scored over a thousand goals lifetime and the first six hundred-plus were in a six-team league. This meant that every night, Gordie Howe was going up against one of the six best goalies in the world. He was going up against four of the twenty-four best defensemen in the world. He was going up against one of the six best **teams** in the world. There were one or two seasons in the '50s when every single goaltender Gordie Howe scored against went on to the Hall of Fame. On a given night, Wayne Gretzky could be facing any one of seventy or seventy-five different goalies. He might get shut out by the best. He might score four against the seventy-fifth best. Where's the comparison?

And Howe kept himself in condition long enough to play from 1946 through 1980—to play long enough to be a threat offensively and defensively while his own kids were playing alongside of him. And while being the greatest goal scorer of his time, he was also the greatest tough guy.

I saw what he did to you last year in that commercial.

Do you know he pulled every one of those punches? Made contact but nothing further? But every time he had to hold on to me, it was like a vice. The man was sixty-eight years old and a half an hour after we finished shooting the spot, just his grip had been so strong that I began to hurt from the tip of my finger to my neck. And talk about carrying a league—the NHL's risky years were not 1979 through 1988. Gretzky may have helped to improve hockey. Howe and the people of his generation saved it. There were a dozen NHL teams in the late '30s and then they started dropping like flies. **Howe** carried the league from that time until expansion.

Something else. I met him when I was ten years old, at the Automobile Show at the Coliseum in New York. He was signing autographs, and I was so scared to meet him that he decided to loosen me up. He signed a postcard and I reached for it, and zoom!, he shot his arm straight up in the air, and I reached up real high to grab it, and zoom!, he shot his arm back down toward my feet. Just to mess with me, just to make me laugh. And when we did the commercial, I told him about it, and of course he didn't remember **me** but what he did remember astounded me. "Oh yeah. Auto Show. 1969. I was there for Ford, with Byron Nelson and Jesse Owens. Kind of a snowy night, I'm surprised you made it."

How the hell did he remember that? Twenty-seven years later? No wonder he was so great. If a goalie made a great move to stop him, he knew never to shoot the puck at him at that level. If some skater got around him, he knew all his moves. Forever. Never forgot a damn thing. And a gentleman, cordial, cooperative, thanked everybody for "letting" him do the commercial with me.

6. **Larry Joe Bird:** I've always appreciated athletes who made it look easy, athletes who are able to make others better, athletes who break the game down to a science—and have fun doing so—athletes who do things not everybody can. We don't see these athletes too often, but Bird was always one of those players. You knew he could go two for eighteen from the floor, but he was still going to win the game, because he loved to have the ball in crunch time, and one of those two shots he would make would be the game winner. He and Magic Johnson are the two best players I've ever seen in finding the right guy. Not just the open man, but the **right guy** who had the best chance of scoring. And Bird didn't care about how much he scored—the bottom line would always be with Bird, winning. I remember being there in 1986 when they won the title, and following the Celtics throughout the play-offs. Bird would always be the last player to leave the locker room. He figured if you **really** wanted to talk to him, you would wait—and he would stay. He'd answer every question, and honestly.

But to watch him play, up close, was to get a true sense of what greatness is in the variety of the things that go into making up greatness: not just scoring, passing, rebounding, but also doing the dirty work—he wasn't a glamour boy, and he talked trash but he backed it, he loved it if a player talked trash back to him. Charles Barkley told me that one time Robert Parish set a pick on him while he was guarding Bird, and Larry went by the pick and went up to shoot, and started yelling at Robert Parish while **taking** the shot. Larry made the shot, but he was mad because Robert turned the wrong way on the pick, because Larry had intended to throw the ball to him. Xavier McDaniel tells the great story that while he was with Seattle, Bird came downcourt and told X where he was going to shoot, and with how much time left on the clock—and he did it from exactly the place he said he would. But after the shot, McDaniel said Larry was upset—because he had left a second on the clock.

I got numerous chances to interview Bird. Probably the most enlightening one was after he retired, and we went up to Boston to do a half-hour special on him, and I knew all the stories, I knew all the people; I just wanted to hear them again. Prior to the interview, I thought well, I'd like to loosen him up, because Larry can be very tough sometimes on reporters. So I called Brad Lohaus, who was one of his friends, and I said, "What do I do to loosen up Larry Bird?" and he goes, "My suggestion would be go out and get a cooler, get a twelve-pack of Lite beer, and give that to him right before you start the interview." And I thought: what a stroke of genius.

Now I don't know if Brad figured that Larry would **drink** the twelve-pack before the interview, therefore be **really** loose. But when Larry sits down, I hand him the cooler, and I say, "Brad Lohaus told me to give this to you," and he says, "What is it, a fish?" He opens it up, sees that it's a twelve-pack, and says, "Can I keep the cooler?"

Obviously he knew your rep on money. Did you fight over the cooler?

Shut up. I said, "Yes you may, Larry. It's a five-dollar cooler."

Five whole dollars, Dan? Did you put in for it on your expense report?

May I continue now? Bird was so honest with his answers. I remember asking him about being able to pay back his mother for having had to raise the family after his father had committed suicide, and I said how do you pay her back and he said, "With money." And he got the biggest kick out of saying that, because that's how he did so, he **literally** paid her back. And Larry's known as a rather frugal guy.

Ahem. Did you discuss advanced methodology in getting your partner to pick up the tab for dinner? You are sometimes **frugal** yourself.

I know, I know. As sad as this is going to sound, living in Ohio, I once took a vacation to French Lick, Indiana. French Lick is known as this resort area, and they have spas there, but I didn't care. I had convinced my girlfriend at the time, "Why not go to French Lick? We can drive there from Ohio." So we drove to French Lick, and I went there for one reason—to see Larry Bird. There's a sign there that says "Larry Bird Boulevard," right outside of his high school. And I thought, how do I find out where Larry lives? Where's his mother's house? I was trying to be very coy: looking in the phone book, asking people in the street. Finally, I just asked the postman: I said, can you tell me where Larry Bird's mom, Georgia, lives? And he burps and says, "Two blocks down, take a right, third house on the left."

So I rented a bike, and I rode over. I did not tell my girlfriend. I was stalking Larry Bird. I figured he'd be outside, shooting jumpers. And yes—he would invite me over: "Dan, c'mon, shoot some jumpers with me." So I rode by the house. I was there for five days. I rode by every day.

Twice a day, once in the morning and once in the afternoon. No Larry Joe Bird. Saw some of his brothers, but no Larry Joe Bird.

Bad vacation.

I was fortunate to see Bird when he won a title when they beat the Rockets. I was there when they beat the Lakers.

We saw them beat the Lakers. I had just left CNN to go to Boston and you had just replaced me, and we both covered that series. You may recall I even felt sorry for you, still being on cable, and put you in a piece I did for the local station there, Channel 5.

You asked me what company I worked for and I said, "Cable News Network," and you said, "What's that?" and then you turned to the camera and said, "That's an inside joke" and I caught hell for that.

First time.

First time for what?

First time you caught hell for something I did.

Yeah, great. Back to Bird. Just being around that whole group made it memorable, because I was able to see one of the greatest players ever. But also a character, too, great sense of humor, great at needling people.

I got to watch him, too. The privilege was seeing this stuff night after night. He would cut the Lakers in half. He would cut the Pacers in half. He would cut the Clippers in half. In practice, he would cut his teammates in half. He's on my list. But my number six is completely out of left field:

6. **Jim Bouton:** One of the best pitchers in baseball for a couple of years, and he gutted out another five or six seasons with his arm virtually Scotch-taped back onto his shoulder. And I thought his comeback with the Braves in 1978 was the essence of sports. Guy hadn't been in the major leagues for eight years, he was thirty-nine, and he went back to the beginning, to the low minors, just to enjoy the whole process all over again before his last drop of ability was gone. And he actually did it, he actually won a game.

But of course he's not on this list because of the pitching. I think the two most important things that have happened to baseball since the breaking of the color line were free agency and Bouton's book, *Ball Four.* I remember my dad reading it, giving it to me, and saying, "This is a very good book but there's some very bad language in it. You're eleven. You've heard every bad word already, so I don't think it'll do any damage to you. Just don't use the words around the house. And learn something from this. There's a lot of truth in here.''

And boy, was there ever truth in there. For the first time, the very first time, there was a book about what it was **really** like to be a pro athlete: the boredom, the practical jokes, the hatreds, the goofing around, the travel, the women. A lot of older people thought Bouton had disillusioned kids about baseball, or even life in general. I think he did exactly the opposite. He showed us that the players weren't superhumans or even gods—they were just grown-ups, and anybody with some talent and some perseverance could become one of them. Or, if they couldn't become a ballplayer, some talent and some perseverance could make them successful in some other field. I doubt Bouton ever thought about it that way, but the book was really very inspirational to kids. There's a great deal in there, in a very subtle way, about working hard and how to overcome adversity. And it's funny as hell. Still. I try to read it at least once a year.

There's something else. After they basically threw Bouton out of baseball for standing up to the establishment, he became a sportscaster in New York. And what a revelation **that** was! I had already decided I wanted to do this when I grew up. And to that point I'd seen Kyle Rote and Frank Gifford and Phil Rizzuto and all these straight-arrow, Pray-to-the-Establishment guys. And here comes Bouton and he's doing things like ripping the Mets for not putting in a waiver claim on Mudcat Grant and letting him go to the Pirates in the middle of the 1970 pennant race, and when his former teammate Jimmy Wynn got stabbed in the stomach by his wife, Ruth—on their anniversary—he says, ''Ruth should know that the traditional gift on your seventh anniversary is not steel, but copper.'' Wow! I mean, highlights **and** jokes **and** substantive commentary.

You remember when we met him?

Emmys, 1995. Sure do.

And he said he loved the show and loved my style and I said, ''You sure should. I've been doing your act since 1975.''

Get me out of this, Dan. Get back to the list.

7. **Arthur Ashe:** He cast a pretty long shadow as a person, and that shadow certainly obscured what he did as an athlete. So I have admira-

tion for the athlete, but something more for the person. I had a chance to interview him a couple of times when he was coaching Davis Cup, and he was always this dignified, refined, gentleman. Every time I spoke to him, he reminded me of royalty. He wanted to make a difference, not just for one or two people—he really had designs on the world, of making it a better place, a more positive place, and you just can't underestimate the task that he wanted to undertake. What he had been through as a person, growing up in Virginia in troubling times, trying to play in a predominantly white sport, being ostracized, and then to emerge on the center court at Wimbledon, and then to win—perhaps the greatest tournament you can win. He didn't return racism with more racism. He tried to explain. "Being a black man in America," he said, "is like having another full-time job." Then to remain a graceful man, and then to have his privacy invaded, because everybody has to rush to tell a story nowadays, which was really a great disservice to this man, everybody falling all over themselves to be the first to say Arthur Ashe had AIDS.

He always wanted to say the right thing, he found it difficult to criticize, because he figured there was a better way to do it, better words to choose, and he just hadn't figured them out yet. I remember asking him what his biggest regret was, as an athlete, and he said, "I don't mean to demean what you're asking me, but how important are athletics? If you ask me as a person, then I'll tell you. But as an athlete, I was in the lap of luxury." And then he just kept talking about how he was fortunate to do what he was doing, because being a successful athlete allowed him to have, no matter where he went in the world, a platform. So, as he kept reminding me, how can I say I've had a bad life? Have there been bumps? Yes, everybody has bumps. Did I grow up with a silver spoon? No. But that makes you greater. He said he felt sorry for the people who grow up in a privileged life—there's nothing wrong with adversity. Here's a man who lived through it, or at least thought he had, until newspapers tried to beat each other to the punch to reveal that he had AIDS. They never thought about what it would mean to a man of dignity to be able to say it on his terms, when he chose to.

When I was at CNN in New York, Yannick Noah opened a restaurant in Greenwich Village. I asked Noah, "Is it assumed that every black tennis player looked at Arthur Ashe as a role model?" And Noah said he was a role model—as a **person.** There were other great tennis players you wanted to be like. But as a person, you wanted to be like Arthur Ashe.

What greater tribute can a man receive?

I'm going to agree with you on Arthur, and I'm going to get us into trouble by picking my next one.

7. **Magic Johnson:** I've never been a huge hoops fan, yet I got to watch Bird every night for most of a season, and Earvin every night for six seasons. There was psychic activity involved in the success of both. And Johnson's big smile was worth sweating through the Laker locker room. And he constantly tried to be nice and accommodating—oops, that's a bad choice of words—to fans and reporters alike. But that's not why he's on this list.

You aren't going to say what I think you're going to say. Not considering how often you bash him for not doing more about AIDS. You're not.

Yes, I am. You're right. I think he bit off more than he could chew when he said he planned to devote his life to being a "spokesperson" about HIV and AIDS. He did a video, held a lot of clinics with kids, did a lot of good things. But he wasn't there on World AIDS Day every November, and he quit the Presidential Commission on the disease, and even when the president changed he didn't do the kind of up-front official stuff that has far more impact on the problem than he could imagine. And he may or may not even have changed his lifestyle. And the endless retirements and comebacks have just worn everybody out. And I'll keep bashing him as necessary.

But he's on this list, and he'll always be on this list, for one reason. One night when I was in Los Angeles, a relative of a prominent local sports figure died. On the news that night, even though everybody in the Southern California media knew that this person had died of AIDS, I read what the family said, that "the cause of death was **announced** as dehydration and complications of pneumonia." Ethically and legally that's as close to the truth as I could come, and I felt sick about it. And the moment I got off the air, I got a phone call from a woman who almost immediately began to cry. Her brother had been in the bed adjoining this person in an AIDS ward and the brother had died about three months previously. And she said that knowing that this person had also died of AIDS but his family wouldn't say so was like reliving her brother's death. "Don't they realize?" she said. "Don't they know? They don't have to do any interviews, they don't have to make any donations. All they have to say is, 'Yes, he had AIDS, it can happen to our family even though we're famous and all-American and all that, and it could happen to yours,' and who knows how many people might have taken it seriously for the first time, or stopped associating it with something that just happened to strangers, or gays, or drug addicts. Why couldn't they just say it? Why did they have to add to the shame? Maybe just saying it might have stopped somebody from getting it. Just one person. Now that person's going to die because they couldn't bring themselves to say, 'He had AIDS.' "

Four months later Earvin Johnson stood up at a podium and smiled and said he was HIV-positive and he was going to fight and we should all be careful. And I thought about that poor distraught woman's phone call and I thought, maybe Magic's no hero for getting the disease or spreading it. But facing up to it, bringing it out in the open—that, that one moment, is a heroic act. And don't tell me he couldn't have kept it a secret. Arthur Ashe did—and people in the media (**responsible** people like Frank Deford) knew about Arthur—and Magic's still healthy enough that he could've played the last six seasons and nobody would've known a damn thing. He **chose** to tell people—and lord knows how many lives he saved by just doing that. How many saved lives does it take to make you a hero? I think just one is enough.

8. **Jackie Joyner-Kersee:** It's only appropriate that she's named after the former first lady, Jacqueline Kennedy Onassis, because she was the first lady of track and field. Just a graceful athlete, and she wasn't in the glamour events—the heptathlon is hardly a glamour event, though she made it so. Nobody had a bad word for Jackie Joyner. Prior to the '88 Olympics, I interviewed her and her brother Al, and just fell in love with both of them, the way they were as people: fun, just smiling constantly. And they had grown up in East St. Louis, and they were grateful that they had, because it taught them the meaning and the worth of everything they had. It taught them about trusting people, having friends, being able to do what you want, coming and going as you want, being free. And as I interviewed them, they were like little kids: They were hitting each other, and goofing around and laughing and poking fun at each other. She was not the celebrated athlete then; it was Flo-Jo who dominated in the '88 games. Jackie Joyner has always had somebody who was

a little bit bigger than her in terms of the spotlight. But if you look at the accumulation of what she's done over her athletic career, nobody can touch her. Longevity counts for a lot. And one of the nicest, sweetest people you'll ever meet. When we finished the interview and I was leaving she said, "This is going to be on CNN. Does that mean that my competitors will be able to see this?" and I said yes, and she said, "I should've been a little bit meaner, shouldn't I?" I said I don't think it's in you. And she said, "No, it's not. But I want to scare 'em—but I don't want to be mean."

Competitiveness and hatred don't have to be the same thing. And competitiveness and compassion don't have to be opposites. Here's another one out of left field:

8. **Jack Twyman:** A six-time NBA All-Star and a Hall of Famer, but that has very little to do with why he's on my list. Late in the 1957–58 season, one of the early power forwards in the league, Maurice Stokes, suddenly went into convulsions on a Cincinnati Royals team flight. Not long after they landed, Stokes's illness was diagnosed as encephalitis, sleeping sickness—he would be hospitalized, virtually incapacitated, for the rest of his life. He and Twyman were teammates, they were rookies together when the team was still in Rochester, and they were friends. But later, both of them would admit that they had hardly been **best** friends, nor even good ones, and this was still just seven years after the color line had been broken in the NBA. Yet Twyman, who was white, had himself appointed legal guardian for Stokes, who was black. He raised funds to pay Stokes's medical bills. He inaugurated the "Big Mo" game at a resort in the New York Catskills—a charity game featuring NBA players that's still held today, nearly forty years after Stokes got sick, more than twenty-five years after he died. And Jack Twyman, who took these responsibilities on himself simply because he felt somebody **should**, continued to play for the Royals for eight more years, including a stretch of over six hundred games in a row. I've always thought that the kind of selflessness Jack Twyman showed was as inspirational and important as anything anybody did on a court or field.

9. **Dick Trickle:** He began as a curiosity in 1985. Perusing through the sports sections in Atlanta—NASCAR town—I couldn't help but notice the name "Dick Trickle." My God! Something went terribly wrong at

birth! How could his parents name him **Dick** Trickle? Better yet, how could he keep the name Dick Trickle as a grown-up? So I began to follow his career. It almost became a passion for Gary Miller and I, since we were both working at CNN at the time. The heck with Bill Elliott, Dale Earnhardt, Dale Jarrett—we followed Dick Trickle. We knew if we were watching a race, we had to watch early, because something would happen to Dick. I remember one night on *SportsCenter*, I think Dick's engine dropped out and I said, "Dick drops a load on lap 21," and he was done: Dick Trickle done for the day. There was some excitement last year in Milwaukee; Dick, back in his home state; Dick, with a chance to win a race; everybody in the entire ESPN complex called me, sent a message via the computer: Dick Trickle is leading.

That's because you said if he'd ever **won** a race, we'd lead the show with it, and then resign. I would've been right there with you, buddy. Right there holding the door open for you and welcoming Rich Eisen to full tag-team partnership status.

I almost felt like a proud father. Of course, as soon as I turn on the race, he crashes. Dick Trickle is Charlie Brown behind the wheel and the rest of the NASCAR field is Lucy, ready to pull the football right out from underneath him, so when he tries to kick it—every year—he falls flat on his butt. But one day, one day Dick Trickle will rise above, and tears will be streaming down my face as I say "and the winner of this year's Daytona 500 . . . is Dick Trickle."

Dan, this would truly be premature jocularity. He's taken a lot of—well, there's no other word for it—**crap** from us.

He's been a good sport about it, too. I did one radio interview with him, and he was down to earth, had fun with it, knew that it was kind of a strange name, had been teased all of his life. And then his daughter called us up and invited us to join the Dick Trickle Fan Club—I'm still a little sensitive that your fan club number is one less than mine.

Just keep telling yourself it's alphabetical, it's alphabetical. Just like the credit on this book.

I'll get over it. The back of my chair at work? There's a Dick Trickle fan club T-shirt. So he's always there.

There are two amazing things about this. You have made Dick so well known (and I've helped, I guess) that we both constantly get Dick Trickle memorabilia sent to us. People have their pictures taken with him—they send us a copy. I'm glad he has a sense of humor about this, or by now, he'd have come to Connecticut and run us over in his car—even if the engine had dropped out of it.

The other amazing thing is that Dick Trickle was one great short-track racer in his native Wisconsin. For all the kidding, he is, basically, the kind of sports figure upon which the whole edifice rests. He's the thirteen-year utility infielder or the guy who played tackle for ten years and coached for twenty more. Two years ago, somebody sent me the final standings for the Wisconsin circuit from 1979. Dick was the champ. The sixty-fifth-place finisher was a Mr. Richard Hed. Now imagine the trouble we'd be in if their fates had been reversed.

Anyway, I completely concur with our friend's place on the list. Nonetheless I have my own entry at this spot:

9. **Ed Giacomin:** What a goalie. To be a hockey fan in New York in the 1960s was to be a fan of Eddie Giacomin. No matter how the Rangers might disappoint in the play-offs, now matter how often they might break your heart, his abilities were a point of pride. For the first five years of his career he basically played 90 percent of the games, and he played without a mask. He flopped, he jumped, he stickhandled the puck to the point where you wanted to scream at him to get back to the crease. He was a tremendous goalie. But once again, this man is on my list for one moment of his career that I think defines what sports is all about.

After ten years with the Rangers, Steady Eddie was sold on waivers to Detroit. Now, by 1975 New York fans had gotten more than a little frustrated with the play-off flops, and the chants of "Ed-die, Ed-die" were more often as not replaced by booing. But Giacomin's first NHL game in a uniform other than New York's just happened to be **at** Madison Square Garden, and one of the most amazing things in sports history happened.

The owners tell us that fans root for teams, not players. That's why the NFL went on with their games during the strike in 1987 and why baseball tried the same thing in '95. I mean, even when Rebecca Lobo returned to the University of Connecticut with the U.S. National Team two seasons ago, the UConn crowd roared for her in the introductions, and then cheered when she had a shot blocked.

But it wasn't that way in New York in '75. The entire Ranger crowd turned on the home team. The Rangers were booed from the moment they hit the ice. And when Giacomin led the Red Wings out of the visitors' tunnel, the fans rose as one and roared and would not stop. The ''Ed-die'' chant rang louder than it ever had before—and it continued for the entire game. And Eddie Giacomin didn't try to play the stoic, emotionless professional. He wept openly. He had to take off his mask a dozen times to wipe away the tears. He won the game, and he wept again in the locker room afterwards. And seven years later, I interviewed him about that game and he was still getting teary-eyed about it. It had been a transcendant moment in sports, and it had had such an effect on him that he never went back to the Garden to play again—not even in any of the old-timers games. ''How could I?'' he asked me. ''The only thing I could give back to those wonderful people who were there that night was my respect and my reverence. How could I ever go back on the ice there again?''

OK, DP, time for your last entry.

10. **Coach Reeves from *The White Shadow*:** I know what you're thinking—great athlete? And I say ''think again.'' If not for that tragic knee injury that he suffered while playing for the Bulls, he could've been Michael Jordan. Coach Reeves, strong to the hole—he was the next Mark Olberding, maybe Mark Iavaroni. He could do it all. But he did something **after** the injury that not many athletes are capable of doing: blending into society, giving something back. And he ran that Carver High Basketball team to perfection—trying to keep Coolidge under wraps, making sure Salami knew how to go to his left. He made us proud. He made us want to play for Carver High, to wear the orange of Carver.

You know that was just a TV show, right?

So? **We're** just a TV show.

I hadn't thought of that. Anyway, I liked Ken Howard better in the movie *1776*.

Thomas Jefferson couldn't go to the hoop like Coolidge.

OK, I have the last submission, and I thought about Curt Flood, who gave up his baseball career at age thirty-two to fight for rights he'd never get to enjoy, and I thought about Fred Merkle—but they're both in the chapter about the Hall of Fame. So now I'll take my tenth pick from beyond even my customary place out in left field:

10. **Grover Powell:** He won exactly one game in a big league career that lasted exactly fifty innings. Grover Powell was a left-hander out of the University of Pennsylvania who signed with the New York Mets, and in his first big league start in 1963 he shut out the Phillies, 4–0. But he hurt his arm in Venezuela that winter, and never made it back to the majors. Given time, Powell might have been not only a fine pitcher but an even finer example of the kind of player we love: gifted, but not too serious about himself. He loved to mess with reporters, telling them his middle name was Demetrius (it was David) and lightening up his postgame comments with references to Greek mythology. He insisted that his hometown of Wyalusing, Pennsylvania, was a garden spot. "Marie Antoinette was going to settle there before she had an accident with a knife." Asked if he saw a line drive off the bat of Donn Clendenon that struck him in the cheek, he said he did. "I saw the ball. I kept telling it to go back."

Grover Powell died of leukemia at age forty-four. On his tombstone is etched an image of him in a Met uniform. And above the epitaph "He achieved his dreams" is a copy of his lone baseball card. I think of Grover Powell just about any time I see a player make his debut, no matter what the sport. I think of the effort and the achievement and the dream which that first game represents. I think of the possibility that the dream may live for only a short time, and I think of how lucky some of us are to see our dreams come true—and stay true.

12

KEITH'S COMPLAINT, PART II:

TO MAKE THE WORLD SAFE FOR ALBERT BELLE TO HATE MY GUTS

When I worked in Southern California, I had a fairly regular schedule: Mondays through Fridays, an occasional Sunday thrown in covering for somebody. In April of 1987, for some reason lost in the floor cracks of history, I had a Monday night off, and I hurried home from an evening out to watch *Nightline* because they'd planned a tribute to the fortieth anniversary of Jackie Robinson's debut with the Dodgers. And I saw Al Campanis, Jackie's old double-play partner with the Montreal Royals, a man I knew, a man I respected, explaining how blacks didn't have the necessities to become big-league managers and executives. And after I picked up my jaw from where it had fallen to the floor, I called the assignment desk at the radio station I also worked for, KNX, and asked them to kill the commentary I had recorded for the morning sportscast. I phoned them in a new one: At five o'clock in the morning and again at eight, the listeners to the top all-news radio station in Los Angeles heard me become the first to demand Al Campanis's resignation as general manager of the Dodgers. I was ashamed of the moment. I was proud to have a platform to take the stance.

233

But in 1987 it was just a stance. I'd grown up in a liberal house-hold, in a liberal environment, mostly white but with just enough of a mix of heritages so that nobody seemed scary to me, nobody seemed beneath me. I went to a liberal college, lived in liberal cities, worked in a liberal business. I never saw outright prejudice; certainly, as as white a white guy who ever lived, I never **felt** it. But in 1990, I moved to a condo right on the border between Beverly Hills and Los Angeles. Then, as now, I worked at night. And usually, just to avoid the crowds, I would do my food shopping after I got home from the job. There was a twenty-four-hour supermarket three blocks away from my apartment, and at 12:30 in the morning, or at 1:00—or at 5:00 if it had been a bad night—I would walk over and trudge back with my armfuls of groceries (OK, armfuls of snack foods).

Perhaps the second or third time I ever did this, I noticed a police car, on the Beverly Hills side of the line, following slowly behind me. I crossed the imaginary boundary into L.A. just short of the corner of Beverly and Doheny, the car hooked a left at the intersection, I did my shopping, and began to walk back. The second I crossed back into Beverly Hills, the police car reappeared from the opposite direction. Only this time one of the officers shined a staggeringly bright light on me. Only for a matter of seconds, mind you. Then off went the searchlight, the driver hit the gas, and off he and I went.

I didn't figure this out the first time. I didn't even figure it out when it happened again a few weeks later. The third time, it finally dawned on me. A rather large man, walking in the shadows of Beverly Hills, after midnight?

They were checking to see if I was black.

You remember the Rodney King beating videotape? It originally aired on the first of the two television stations I worked for in Los Angeles, KTLA. KTLA's News at Ten was, and remains, one of the news-heaviest hours in the country. There is the occasional dog-mothers-the-cat story and the random fluff piece. But for years, it's pretty much been four minutes of sports, three minutes of weather, twelve minutes of commercials, and about forty-one minutes of honest-to-God news. It doesn't always leave you aroused, amused, invigorated, or titillated, but it gives you at least a sense that you just received some vague idea of what happened in Los Angeles and everywhere else that day.

The night they got the Rodney King tape, KTLA did not lead its newscast with it. It didn't even run in the first fifteen minutes. It was aired about half an hour into the show, not because of some psycho manager's idea of when the maximum audience hit or anything like that. It was because, as shocking as were the images on the tape, there was an instinctive understanding on the part of the producers that the audience was all too familiar with what they'd be seeing. This **was** atrocious; it was not necessarily **breaking news.** We'd all—white, black, Hispanic, Asian—we'd all seen something like this in Southern California, or heard about it.

Let me take you back to that intersection of Beverly and Doheny in Los Angeles. One afternoon I was walking up to the video store when I happened to notice a few police cars sort of filling up the intersection. Say, about twenty of them. There was a big old tree in front of the apartment building on the northwest corner. And there was a dark-skinned gentleman whom I might best describe as being "attached" to that tree. He seemed to be handcuffed to it, or around it. And his feet were dangling a few inches off the ground; I can't remember if he was legcuffed or not. It's just that the tree had to have been eight or ten feet in diameter. However they had hooked him up to that tree, he had to be mighty uncomfortable. And I don't think the twenty or thirty cops with their weapons pulled made him feel any better.

Now, I don't know what this guy did, if anything. For all I know, he had just wiped out a mosque. But I couldn't help thinking about my midnight forays to the supermarket, often going right past that tree. I edged around the scene wondering if, one dark and foggy night, if I ran into a couple of legally blind cops, and I couldn't prove I was white, might I wind up embracing that same tree?

I should mention here that I have no idea if the scenes I witnessed and the other stories I heard about were typical of law enforcement in Southern California. I'll defer to the assessment of the great former Los Angeles district attorney Vince Bugliosi, who said that he had seen enough racism by cops to always presume it was possible but not enough to always presume it was fact. All I know is I saw enough that I didn't sneer when O. J. Simpson's defense team suggested racism played a role in the investigation of the case. I found it an awfully huge and dubious jump from the racism I saw and heard about, racism in terms of violence and degradation, to racism in terms of a meticulous, secret, intricate, precise frame-up from the same cops whom the defense attorneys were otherwise asserting were sloppy morons. But I didn't dismiss the idea as so many did because it was unthinkable.

But back to sports, and that infamous Ted Koppel interview with Al Campanis and my insistence that he quit. It wasn't that Al Campanis was a bad man. It wasn't as if his bigotry was irredeemable. Hell, he **wasn't** a bigot. He came from a family of first-generation Greek immigrants in New York, like my own grandfathers had come from families of second-generation German immigrants in New York. And in that environment of suspicion and class and race hatred—especially distrust, even revulsion, of blacks—Al Campanis had not merely grown up: He had **risen.** By the time he was twenty-nine years old, he had befriended an African American—the first to play in the minors since six months before Campanis was **born.** Played alongside him. Helped him. Became his friend. Stopped thinking of him as a black man. And by the time Al Campanis was thirty-nine years old, he was scouting players for the Dodgers, looking not for the color of a kid's skin but merely for his talents. And by the time Al Campanis was forty-nine years old, he was hiring African Americans to scout players—black players, white players, whatever—for the Dodgers. Al Campanis came a long way, and in his own corner of the world, he helped to wipe out an incredible amount of bigotry.

But we all stop growing, eventually. Al Campanis had outgrown the blank wall of unthinking racial prejudice next to which he'd been born. He'd outgrown his fears of sharing a double-play—or a locker room—with a black man. He'd outgrown his fears of turning his own previous job to black men. And then he stopped. And when he stopped, it was necessary for somebody else to take his place—someone for whom the trip was not from a starting point of racial hatred to a concluding point of "blacks are equal (except for management)"—someone who would begin where Al Campanis left off.

And that's what the next generation of athletes and sports reporters has to do. We have gotten to the point where a white executive of a baseball club—Lee Thomas of the Phillies—can look on the field and suddenly realize he doesn't see anything but white faces in his lineup, and be confused by that fact, and be surprised by it, and be shamed by it, and decide to do something about it because it suggests, in equal measures, that (a) there's racism afoot, and (b) that some idiot in his organization may have thwarted the career of a good ballplayer because he didn't like the color of the man's skin. We have gotten to the point where biases like Al Campanis's are anathema in sports: The appointment of black coaches, black general managers, black executives just isn't ground-breaking news anymore. We have gotten to the point where I can make a list off the top of my head of the top ten most visible sportscasters in the country, and find that five are African Americans. We have gotten to the point where with top African American athletes earning tens of millions of dollars over the courses of their careers, they—like Earvin Johnson—have, or shortly will have, the unforced, unaffirmative-actioned, unmanipulated opportunity to become franchise owners.

And now we need to go to the next stage. We need to make the world safe for Albert Belle to hate my guts and for me to hate his. Not because I'm white and he's black, but because I think he's hurting his business and mine, or because he thinks I'm hurting my business and his. We need to get to the point where I can accuse him of trying to separate Fernando Vina's head from his shoulders and have neither him nor anybody else accuse me of racism. We need to get to the point where he can call me a bad reporter and a lousy judge of his character without being accused of reverse racism.

I started this thing on The Big Show in 1995 when touchdown dances got out of hand: "Real men don't taunt." It hit a real nerve. It hit a couple of real nerves. A lot of fans and even players have been very pleased to see it. And a lot of fans and even players haven't. I've been accused of not being in touch with the modern athlete who is just "expressing himself." It has been suggested, politely but firmly, that my comments are racially motivated. I point out, just as politely and just as firmly, that the first ballplayer I ever ripped for taunting was Mark Gastineau of the New York Jets, an extremely white fellow, and that I am as fervent about blasting all-white NASCAR pit crews who start taunting each other and doing victory dances as I am about knocking Keyshawn Johnson for taking off his helmet and parading around the end zone after a touchdown.

I don't like taunting. I think it's poor sportsmanship. I think it takes the focus away from the concept of sports: challenge, skill, accomplishment. I don't care if it's Dick Trickle taunting. Or Keyshawn Johnson. If Cindy Crawford played football and did a striptease after she pulled down a Steve Young pass for a thirty-five-yard touchdown, I'd blast her, too.

Of course, as I write this, I think back to my nocturnal trips to the supermarket, and those cops with those bleaching searchlights, and that guy involuntarily hugging the tree at Beverly and Doheny, and I think I get a momentary glimpse into the other side of the mirror. I think those of us who are white see a line of demarcation in the past, a point at which most of the members of our race stopped making things worse and started making things better. I don't think that that supposed line of demarcation is visible for minorities in this country. If it's gotten fifty degrees warmer in your house since the furnace went on, that's great if it was eighteen degrees before you fixed the damn thing. If it was -273, that's another story.

How much racism is there in sports? Probably less than there is in the real world. And the strides in the last ten years since Al Campanis's remarks have been faster than that in the real world. In 1987, I think it was, I did an analysis of the roster history of the Boston Red Sox, the last team in the majors to integrate. Even though I had gone in with a presumption that there had been racism in their player selection, I was stunned to discover that until the late '80s, only **once** had the Red Sox had more than six African American players on their team at a given moment. This was in 1966. They had opened the season with Joe Foy, Lenny Green, George Scott, George Smith, Earl Wilson, and Joe Christopher, who was from the Virgin Islands. On June 13 they made a trade to get John Wyatt from Kansas City. He became their seventh African American. The **next day** they traded Christopher and Wilson away to Detroit and got back down to five. In September they called up

Reggie Smith. It was there—thirty years after Jackie Robinson, it was there. A quota system. The Red Sox don't have that system anymore.

Then there was a more insidious form of racism: an institutional, developmental kind: You know—this guy has no experience so how can we give him this job (of course, we were responsible for never giving him the experience in the first place). The absence of minority managers in baseball, for instance, probably stemmed less from active, current, intentional racism than it did from residual opportunity racism. Minorities, especially African Americans, were either big-league stars, or they dropped out of the game. The utility infielders and the journeyman pitchers and the back-and-forth-to-the-minors catchers from whom the vast majority of **minor**-league managers came had all been white guys. Simple as that. Reggie Jackson had no desire and no need to go manage the Oneonta Yankees for $27,000 a year. Wendell Alston, who probably lost his shot at playing every day in the majors because the Yankees signed Reggie, might have been delighted to manage the Oneonta Yankees for $27,000 a year, only he didn't get to stay in the majors long enough even as a backup to get into the old-teammate network that fills virtually all of the minor-league jobs. Now, that's changed. Twelve teams in the minor league, the New York–Penn League. Last year: eight whites, two blacks, two Hispanics. The Phillies had six farm clubs last year, two of them managed by African Americans. The Marlins had seven farm club managers: four Hispanics and an African American.

Case closed? Hardly. Look at the highest rung of the minors last year: triple-A ball. Jerry Royster managing the Las Vegas Stars—and twenty-seven white guys, nearly all of them from that Marvis Foley/Pete Mackanin/Brad Mills group of fringe major-leaguers of the late '70s and early '80s. But it may be time to close the case on the formerly correct assumption that every time something stood in the way of an African American's progress in sports, that that something was necessarily racism. That's where our next generation of athletes and media—and fans—come in. The presumption of the hidden agenda has to be eliminated. When I suggested on the radio and on our computer network that Albert Belle deserved to be suspended for a period of weeks or even months, I got complaints from listeners and readers who genuinely believed I was a white man trying to suppress a black man. I also got even more complaints from listeners and readers who genuinely believed I had something in for the Indians or the city of Cleveland (this was before he left for the White Sox, and Indians fans got to stop pretending he wasn't misbehaving). It hadn't mattered that the two baseball figures I had used as historical comparisons to Belle were Ty Cobb and Billy Martin, or that I had a track record of having constantly attacked racism in sports.

I just think that in sports we need to get to the point where every controversy involving any member of a minority group has not just one explanation, but at least a series of possible explanations. Take the Belle stuff as an example. I pound him on the air. Why? All I want—until such time as there is genuine equality in sports and in life and somebody at home has to stop and think and double-check and not quite be sure if Keith Olbermann and Albert Belle are both white or both black or what—is for there to be five possible answers to that question:

1. Maybe I'm a racist.
2. Maybe Albert Belle's genuinely wrong and race has nothing to do with it.
3. Maybe I'm genuinely wrong and race has nothing to do with it.
4. Maybe the critics of my criticism are genuinely wrong.
5. Maybe the critics of my criticism are racists.

I don't want African American leaders to stop pounding this country about racism. There will always be too much of it to go around. And I'm not going to stop pounding the sports world about racism. And I'm not going to forget the police car's blinding light in Beverly Hills, either. It's just that when racism is accused in a case where it didn't exist, it is sometimes **created**, either by the accuser or in the accused. And it's stuff like that that threatens to undo whatever amount of progress we've achieved, and how quickly we complete the progress we **must** achieve.

13

PLAYS OF THE WEEK

''The Plays'' have been a part of *SportsCenter* for ten years now, a regular feature on the Sunday Night edition of The Big Show. And we enjoy them just as much as you do: the great sliding catches, the amazing football runbacks, the length-of-the-court baskets, the occasional shot of the deer invading the Australian racetrack and one of them charging and knocking over some idiot who tried to pet one of them.

Face it: They're our version of *America's Funniest Home Videos* only without all those shots of baby's butts and big fat guys falling over at weddings. But as much as we love the plays themselves, our real fun is writing the introductions to them. There's always a theme and we always try to select four, five, or six players who fit the theme but who . . .

. . . You won't be seeing. We don't want to make this job sound more difficult than it really is. But honest to God, we've sometimes spent an hour looking for the names, combing through the encyclopedias, combing through Dan's hair . . .

Just get to the list or I'll turn this into a chapter about **your** hair. You won't win that fight.

Ahem. The theme for The Plays of the Week is the best lead-ins we've ever done. And among those you won't be seeing: hockey goalie Allan *Best*er, former Cornell soccer coach Jack **Writer,** and boxing's Bundini "Don't Call Me **Pun**dini" Brown.

You won't see soccer's George **Best,** ex-Braves pitcher Bob **"In" Tro**bridge, or the former Houston outfielder Johnny **Weekly.** But you will see . . . the best lead-ins for The Plays of the Week.

June 23, 1996. Theme: "Deion Sanders Goes Fishing Edition": Former Mets pitcher Jay **Hook,** ex-Astro catcher John **Bate**man, veteran pitcher Steve **Trout** (Dan). Twins' pitcher Bob **Kipper,** basketball announcer Steve **Snapper** Jones, Padres' first baseman **Walleye** Joyner (Keith).

September 6, 1992. Theme: "Labor Day Telethon Edition": Baseball's Mark **Lewis,** basketball's Reggie **Lewis,** or football's **Louis** Lipps (Dan). **Giff**ord Nielsen from the Oilers, receiver Ernest **Givens,** or Lakers coach Randy **Pfund** (Keith).

September 17, 1995. Theme: "Miss America Contest Edition": NFL quarterback Jeff "Don't Call Me **Phyllis**" George, or former 49ers Dwayne Board **Walk** and Dave "Don't Call Me **Bert**" Parks (Dan). Former Giants catcher Bill **Bathe**-ing suit, and your genial Contest hosts Gerry "Don't Call Me" **Regis** Philbin and Frank "OK, Go Ahead and Call Me **Kathie Lee**" Gifford (Keith).

February 28, 1993. Theme: "Beat the Clock Edition": The NBA's **Tick**y Burden, and hoops coach Bob Spoon**auer** (Dan). Football's Buddy **Dial,** great Pirates' reliever Elroy **Face,** and former Cub Bill **Hands** (Keith).

November 19, 1995. Theme: "We Never Got the Memo About What the Theme Was, but the Music This Week Is the Stuff They Used to Play When That Guy Came on the Ed Sullivan Show and Spun Plates on Top of Sticks Edition": Former Buffalo Sabre Brian **Spinner** Spencer, the Oilers' Cris **Dish**man, and minor-league legend **Crash** Davis (Keith). Bronco Mike Lo**dish** and former Redskin Todd **Bowles** (Dan).

June 4, 1995. Theme: "The Staff's on Vacation So There's No Theme Edition": Infielder Junior **No**boa, Hideo **No**mo, musician Yoko O**no** (Keith). Cowboys tight end Jay **No**vacek, tennis's Jana **No**votna, and Red Sox farmhand **No**mar Garciaparra (Dan).

June 25, 1994. Theme: "Would You Buy a Used Car from Dan Edition": Pitching coach Cot **Deal,** baseball's Chet **Lemon,** and the

NBA's **Rex** Chapman (Keith). Whitey **Ford, Mercury** Morris, and **Lincoln** Kennedy (Dan).

December 10, 1995. Theme: "Outer Space Edition": Former 76er **World** B. Free, tennis phenom **Venus** Williams, and football immortal Bart **Starr** (Dan). NFL receiver Al **"Nep" Toon,** sportswriter Terry **Pluto,** and the familiar chant at college football games: "Up Mars, Up Jupiter, Up Uranus" (Keith).

July 21, 1996. Theme: "Olympic Edition": Former big-league pitchers Dave **Goltz,** Jim **Brons**tad, and **Silver** King (Keith). The Colorado **Silver** Bullets, former Cowboy **Golden** Richards, or former Twin Steve Braun and his family, the **Brauns** (Dan).

June 11, 1995. Theme: "The Philosophy of the Far East Edition": St. John's basketball player **Zen**don Hamilton, any football kicker named **Zen**dejas, or the San Jose Sharks' Jeff Frei**sen** (Dan). Buffalo Bills' great **Fortune Cookie** Gilchrist, senior golfer Larry "Chairman" **Mow**rey, and **Chaing Ki** Shaq O'Neal (Keith).

February 4, 1996. Theme: "The Dan Patrick Has the Night Off Edition": Boxers Juan Rol**dan Patrick** and Marcel Cer**dan Patrick,** and New York senator **Daniel Patrick** Moynihan (Keith).

January 21, 1996. Theme: "The Long Distance Edition": Former Detroit Lion Mel **Farr** and former Detroit Piston John **Long** (Dan). Former Detroit Pistols Eddie **Miles** and George **Yard**ley, and ex-catcher Barry **Foote** (Keith).

August 11, 1996. Theme: "The 'We've Been Sued' Edition": The Braves' David **Justice,** former Cleveland Brown **Lawyer** Tillman, or softball legend Eddie Feigner from "The King and his **Court**" (Dan). Former Washington Senator Joe **Judge,** ex–White Sox center-fielder Rudy **Law,** and tennis great Margaret **Court** (Keith).

September 24, 1995. Theme: "The Old TV Show 'Wild Kingdom' Edition": The Mascot Billy the **Marlin Perkins,** Marlin's assistant host Jim "Don't call me Chris" **Fowler,** or Joe **Muich** of the 1924 Braves, which is the closest we could get to the show's sponsor "Mutual of Omaha" (Keith). Former Jet Marty **Lyons,** Stanford golfer **Tiger** Woods, and ex-Knick Ken "The **Animal**" Bannister (Dan).

October 8, 1995. Theme: "The Variety of Strange Gutteral Noises Edition": Former NHL defenseman Doug **Mohns,** ex–Red Sox pitcher Bill **Rohr,** and from the Mariners, Tim **Belcher** (Keith).

The Reds' Dave **Burba,** the young Red Sock Brian **Bark,** or tennis's Sabine **Hack** (Dan).

May 5, 1996. Theme: "The May Showers Edition": Former Royals John **May**berry, Brent **May**ne, and Lee **May** (Dan). Pitcher **Storm** Davis, ex-NFL quarterback Steve **"Daffo" Dils,** and the Yankees' Tim "I'm Only Happy When It" **Raines** (Keith).

June 18, 1995. Theme: "The Batman Edition": NHL Commissioner Gary **Bettman** and future baseball Hall of Famer **Robin** Yount (Dan). Caps' goalie Jim **Carey,** Val or Billy **Kilmer,** or early-twentieth-century sportswriter **Hype** Igoe (Keith).

September 3, 1995. Theme: "The Back to School Edition": Former Indiana Hoosier Keith **Smart** and Marlins general manager Dave **Dom**browski (Dan). NBA great Alex **English,** boxer Buster **Math**is Jr., or 1930 Chicago Cubs pitcher Bud **Teach**out (Keith).

July 8, 1996. Theme: "The Baseball Plays of the First Half Edition, Hosted by David Letterman": NFL player Leon **Lett,** Dodgers' team physician Dr. Michael **Budd** Melman, and racing's Dan and/ or **Hal** Gurney (Keith). Catchers Danny "Don't Call Me **Paul**" Sheaffer and **Biff** "Henderson" Pocoroba (Dan).

February 11, 1996. Theme: "The Show Business Edition": 76ers owner Harold **Katz** or his team, **Les Miserables** (Dan). Hockey's Curtis **Joseph** and the Technicolor Dream Coat, or Gordie **Howe** to Succeed in Business Without Really Trying (Keith).

November 5, 1996. Theme: "The Rhythm and Blues Edition": Former A's infielder Keith **Drumright,** Steve and Dave **Sax,** and former Orioles manager Joe **Alto**belli (Keith). Ex-Falcon Jeff Van **Note,** or any of the Blues Notes: Vida **Blue,** John **Blue, Blue Moon** Odom, and **Blue** Edwards (Dan).

March 10, 1996. Theme: "The March Madness Edition": Edmonton Oiler Todd **March**ant, former Flyer Brad **Marsh,** or Baltimore coach Ted **March**ibroda (Dan). 1890s National League pitcher **Crazy** Schmit, former Cardinal twirler Memo Luna**tic,** or ex-Pittsburgh Steeler Buzz **Nutter** (Keith).

August 4, 1996. Theme: "The Sports Fantasy Camp Edition": Former Expos manager Jim **Fan**ning, tennis badboy Ilie Nas**tase,** or former Braves pitcher Rick **Camp** (Keith). Oilers great Earl **Camp**bell, A's shortstop Bert **Camp**aneris, or ESPN's own Dave **Camp**bell (Dan).

May 12, 1996. Theme: "The Mothers' Day Edition": NHL forward Sergio **Mom**esso, or former big-league center-fielder Jerry **Mum**phrey (Dan). Big league catcher Mark **Parent,** Marlins' reliever Rob **Natal,** or former NHL referee Bruce **"Mother"** Hood (Keith).

October 22, 1995. Theme: "The Channel-Surfing Edition": 1914 Yankees outfielder **Les** Channell, Dave **"Re"** Moates of the 1977 Texas Rangers, and wheelchair marathoner Candace **Cable-Brooks** (Keith). Enos **Cabell** (Dan).

April 1, 1996. Theme: "The Athletes Who Won't Go Down Without a Fight Edition": Allen **Battle** of the A's, from the 1959 Cubs outfielder Bob Will **To Win,** and former Roller Derby queen **Toughie** Brashun (Keith). Knicks coach Jeff Van **Gun**dy, golfer Tommy **Armour,** or the NBA's Chuck "The **Rifleman**" Person (Dan).

August 6, 1995. Theme: "The Keep Your Eye on the Ball Edition": Georgetown star Allen **I**verson or Phillies outfielder Jim **Eis**enreich (Dan). Saturday Night Live character Chico "Keep Yo Eye On De Ball" Escuela, former Cleveland pitcher Hooks **I**ott, or New Jersey Nets announcer **I**on Eagle (Keith).

February 14, 1993. Theme: "The Valentine's Day Edition": Golf's Davis **Love,** football's Duval **Love,** Chicago Bulls great Bob **Love** (Dan). Baseball pitcher Vance **Love**lace, Cincinnati hoops coach Bob **Hug**gins, and hockey's Kelly **Kis**io (Keith).

February 18, 1996. Theme: "The Valentine's Day Edition": Former major-league baseball players Greg **Harts,** Ben **Flowers,** and Slim **Love** (Keith). Colgate basketball player Milik **Cupid,** Cincinnati hoops coach Bob **Hug**gins, or referee Ted **Valentine** (Dan).

November 12, 1995. Theme: "The Look at Milestones Edition": Cardinal quarterback **Stoney** Case, former high jumper Dwight **Stones,** and Cubs announcer Steve **Stone** (Dan). Great Washington outfielder Clyde **Mil**an, announcer **Milo** Hamilton, or Karl "The **Mile**man" Malone (Keith).

March 17, 1996. Theme: "The St. Patrick's Day Edition": Sacramento Kings coach Garry **St.** Jean and San Jose State hoopster Olivier **Saint** Jean (Dan). Former Knicks president Ned **Irish,** Colorado hoopster **Erin** Scholz, or the NBA's A. C. **Green** (Keith).

August 30, 1992. Theme: "The Back to School Edition": Baseball players Dave **Chalk,** Rod **Book**er, and Dan **Quis**enberry (Keith). Pitchers John **Tudor** and Mike **School**er (Dan).

July 2, 1995. Theme: "The Genie in the Bottle Grants Us Magic Wishes Edition": Lakers executive **Jeannie** Buss, **Magic** Johnson, and 1912 Detroit Tigers strikebreaker Alo**ysius** Travers (Keith). Former Cowboy **Jean** Fugett, ex-Brave **Gene** Garber, or Billie **Jean** King (Dan).

July 28, 1996. Theme: "The Postcards from Summer Vacation Edition": Canadian Football League team the Calgary **Stamps.** Duster **Mails** of the 1920 Indians, or Dickie **Post** of the 1970s Chargers (Keith). Former Falcon Sylvester **Stamps,** or the combination: outfielders Wally **Post** and Rowland **Office** (Dan).

July 10, 1994. Theme: "The 'We're Moving' Edition": Outfielder Andy **Van** Slyke, football's Leon **"Sub" Let**t, and Rangers pitching coach Tom **House** (Dan). Basketball's Robert **Pack,** Florida Marlin Rich **Rent**eria, and women's golfer **Lisolotte** Neumann (Keith).

March 24, 1996. Theme: "The Spring Break Edition": Phillies' pitcher Russ **Springer** and former Cowboy Ron **Springs** (Dan). The old USFL team the Boston, later Portland **Breakers** and famous NFL coach Chuck **"Vernal Equa"** Knox (Keith).

September 10, 1995. Theme: "The Cal Ripken Edition": Former Phillie Johnny **Cal**lison, America's finest actor **Rip** Torn, or Angels coach Bobby **Kn**oop (Keith). Former ABA star Mack **Calvin,** ex-Pirates pitcher **Rip** Sewell, or Notre Dame running back Randy **Kin**der (Dan).

March 7, 1993. Theme: "The ESPY Awards Edition": Ex-Yankee **Oscar** Gamble, Braves pitcher **Tony** Cloninger, and songstress **Emmy** Lou Harris (Keith). Baseball's Cecil **Espy** and Alvaro **Es**-**pi**noza (Dan).

July 16, 1995. Theme: "The We're Going to Disney World Edition": Former Giants pitcher Cliff **"Mickey Mouse"** Melton, and sportswriter Jack **Disney** and Terry **Pluto** (Keith). Football coach **Mouse** Davis, Joe Tinker **Bells** from Tinker to Evers to Chance, or any of the dwarves: **Sleepy** Floyd and **Doc** Medich (Dan).

September 20, 1992. Theme: "A Trip to the State Fair Edition": Hockey great Brad **Park,** two-time batting champ **Ferris "Wheel"** Fain, and former Cleveland Brown **Fair** Hooker (Keith). Announcer Ron **Fair**ly and football coach Chuck **Fair**banks (Dan).

July 30, 1995. Theme: "The Silent Movie Edition": Racehorse Sunday **Silence** or Angels manager **Marcel Marceau** Lachemann

(Dan). Former Seattle Supersonic Garfield **Heard,** Cornell football defensive coordinator Pete **Noyes,** or baseball immortal Tris **Speaker** (Keith).

June 25, 1995. Theme: "The Summer Camp Edition": Former Braves pitcher Rick **Camp,** the MLB's Vince Coleman **Stove,** or Astro slugger Jeff **"Sleeping Bag**well (Dan). **Knu**te Rockne, nor **Art** Mahaffey, **Art** Howe, Harry **Craft** or Bob **Kraft**—the Arts and Crafts guys (Keith).

Dan and Keith's Top Ten Pleas To Athletes Who Are Being Interviewed:

1. Stop referring to yourself in the third person. A Keith Olbermann just wouldn't refer to himself in the third person or do anything else that a Keith Olbermann wouldn't do. And neither would a Dan Patrick.

2. Look at us while we're talking to you! Don't look into the camera if the reporter is standing next to you. **We** look into the camera. **You** look at the reporter. Thank you.

3. Watch your language. You get real ticked when a fan swears at you from the stands, right? Why are you swearing at him? Besides which, bleeping you takes time and effort.

4. Inquiring about Dan's kids would be a nice touch now and then.

5. Put your pants on. We know we really shouldn't be in the locker room to begin with. But if you're willing to put your pants on first, we're willing to not ask any questions until you do. If you want, we'll even wait till you put your **shirt** on.

6. But take your sunglasses off. We know the lights are bright. They blind us an hour at a time. Take a couple of minutes so we can see what you really look like.

7. If you're one of those thirty-seven sponsors per athlete sports like auto racing or skiing, please don't refer to each of them during your interview. Those logos, emblems, caps, name-brand turtle-necks, and forehead tattoos are plenty as it is.

8. Limit the God stuff. We're not criticizing anybody for being devout, and nobody minds if you make a reference now and again. But

even the pope would get a little edgy if you insisted that Jesus knocked the wide receiver down and that's why they didn't call pass interference on you.

9. Don't use a reporter's name when answering his question. There's nothing sillier than having one of us lead in to your sound bite and then you say, "You're right, Jim."

10. Come to think of it, why don't you **always** answer questions by saying, "You're right, Keith," or "You're right, Dan," or "You're right, Dan and Keith." Thank you.

OUR GREATEST GAMES
(WATCHED, THAT IS, NOT PLAYED)

Dan and I are approximately the same age—of course, that doesn't change the fact that he's still **older** than I am. But given the fact that I skipped the first grade and he transferred in college so that took a little longer, we graduated into the "real" world within days of each other. So, sportswise, we should have the same interests, the same memories, the same milestones.

Yet when we put together our lists of the top sporting events we actually attended and/or covered, we had only one overlap. Our mix of sports isn't even close.

This is a product, we think, of something that is beginning not to exist anymore: regionalism in sports. I grew up outside New York in the '60s and '70s. The Jets won a Super Bowl, the Giants stank. Until the very late '60s, the Rangers always outdrew the Knicks. There was no college basketball or football. Tennis got interesting for two or three weeks a year, there were some golf fans. But baseball was still king in New York, certainly through the year I graduated high school; probably even into the '80s.

And it was different in Ohio. College sports: huge. The NBA: dominant. As much as Ohio loved The Big Red Machine, bad Bengals teams were sometimes just as interesting as good Reds ones.

Now it's a different world. NASCAR can draw 100,000 fans at Louden, New Hampshire. Cable TV puts Utah Jazz caps on kids on the street where I grew up. I mean, the night the Knicks won their first NBA title in 1970 **the game wasn't on live television in New York.** Tape delay! Local blackout! They figured if they showed the decisive game, Wilt Chamberlain versus Willis Reed, on local TV, they might not get fifteen thousand people to actually go. The Knicks were just fifteen years removed from having played regular-season home games at a Manhattan armory, for crying out loud.

The point of this is, the way we're going, sports won't be regionalized anymore. We've already seen hockey succeed in Florida and people promoting a Formula One race to be held in New York. But Keith and I are from the last generation. Look at our lists of the greatest thrills we've witnessed in person and you'll see. Keith gets to start.

1. **Yankees–Red Sox Play-off, October 2, 1978:** Easily the greatest sporting event I've ever attended, and it happened when I could still be 100 percent fan **and** 100 percent reporter. Instead of vacations, we used to buy Yankee season tickets, so for the preceding seven seasons I'd been to nearly every home game. I lived and died with the Yankees. Sparky Lyle blows a game in Chicago in 1972? I was so angry I threw my radio out the window. I cut college for weeks at a clip three years running to go home and cover them in the play-offs and the World Series. It still **mattered** to me. Desperately.

You must have **really** enjoyed the 1976 World Series. Reds: four wins. Yankees just watching.

Shut up. And then comes the fall of '78. I'm just starting my senior year in college, just finished an internship at a TV station in New York, so I'm seeing all this not just as a Yankee fan but as a near-reporter. The Yankees put on this comeback from fourteen games out, they actually jump ahead of the Red Sox, and I go home to watch them polish off Cleveland and take this historic title. Only, they **don't** polish off Cleveland. Rick Waits beats them on the last day of the regular season, and Luis Tiant beats the Blue Jays in Boston—and it's a tie. First time ever, the division ends up in a tie. Well, who's been in Boston all weekend watching the Red Sox but my best friend, Jim Burger, an arch-Boston fan whose wife had gotten him tickets for the series against Toronto when it was just a meaningless wrap-up to the Red Sox title. So I had said to Jimmy, if they put play-off tickets on sale, get three. I'll come up from New York.

Of course it happens that way. And that Sunday night, the Yankees TV station televises *Pride of the Yankees*—which you saw on TV in those days maybe once every two years—and I get out to the airport at the crack of dawn to take the hourly shuttle to Boston. It was Eastern Airlines, and they had a policy guaranteeing you a seat. If their plane sat 125 and 126 people wanted to go, they'd roll out another plane and fly the 126th person up by himself. So they've got more passengers than seats and they roll out another plane and there are maybe five of us on it: Dick Schaap, American League president Lee MacPhail, and me. This just keeps getting better and better.

We get into Boston and the day is perfect. The quintessential New England fall day: crisp but still warm; classic angles of sun and shadow. And Jim, in his Red Sox cap, and Jim's wife Gloria, and me in my Yankee cap go to our seats in the very last row behind first base. And starting two or three hours before the game we take turns phoning in reports to our radio station from the pay phone just behind us. On top of this, we're sitting behind these two guys who had been at the **last** play-off game involving the Red Sox, against the Indians, in 1948. They're talking about how Lou Boudreau, the Cleveland shortstop, beat the Sox for the pennant with a couple of homers, and how they, then kids, cried all the way home. It's just classic.

Then Yastrzemski homers off Ron Guidry and all of a sudden it's not so classic anymore. And Jim's smiling, excited, and I'm getting worried. My friends and I had been hiking up to Boston nearly every summer to see a Red Sox–Yankees series and I think the Yanks were 2-and-9 at Fenway with me in the house. And I'm remembering one night in '74 when I see Terry Hughes taking infield practice at third base for the Red Sox and I turn to my friend George Goodman and I say, "**There's** somebody who's not going to have any impact on this game," and all of a sudden Rico Petrocelli gets scratched from the lineup and Hughes plays instead and drives in the winning run and George threatens to push me under a train.

George, you reading this? I understand your pain.

Now Boston gets another run. And Mike Torrez has been getting away with murder against the Yankees. He's not sharp; it doesn't matter. They've shot their wad. Made up fourteen games in the standings, scored forty-two runs in four games in Fenway in September. Now the guy they couldn't re-sign as a free agent the winter before is going to make it all go up in smoke. Finally, in the seventh, the Yanks put two guys on and send up Jim Spencer to pinch-hit. And Torrez strikes him out. And my buddy Jim looks at who's coming up off the on-deck circle and sighs and sits back in his seat and says, "Whew. Thank goodness. Dent's no home run threat." I turned and gave him a look from a movie. "Are you nuts?" I say to him. "Have you learned anything from life? Anything from being a baseball fan? From being a **Red Sox** fan? Don't you know what you've just done? Don't you **know**? Bucky Dent **has** to hit the homer now. Because you're not worried. Just because you're convinced it can't happen."

This was only the start of my diatribe. Dent fouls a pitch off his instep and goes down in the dust and we don't even notice Mickey Rivers coming out of the dugout and exchanging bats with Dent. Rivers said the first bat was "broken." The Red Sox have since suggested the second bat was corked. Whatever the truth, I'm invoking words like hubris and arrogance and fate and *Sturm und Drang* and my poor friend Jim's going pale. And I bring up Terry Hughes and George threatening to throw me under a train and my guilt, guilt, guilt. And of course I know I'm right—in that situation you have to keep your yap shut because whatever deities there are they aren't **always** listening but they **are** always listening at Fenway Park— but I seriously doubt Bucky Dent's going to hit a three-run homer right then, merely because Jim's offended something somewhere.

And then Dent hits the ball. And this moan grows throughout the ballpark. Remember, the seats for the play-off game had gone on sale only two days before and only at Fenway, so there can't be more than thirty Yankee fans in the place. And each of us rises as if levitated out of our seats. Down in the first base boxes, I can see Harry Friedman, a kid I went to high school with, his arms coming up from his sides as he stands, looking like a ballet dancer. All of this is happening in slow motion, in black and white. I swear I can see the stitches turning on the ball as it climbs up, up, up. I can see the smiles of anticipation on the faces of individual Yankee fans sitting four hundred feet from me. The collective moan gets louder. Now it's a shriek of pain—except for the thirty of us screaming our heads off. And I turn and look down at Jim and I swear the skin has peeled off his face.

He think's he's **caused** Bucky Dent's homer.

So now I have to spend the rest of this game consoling my best friend. And Gloria and I can't even get him to speak. When Piniella cuts off the ball in right field in the ninth and they fake Burleson into holding at second, I tell him how lucky the Yankees are. But I know it's over. Rice won't get him home. I tell him if Yaz doesn't get him home, I'll eat my cap. Yaz doesn't get him home. I mime a bite out of the cap. Jim looks like he's been stuffed by a taxidermist. And still he doesn't say anything. Curse of the Bambino? Curse of Jim Burger, more like.

Needless to say he can't phone in the reports to our radio station. He's still sitting in his seat while all of these crushed Red Sox fans file out past me. They're not really moving; they're being swept along like bubbles heading to a drain. They don't care. They have no will. They've been destroyed—again. I'm on hold in Ithaca waiting to go on the air and talk about the Yankees heading to Kansas City for the play-offs and I'm enjoying what I saw as a fan when I see the two guys who had been sitting in front of us, the ones who had been at the play-off game thirty years before. And they're crying again. "Marty," the one says to the other. "Maybe we're a jinx."

Finally we file out and find Jim's car and we're driving back to Ithaca. Seven hours maybe. And he's up to grunts and the occasional question about directions. But he's still not saying anything about it. And to this day, nearly twenty years later, you can't convince him he didn't cause it. When Bucky Dent opened his baseball school in Florida and put up a Green Monster in left field with a scoreboard duplicating the exact moment after his homer, Jim called me in Los Angeles, and his usually mild-mannered voice was full of evil predictions and guttural threats. I don't know that Bucky Dent has a true enemy in this world, but if I were him and a man ever came up to me and introduced himself as Jim Burger, I'd cut out of town in a hurry.

And the irony, of course, is that truly, that game marked the day I stopped being a Yankee fan. First off, nothing could ever top that. They won the World Series three weeks later and it was great. But it wasn't close. So, as a Yankee fan, I have nothing more to look forward to. And moreover, as I'm walking out of Fenway, listening to these Sox fans making sad, pathetic threats about "lookin' fah cahs with New Yawk license plates to tuhn ovah," I begin to think about all the times they've been through this before, and of what nameless horrors await them in the future (I see a problem. A man with a mustache. A man with bad ankles. A silly manager. Something called "Mookie."). So, it's obvious I'm rooting for the wrong ballclub here. But I certainly can't root for the Red Sox—you don't make **that** kind of switch in just one lifetime.

So. Greatest game I ever covered. End of me as a fan. Not a bad way to go out, I suppose. But don't tell Jim that.

1. **World Series Game Six, October 23, 1993:** I'm covering the game with Peter Gammons and Dave Campbell, and we're probably a hundred feet away from the left-field foul pole, sitting in the press box at SkyDome. The Phillies take a 6–5 lead into the bottom of the ninth, Mitch Williams is on, first batter he faces is Rickey Henderson. He walks him. Two batters later, he faces Paul Molitor and gives up a base hit, and that set the stage for Joe Carter.

I remember turning to Peter and saying, "It looks like we're headed for extra innings." And I turned back, Mitch delivered the pitch, Joe swung, and the next thing I know, the Toronto bull pen is doing synchronized aerobics. Joe Carter has just ended the World Series. I immediately thought of how happy I was for Joe Carter. Because here's a guy who was once traded from the Cubs to the Indians for Rick Sutcliffe; Sutcliffe went on to win the Cy Young and the Cubs went to the play-offs. Carter went to the Padres in the trade that got the Indians off the floor. And finally the Padres traded him to the Blue Jays, but he'd never had an opportunity to really show what he could do in the postseason.

And as he said afterwards, there's a little kid in all of us, we all want to be a hero. And I remember going to the Phillies locker room, and Mitch Williams did not shy away from the media. He answered everybody's question. He was brutally honest. He said he thought he slipped off the mound, which the replays show he did, but he said, ''Give credit to Joe Carter. He hit an ugly pitch. He hit a pitch that he should have hit out.'' He refused to go and take a shower, and Curt Schilling and some of his other Philly teammates were trying to shoo away the media, but Mitch said, ''I gave up the pitch. I'll sit here and answer the questions. Because if I'd gotten him out, I'd be sitting here as well answering questions about what I did right.'' And I had great admiration for what Mitch did after that game.

A couple of months later, I visited Mitch on his ranch just outside of Arlington, Texas, and I also went to visit Joe Carter in Kansas City. The point of the story was to find out what had happened to these guys since the home run ball. Well Mitch, laid back, riding horses, on his tractor, getting ready to get married, didn't have any problems with it. He said, ''It's baseball. I threw it. He hit it. He's the hero. I'm the goat.''

I visited Joe at his home the following week, and I asked him if he was curious about how Mitch Williams was feeling. And he said, ''No, not really. If Mitch had gotten me out, I would've been the goat, he would've been the hero.'' He said the same exact thing Mitch did. ''It's baseball.'' I asked him if I could see the home run ball, or if it was in a safe-deposit box. And he said, ''No, it's right in here.'' We turned a corner, right around from the front door, and there it was, in his office, out in the open. He'd put down the time and the date, and the event, and I asked him if he realized how much that ball was worth. And he said, ''I don't care. It's not for sale. It's my wife's.''

And you dropped him with one punch, stole the ball, fled for the Missouri border, and phoned Charlie Sheen . . .

Never mind. My turn.

2. **Providence Hockey at Cornell, March 5, 1979:**

Wait. You're picking a **college hockey game** as the second greatest sporting event you ever covered?

I told you we had different backgrounds. There are two things you have to understand as background to this one. First, at Cornell, hockey was **the** sport in the '70s. The Ken Dryden era was recent history; one of his teammates was still the head coach. The year before, Cornell had been ahead 9–0 over Yale **with a minute to go in the first period.** The arena, Lynah Rink, was as noisy as any sports stadium ever and the fans had rituals that would impress English soccer hooligans. Second, the squad from the year before was national championship caliber and they'd been upset, in the first play-off game, at home, by the lowest-seeded team in the conference tournament—Providence.

So who does Cornell draw in the 1979 opener? Providence again. This was a pretty good team: The goalie, Brian Milner, went on to the Red Wings for a time, and they had a defenseman named Jim Korn who spent years in the NHL. The coach was Lou Lamoriello, who became the GM of the Devils. This wasn't some pickup team. And boy, did we know it. Cornell's losing 3–0 after two. First minute of the third period, the Friars score again. Cornell gets one back; Providence scores immediately—it's 5–1. I'm the sports director of the Cornell station, WVBR, and I've got four reporters with me and I know we're going to have to go into that locker room and do this same brutal postmortem we'd done the year before. And the Cornell hockey team was covered with all the zealousness and venom the New York papers reserve for the Jets and Giants—we're going to have to go in there and carve up these classmates of ours and I'm wondering if I'm going to have to go on the air and call for the coach's firing.

You? Worried about **that?**

I was nineteen at the time. Stop interrupting. Suddenly, a bank of lights at the Providence end of the ice goes dark. And we see electricians scurrying among the rafters and big bulbs being moved around and a minute goes by, and then two, and then five, and the Providence players are just skating around trying to stay focused while the Cornell guys are all over at the bench. And they fix the lights and the electricity comes back on. Cornell scores: it's 5–2. Again. It's 5–3. And they are peppering the net. Each rush, they get five or six shots. Five minutes left, a kid named John Olds makes it 5–4 and now it's like the ice isn't level any more. Providence can't get out of its own end; Cornell can't score. With a buck-nineteen left, the freshman Cornell goalie, Brian Hayward, gets pulled. And that's when Providence finally breaks out. A fellow named Randy Wilson busts past the Cornell blue line and has an uncontested shot on an empty net with twenty-nine seconds left.

And he misses.

And Lance Nethery, the Cornell captain who, like Hayward, later played in the NHL, picks the puck up behind his own net and weaves through every Providence player, unloads a slapper on Brian Milner and ties it with thirteen seconds to play. The overtime was academic; Cornell scores exactly four minutes in.

Down 4–0 a minute into the third period, they win 6–5 in OT. Damndest thing I ever saw. And I'm still wondering if somebody deliberately shut those lights off above the Providence net.

2. Game Six, NBA Finals, June 17, 1996:

Wait a minute yourself, buster. You're picking the anticlimax of all anticlimaxes as **your** second greatest game? Take me back to Lynah Rink!

All right, I admit it. The game itself was not memorable, but the coronation afterwards was. Michael Jordan told me this was probably the toughest time he'd ever gone through in trying to play basketball. His father, the late James Jordan, celebrated with Michael in his three previous championship runs. But his father was killed less than two months after Michael had won that third title. After winning this one—on Fathers' Day no less—he told me he couldn't help but think of his father and that he should've been there celebrating that win.

Throughout the regular season the Bulls were hailed as the greatest team of all time, and, statistically speaking, they were. They went 72-and-10. But their armor suffered a couple of dents during the NBA Finals when they lost back-to-back games in Seattle. Jordan would later say, "It's up to the historians to decide where we rank among the great teams of all time. All I know is, we accomplished everything we set out to do."

Jordan was named MVP, but if you ask Seattle head coach George Karl, that honor should've gone to Dennis Rodman. Karl told me that Rodman singlehandedly won two of the games with his rebounding, his defense, and his theatrics. He took Seattle out of their game plan on numerous occasions. We had Dennis on ESPN after they won the title, and he said to me that he loves to surprise people, that people continued to count him out and not take him seriously, but that he was still a great basketball player. And then he got up to leave, and he leaned over to me, and I thought he was going to kiss me. As soon as we went off the air, and the interview was over, I said to Dennis, "You were going to kiss me, weren't you?" and he turned and just laughed. And I felt bad that maybe I'd misinterpreted, maybe I'd blown this out of proportion, given Dennis's track record, and then I see Dennis show up three months later in New York in a wedding dress, and I realize: He **was** going to kiss me.

Oh, the regrets of romance. I know it well. And you thought the pangs would stop the day you got married. Sue **is** seeing this for the first time, isn't she?

No comment.

3. **USA–USSR Hockey, 1980 Winter Olympics:** I was about a week past my twenty-first birthday and I'm in Lake Placid covering the Olympics for UPI Radio and they've been sending me out to cover this nondescript U.S. hockey team that the experts say has about a one-in-three chance of just making the medal round. And there were more reporters at the Tai Babilonia–Randy Gardner skating practices than at the early games. But the U.S. keeps winning, and all of a sudden they're in the position to clinch a medal and virtually clinch the gold—all they have to do is beat the Russians.

Now my boss, Sam Rosen, has been assigned to cover the relevant medal games, so this game is his baby. Besides which, he's the backup play-by-play man for the Rangers and he knows his stuff. The demand for credentials is now huge; we have just the one for the radio network. So I content myself with going back to our studios and watching from there. And that afternoon Sam calls me into an anteroom in our office and he says, "Change of plans. I'm covering the game. You"—and with this he produces a ticket to the game—"You are covering the crowd."

I got to sit in the stands for the greatest upset in modern Olympic hockey history. And the only time I had to work was **after** the game, interviewing fans. Tough life, huh? And I'll always remember the **next** day inside the Olympic press center. Next to the cafeteria were the offices of the Russian news service, TASS. I go past their door, the lights are all out, and on the window is a hand-lettered sign reading "Today Closed We Are." Sort of summed it all up.

Somebody pointed out that that game might have been the beginning of the end of the Soviet Union.

Thinking back on it, I wouldn't be surprised. Not just because of the U.S. victory. Think about it: Here was an entire Russian Olympic team in this country for the first time since 1960. Color TV. Electronics up the wazoo. The first Walkmans. Jeans. The Russians were buying the stores out of them. Lake Placid had **cable**, for crying out loud. You let people play with material things their system can't produce, and they don't want to give them back.

So Jimmy Carter won the Cold War.

You are correct, sir! Anyway, back to the ball games.

3. **Final Round, Masters Golf Tournament, April 14, 1996:** In any other year we would've remembered Nick Faldo's closing 67 as one of the greatest final rounds ever by a Masters champion, as he became the seventh player in history to win three green jackets. But instead of the 67 by Faldo, we will never forget the 78 turned in by Greg Norman.

Through the first two rounds, the media kept talking about how composed Norman was. He was letting the golf course come to him. He wasn't attacking it as much as he was being patient. He was brilliant with his putting. Following the second round, I was in my hotel room, and Rick Reilly of *Sports Illustrated* called me up to talk about perhaps playing golf on Saturday morning. And after we had discussed a couple of scenarios of when we could play, I said, "What do you think of Norman?" And he said, "He always seems to find the banana peel." I said, "You don't think he's going to win?," and Reilly said no.

After the third round on Saturday, Norman held a six-stroke lead. This marked the sixth time he had taken a lead into the final round of a major—he'd lost the other five. I began to think Norman was finally going to exorcise his demons; he was going to finally show the world he **was** the greatest player and he was going to run away from the rest of the field at the Masters. He had played three perfect rounds—why would we expect the Augusta course to come back and bite the Great White Shark?

But on Sunday morning, I started to have doubts. Jim Colbert, who plays on the senior tour, was working with our ESPN reporting team, and Jim and I began discussing what Norman had done in the first three rounds. And Jim said he was getting the sneaking suspicion that Norman would try to attack the course in the final round; that he would try to force that exact scenario I mentioned before: that he would go out and try to run away from everybody. And Jim said, "If he does it, he could have problems. If he lets the course come to him as he's been doing the first three rounds, he should be the winner." And while we were doing *SportsCenter* on Sunday morning, I said to Jim, on the air, "If Norman loses **this** it will be the biggest collapse in modern history."

Rule One: Always listen to the golfer wearing the silliest hat.

You're learning. I watched the first nine holes on TV in a broadcast facility across from Magnolia Lane, and then the morbid curiosity started to settle in for me. It was like I was driving by a car accident, and knew I shouldn't look, but knew I couldn't help but do so. I went across the street and decided to follow Norman and Faldo.

If you've been to Augusta, you know that the roars in there are as loud as you'll hear at a sporting event—even at Keith's little hockey rink—because they echo off the trees. But there were no roars. Very little cheering. It was almost as if you were at a wake. It was as if the greatest player in the world had suddenly become a 19 handicap, and people began to wonder, "Who is **in** Greg Norman's body?"

Norman started to press a little bit; Norman started to attack a little bit more. Meanwhile Nick Faldo continued to play his regimented, robotic style, which has made him one of the greatest players of all time. Faldo could sense the wheels were starting to fall off Norman, so he didn't take chances—he didn't have to. I couldn't help but think of the irony watching these two golfers on the back nine. Here was Norman, the greatest player in the world, collapsing. And here was Faldo, who in previous years had been skewered by the British tabloids as "Nick Foldo."

By the time Norman and Faldo had gotten to the eighteenth green, I felt like I was witnessing a bad vaudeville act, one you just wanted to have pulled offstage. I felt bad for Greg Norman; he wanted to hide—but how do you hide at the Masters? The first person to comfort him just happened to be Nick Faldo, who would later say, "I just wanted to give Greg a hug." I couldn't wait to hear how Norman would answer questions **after** the collapse, but when he met the media, he was very honest and forthright, saying, "You can call it whatever you want. You can call it a choke. Use any term you want."

But he said there wasn't a whole lot of anguish. I figured that would come later. He went on to say that you always learn, you try to understand why and what happened, but in the situation like that, "I may not want to learn about this one. Maybe this one I just screwed up enough with my own mistakes."

4. **Game One, World Series, October 15, 1988:** I still don't know how the Dodgers had even gotten **into** that World Series, let alone put us in the position we were in. I mean, the 3-4-5 hitters for every game of that series against the A's were Mickey Hatcher, Mike Marshall, and John Shelby. But the Dodgers are still losing 4–3 in the bottom of the ninth when all of us TV types go downstairs to prepare to muscle our way into the locker room. And we're watching the game on monitors out by the hot dog stand in the basement

of Dodger Stadium and I can remember a producer from CBS News who worked out of our office sidling over to me and saying, "So what would you like to ask Dennis Eckersley? If they're going to **sweep**?" And the same sort of thing came over me that came over me at the Dent game. "Oh no," I said matter-of-factly. "You watch. Old Gimpy's gonna come up and pinch-hit a homer." And she laughed and I said, "Just watch."

And we did. And if you ever want to be frightened at a sporting event, be in the basement of a ballpark in earthquake country when Kirk Gibson hits an impossible game-winning homer. Sounded like an 8-point-2. And this producer and her crew and I and my crew are rushing to get into position to get the Dodgers storming up the runway to their clubhouse and she just looks at me and said, "How did you know?" And I said, "Because I wasn't out in the stands to see it. Same damn thing happened to me at the Chris Chambliss game."

There's a postscript to this game that I love, too. Josh Kaplan, who was one of our great producers at KCBS in L.A. and for a long time produced *SportsLook* for Roy Firestone, pointed out that the greatest instant of the Gibson home run is actually out in the parking lot. Watch the tape sometime that has Jack Buck's radio call on CBS. The moment he says, "This is gonna be a home run!" some yahoo who has just left the game in the time-honored tradition of Dodger fans slams on his breaks—you can see the break lights go on.

I've always wondered how **he** felt.

Speaking of wondering how a guy felt:

4. **Final Round, Masters Golf Tournament, April 9, 1995:** Ten days before going down to Augusta to cover the Masters for ESPN, I was asked by our producer Mike McQuade who I thought could win that year, and I blurted out Ben Crenshaw's name. Well, Mike being the golf fanatic that he is, got a good laugh out of this. Ben had not exactly been on a winning run. Mike proceeded to tell anybody and everybody who came by in the next fifteen minutes that I was picking Ben Crenshaw to win the Masters.

We miss Mike on the show. Some of the time.

Three days later, Crenshaw's lifelong teacher, Harvey Penick, the man who first placed a club in Ben's hands at age seven, died at the age of ninety in Austin, Texas. Crenshaw chartered an airplane with Tom Kite to attend Penick's funeral on Wednesday, the day before the Masters opening round. Crenshaw played well for the first three rounds—much to the chagrin of my fellow ESPN employees, who didn't care who won, just as long as Ben Crenshaw didn't win, because they knew I would never let them forget that that's who I had predicted.

Going into the back nine, it looked like it was going to be a three-man chase: Crenshaw, Davis Love III, and Greg Norman. The other contenders, names like Fred Couples, Scott Hoch, Curtis Strange, Brian Henniger, and Phil Mickelson, had fallen by the wayside. But imagine the mixed emotions Davis Love had to be entertaining. He didn't qualify for the Masters until the previous week in New Orleans. In fact, he won the Freeport MacMoran on the day Harvey Penick died. Keep in mind that Love's late father was coached by Penick at the University of Texas; Davis was close to Harvey as well.

But Ben Crenshaw called Davis during the week and said, "You don't need to go to the funeral. You need to stay here and practice and get ready for the tournament." As Davis would say afterwards, "Once I found out I couldn't win it, I was thrilled for Ben. He lost one of his closest friends, but his thoughts had been about me, hoping I would get ready for the Masters."

Crenshaw came to the eighteenth armed with a two-stroke lead. He needed to make a putt from eighteen inches away for bogey to win it. And he said he had a little talk with himself. He said, "Make this eighteen-inch putt, and then you can have yourself a good cry." The result was one of the most emotional moments in golf history: Crenshaw making the putt, and then collapsing into the arms of his caddy, Carl Jackson, who had been with him at Augusta since 1976.

Crenshaw later said he was crying for joy, crying for relief, most of all, he was crying for Harvey Penick.

5. **Game Seven, NBA Finals, June 12, 1984:** This was almost the end of the Celtic dynasty, not that anybody knew it then. And considering what a seesaw series this had been, this should've been an epic last game. But the Celtics won it by nine, and there were very few moments when it was truly in doubt. My memories of this one were all the events **surrounding** the game. I had been with my station in Boston for barely six weeks and this was only the second time they had actually sent me to the Garden. We were **all** there:

My job was to do some kind of feature before the game for our six o'clock news, and then help out in the locker rooms with interviews.

So I did my feature on all the other reporters. This is when I interviewed you and got you into trouble by asking what Cable News Network was . . .

Thanks for reminding everybody. Again.

Always glad to be of service. Anyway, there was a premise to this. I couldn't, for the life of me, think what questions were **left** to ask before the decisive game. Nobody was hurt, nobody was changing plans, so I just went around asking questions about questions. I asked Pat Riley if he could think of anything left to ask. "Just how you guys are holding up. You guys holding up?" And I asked K. C. Jones the same thing and he said, "That's the only question I haven't asked myself since I woke up at four this morning." And there was a real feeling that day and night of this being a championship game—that big-game feeling that you can't put into words.

As I said, I'd only been in the Garden once as a reporter to that point. That had been on my first week on the job, and I interviewed Dick Vitale of all people. One question, and then back to the studio. And one or two people in the crowd had recognized me, wished me luck. So here it is six weeks later and I'm figuring it's the same thing. We do our live shots at six, I'm hungry, I go to get a hot dog. And I get **mobbed.** I mean, two hundred people must have said hello or asked for autographs or something. The guy wouldn't let me pay for the hot dogs. First time I realized the impact of actually being on TV. I hadn't gotten two hundred **letters** from viewers in three years at CNN.

Earth to Keith's ego. Earth to Keith's ego. Come back . . . we miss you.

Honestly, there was a point to this.

Yeah, and the reader and I both know what it is.

Hear me out. There's a punch line.

There always is.

The Celtics win the title, and the Lakers get jostled by the crowd on the way off the court, and somebody hits Kareem in the shoulder with a bottle, and here are the Lakers—who had won game three by 33 points—going home from Boston, losers again. And after all the interviews and all the celebrations, by the time everybody's clearing out it's nearly two in the morning. And as I'm heading to our truck, my head still swirling from all the work, and my first realization that people were actually **watching** this crap I was doing, here comes Swen Nater, the backup center for the Lakers, walking down the hallway in the opposite direction. And just as I'm thinking how rotten he must be feeling, he stops and points at me and says, "Hey, Keith," and now I'm thinking I have a sign around my neck with my name on it because how the hell else does Swen Nater know who I am? And he says, "That was a hell of a piece you did on the six o'clock news about 'no more questions to ask.' It's nice to meet you."

You could've knocked me over with a feather. Championship game, the whole thing on the line, and what are these guys doing at 6:35 that night? Watching my damn silly feature piece on the local news. I'll never get over that.

5. **Game Six, NBA Finals, June 8, 1986:** Your Garden story, now **my** Garden story. Boston, one win over Houston away from their six-teenth championship banner. I made it a point to always arrive early at the Boston Garden, because it gave me an opportunity to just sit and watch Larry Bird shoot. Bird would be the first player on the floor, and he would usually spend thirty minutes, shooting, all by himself. Nobody said a word to him; he would have a ball boy rebound to him, and it was his way of getting his rhythm, getting his game face on.

Getting his breath back after he had spent an hour running up and down the uneven aisles in the Garden stands.

I didn't get there **that** early. Anyway, I just marveled at the fact that here was the best player in the game, and **he** practiced the most.

There was heightened security going into game six, because in game five, Ralph Sampson had taken a swing at Jerry Sichting. Sampson had been ejected from the game, and with the series shifting to Boston and memories of the Lakers and '84 still fresh in their minds, the NBA was aware of the fact that Ralph would be Villain Number One. Every time he touched the ball, he was booed. He missed his first seven shots. There was a banner that was unfurled that read, "Sampson Is a Sissy." Ralph was never a factor in this game.

Larry Bird, on the other hand, was. Bird put up a triple double plus three steals; I would later find out that he did this even though he was extremely upset with his teammates at halftime because he wasn't getting the ball enough. He would later say, "If they would've given me the ball in the first half, this game would've been over then." As it turned out, the Celtics built up a comfortable lead and were never challenged and they won it 114 to 97. I felt privileged to see perhaps the greatest front line to play in the NBA: three Hall of Famers, Bird, Kevin McHale, and Robert Parish, plus a very underrated Dennis Johnson and Danny Ainge, and Bill Walton—who had taken less money, less playing time, for a chance to be on the same team with Larry Bird.

Little did we know that Celtic fans would have to live off these championship fumes for at least a decade. After winning the championship, the Celtics had the number two pick in the draft. And that year, they took Len Bias. Bias died of a cocaine overdose while celebrating his selection, and of course never played a game in Boston.

But that was in the future. When I went into the locker room, I couldn't wait to hear what Bird would say. But Bird would take so long to get dressed that you had to wait. Even in victory, even in a championship game. So while I waited for Bird, I asked Red Auerbach his thoughts on Larry's performance and he said, "The difference between Bird and everybody else in this league is Larry comes to play every single night." I later asked Bird if winning defined who he was. And he said, "I never thought winning could make me feel so good about myself."

Bird was never about statistics. He was never about individual awards. He knew the bottom line was always, "Did I win a championship. And if I didn't, how could it be a successful year?" The argument comes up at least once a year in the newsroom: Who's the greatest player of all time? I still maintain Michael Jordan and Magic Johnson are the two greatest players I've ever seen, but Larry's not far behind. And on that day, with that team, in that year, Larry would've taken on anybody, and won.

Except for my next one.

6. Game Six, NBA Finals, June 9, 1985:

We're on quite a Celtics run, huh?

We've got everything in here but the last fight Ainge started before he became coach of the Suns. Anyway, by this point, I had just signed to join a Los Angeles station and they sent me up to Boston, free-lance, to cover games six and seven of the finals. And remember, (a) after I had left my employers in Boston the previous fall, they had made a few ill-chosen remarks about how I'd never work in the business again, and (b) after the Celts had won the year before, Bird had made a few ill-chosen remarks about how the Lakers could've, or should've, won in four, but they'd choked.

Problem was it was probably true.

The Lakers part. Not the you-not-working part.

Thank you for that. The Lakers part. Byron Scott and James Worthy had vanished the year before. Kareem had looked like the Exxon *Valdez* out there. And it had always been thus. Jerry West used to disappear against the Celtics in the finals. Or Elgin. Or Wilt. Or Rod Hundley. The Lakers had never beaten the Celtics for the title.

But this time, Kareem ate Robert Parish for lunch. There would be no game seven. And in consecutive years, I got to cover a Boston victory over Los Angeles for the benefit of a Boston audience, and then a Los Angeles victory over Boston for the benefit of a Los Angeles audience.

6. **Atlanta Hawks at Cincinnati Royals, March 13, 1971:** This was my first chance to see Pete Maravich in person. The greatest college scorer of all time. He was facing my favorite player, Nate Archibald, the only man to lead the NBA in scoring and assists in the same season. Nate was a brilliant player on a bad team. Some friends and I decided that we were going to drive down three hours before the game. So Zeke Campbell and I piled into Bill Richardson's 1967 blue Mustang and headed off to Cincinnati.

We had a '66 midnight blue Mustang. This is getting eerie.

No it's not. They made thousands of them. Anyway, we had this vision in our heads that we would arrive, that Maravich would be shooting by himself, and need somebody to rebound for him. When we got there, we found Tom Payne shooting by himself. He was the seven-foot-two center for the Hawks out of the University of Kentucky, who would later go to prison for rape. Tom—less than politely—informed us that he didn't need anybody to rebound for him that day. We obliged, and heeded his warning.

Two hours later Maravich finally came out. I couldn't take my eyes off of him. The ball looked like it was on a string every time he dribbled. The ball looked like it was meant to be in his hand every time he shot it. He knew he was a showman; he was paid to be a showman, and he was going to be a showman that night. This turned out to be an "anything you can do, I can do better" night between Maravich and Archibald. Maravich ended up with 44. Archibald ended up with 47, and the Royals won 136–127.

Afterwards the three of us waited for Maravich outside of Cincinnati Gardens. We were hoping to get his autograph. There were probably seventy-five to a hundred people waiting outside with us, hoping to do the same. Maravich finally came out and you would've thought the Beatles had just landed in New York. Men and women **screaming,** shoving programs in his face. My friend Zeke Campbell actually reached in and grabbed a lump of Pistol Pete's **hair** and to this day he's still not sure why he did it. Pete would sign my program. Zeke got his clump of hair.

Should we call Sy Sperling? Clone that stuff and you've got a hell of a memorabilia item—and it'd be **undetectable!**

At this point, Walt Bellamy, the future Hall-of-Famer, pulled up in a white Cadillac Eldorado. He pulled Maravich from the crowd, he put him in the car, and they drove off.

That was the only time I saw Maravich play in person, but I ran into him fifteen years later in Springfield, Massachusetts. I was working for CNN at the time, and I was covering Maravich's induction to the Basketball Hall of Fame. And if you've been to the building, you know that you can shoot hoops at the end of the tour. I'd just done the interview with Maravich, he took the tour, and then started shooting free throws, and I walked up next to him, and I said, "Do you realize I've been waiting fifteen years to rebound for you?" And he said, "You can rebound all you want. But I don't miss many."

There's going to come a time—as I think of it, maybe the time's already come—when it's going to be impossible to explain to current fans why Maravich had this appeal to people. This was a guy with a gift like Jordan has a gift or Magic had a gift. But this wasn't passing or driving to the basket or aerial work or slam dunks. This was magic on the elemental level of the game.

This guy gets the ball, he's going to score. And he's going to take the shot from anywhere. And he's going to come back down and do it again.

And he only played ten years as a pro, he was never with a good team or in a good media city, and he only got to play in twenty-six play-off games. And he died so young. This is one of those word-of-mouth guys I'm always telling you about in base-ball. You make a list of the five greatest basketball players ever, and he's on it, and somebody who is less than thirty years old is going to say "Pete Maravich?" and you can go to the statistics and you still can't put it across.

I give. Sometimes you have to accept word of mouth.

Buck Ewing: greatest catcher of all time.

I won't go that far.

We have this argument all the time, Dear Reader. Dan just proved my point.

Shut up. Your turn.

7. **Game Four, World Series, October 15, 1969**: I wasn't much of a reporter for this one. I remembered to bring my binoculars, but I forgot to my father's eight-millimeter movie camera. But it didn't matter. I was going to see a World Series game. And I **hated** the Mets. We were Yankee fans. Earlier that year, when the Mets had started to close on the Cubs and the Yankees were sinking further and further behind the Orioles, I had announced to my folks at the dinner table that I'd become a Met fan. And the conversation stopped. Even my sister Jenna, who was barely a year old, went silent. My mother, who was the real fan, just looked at me. My father said, "You don't just **change** teams because yours is losing and the other one is winning. That's not being a **fan.** That's being what we call a front-runner."

So I did not go to see Tom Seaver and the Miracle Mets face Mike Cuellar and the Orioles as a rabid Met fan. But it didn't matter. It was a **World Series** game. It could've been two teams I'd never heard of. The World Series **counted** in a way nobody under the age of thirty can really appreciate. And it was a fantastic game: Donn Clendenon homering in the second and Seaver making it hold up until the ninth, and then a wonderfully controversial finale in the bottom of the tenth when J. C. Martin dropped a bunt, and ran so far out of the baseline that the Baltimore reliever, Pete Richert, threw a strike to first base and still managed to hit Martin in the back. The ball bounded down the right-field line and Rod Gaspar scored the winning run from second. My Dad and I hustled onto the subway, sat on the floor of the train all the way back to Manhattan, then got caught up with Vietnam War protestors shouting, "Hell

No, We Won't Go" in the middle of the Times Square station. Oh, and we went to Barney's and they made me buy a suit.

But what I remember most was the incredible excitement of just being there. It was a beautiful fall day, just enough of a haze to give everything a kind of glow. And these binoculars I had—I always wondered what happened to them, they were better than a television lens—I could see Joe DiMaggio and Stan Musial and a dozen other heroes sitting behind home plate as clearly as if they were in the next row. They weren't—my father and I were in deep left field.

Anyway, the real point to this one that has stayed with me for more than a quarter of a century is a very simple, very sad fact. The World Series today, through the genius of the game's leaders, is just another championship. It might still carry a little bit of a ritzier imprimatur than the Stanley Cup or the NBA Finals or even the Super Bowl (that's an adjective, not a brand name). But the difference is slim, indeed. In 1969, the World Series was so important that when I went to my seventh-grade home-room teacher, Miss Barton, who had been there, we thought, since before the school had been built in 1911, and I told her why I wanted to take the day off from school, she looked at me like I was crazy. "You have to **ask** if it's OK to skip school to go to the **World Series**? Have you got a ticket for **me**?"

That's what we've lost. Instead we have hype and games that go to midnight and owners who can't figure out why baseball's number three now. And we have Super Bowls that never live up to their advance billing.

Except one:

7. **Super Bowl XXV, Bills vs Giants, January 27, 1991:** This was not only the best Super Bowl I've ever covered, but perhaps the best NFL game I've ever witnessed. The lead changed hands four times, and the outcome was not decided until the last four seconds when, of course, Scott Norwood's field goal went wide right.

But the game had an eerie backdrop because our nation was at war in the Persian Gulf at the time, and as a result, the most extensive security ever mounted for a sporting event was on hand, including a pregame flyover by four F-15 jets.

And as great as the game was, as strange and uncomfortable as all the security was, what happened **after** the game was the strangest of all. When you go into a winning team's locker room you expect to see the same thing every time: guys going crazy, champagne flowing, hugs, kisses. But I couldn't help but notice, all the way at the end of the Giants' locker room was O. J. Anderson. He had spent the good years of his career playing for Cardinal teams that had no chance of getting to a Super Bowl. He had finally gotten his chance. But he wasn't celebrating. So I walked back and I was listening to some of his comments to the media. And I remember him saying, "Nobody picked us. None of you guys picked us." I was thinking, this guy's just won the Super Bowl, and he's upset because nobody in the media picked the Giants to win? He turned toward me, and he was going to walk out of the locker room, and I said "O. J., I can't believe you're letting this bother you." And he said, "It's all about respect, man. A couple of people picked us to win. You and Tom Jackson did." And earlier in the week, Rudy Martzke from *USA Today* had asked us our Super Bowl opinions. Chris Berman and Joe Theismann said Buffalo would win, and Tommy turns to me and says, "Maybe we should be different. Giants are gonna win," and Rudy reacted by saying, "Great, great. **Somebody's** going to go with the Giants." Tommy goes "21 to 19, Giants." I said, "Giants by three." Final score was 20 to 19.

But it got even stranger. After leaving O. J. Anderson's locker, I walked around the corner, and noticed that Jeff Hostetler had just come in from the interview area. We both arrived at his locker at the exact same time, and we both saw his suit, ripped to shreds. Somebody had gotten in there, right after the game, and ripped his suit to shreds. He left that locker room, that night, the greatest triumph of his career, upset because somebody had ripped up his suit! He didn't know if it was a joke or not. He thought that maybe Phil Simms had done this; Hostetler had taken over for Simms late in the season, when Simms got injured.

You're not saying one teammate would do that to another? Heavens! Are you sure it wasn't Saddam Hussein disguised as a clubhouse attendant?

To this day, I don't know if he ever found out who did it. But Jeff Hostetler had to leave the Super Bowl winners' locker room that night . . . in his **uniform.**

8. **Game Five, World Series, October 14, 1984:** Flatly, the Tigers and the Padres in 1984 wasn't much of a series. Everybody

had been anticipating this great Tigers–Cubs showdown and instead here come these Padres in these brown-and-yellow softball uniforms. But this was one where the ambience made up for the lack of competition. Firstly, there was Tiger Stadium. If you have never been there, go—go **now**, the Luxury Box Police are about to tear it down. Tiger Stadium may be the most underrated sports facility in America. The TV camera angles blow it all out of proportion. It seems very big and very spacious; in fact it's just Fenway Park with an extra deck of seating and the outfield filled in. And you can sit there and out of the corner of your eye you see some different angle to the place and you can imagine you're in Ebbets Field in Brooklyn or Forbes Field in Pittsburgh . . .

Or Crosley Field in Cincinnati . . .

Exactly. It's the survivor. Fenway and Wrigley are living monuments. Tiger Stadium is the old, functional, respectable school building, or the office building with the push-out windows and the gargoyles on top. So while the Tigers and Kirk Gibson are beating up every pitcher in Padre history except Vicente Romo, I'm soaking in the ambience in the press box. And there were only two local TV reporters covering the series for cities that weren't involved in the games. And they sat us together. From Channel 5 in Boston, there's me. From Channel 7 in Boston, there's . . . Carl Yastrzemski.

You're kidding. You sat through a World Series game with Yaz?

Amazing. He was the buddy of the station owner and at that guy's insistence he dabbled in TV for the first two years after he quit. So now here's Yastrzemski, who I'd always hated because he used to plow the Yankees every damn game, on top of which, on my ninth birthday, my dad and I had gone all the way out to Long Island in a snowstorm to see him at a banquet, and he didn't show, and the only other ballplayer there was Chuck Schilling, of all people. So I didn't particularly care for Yaz.

But one on one, with nobody bothering him and him feeling like the rookie and thinking I'm the veteran, he loosens up. He starts telling me stories. Tiger Stadium stories. "I hit a ball there," he says, and he points to the roof over right field. "I hit one **there**," he says, and he points to the roof over center field. And on and on. And then he starts talking about 1967. And he's chain-smoking cigarettes and talking about how the '67 Series still hurt, and '75, and how sorry he was to be retired, and I'm thinking, ''Why the hell bother to do a story on this game? I should just be interviewing this guy for four hours.''

Well, the Tigers eventually win and we make our way downstairs just as the entire crowd storms on to the field and Kirk Gibson socks some guy square in the jaw just to get past him into the dugout. And we do the postgame interview stuff and duck the champagne squirting, and we're about ready to get out and go back to the Detroit station where we were editing our stuff and Yastrzemski says, ''We're not going anywhere. There's a riot out there.''

So we go up to the roof of Tiger Stadium, and it's true. Michigan and Trumbull Avenues are packed with people. And some poor guy tries to get through in a cab, and the crowd stops him, some fellows politely invite him and the driver to step out, and fifty people pile on the cab and start jumping on it. Then they turn it over. Then they light it on fire. Then the cops come in on horseback and all of a sudden it's the streets of St. Petersburg during the Russian Revolution. I'm figuring I'm going to see people **killed** because of a lousy sporting event! Fortunately, the crowd wasn't quite that rowdy—they start running and nobody gets hurt. But as soon as the cops go through, the fans come right back. And at this moment, a helicopter takes off from inside the stadium. A big Detroit ''D'' logo on the side. It's Tom Monaghan, the owner of the team. And Yastrzemski turns to me and says, ''There goes our ride.''

So Yaz, who I am really beginning to like, says all the players and their families are downstairs waiting out the riot. And he takes me and my cameraman Donnie Mitchell down into the basement, and we wait it out down there. And I get to meet Dan Petry's parents and Alan Trammell's folks and now it's the damn London Blitz and we're in the Underground, waiting for the bombs to stop.

Here's the punch line. The revelers finally go home about 3:00 A.M. and we go out in search of our car and the streets are covered with debris. And there, with one full giant lawn-size Hefty Bag slung over his shoulder and another half-full one in his hands, is this guy, picking through the broken glass: looking for unbroken bottles he can bring back for the deposit.

And that guy grew up to be . . . Bill Clinton!

Right. Lousy game. Great postgame show.

8. **NCAA Championship Game, Kansas vs. Oklahoma, 1988:** Twice during the regular season, Kansas lost to Oklahoma, each by eight points. Kansas, in five of their losses that year, lost by at least ten points. There was a six-game stretch during the midpoint of their season where they didn't beat a Division I opponent. The only win they had was against Hampton of Virginia. I arrived at the title game probably two hours before tip-off and one of the first people I met was Sonny Vaccaro, who was working for Nike at the time—he's now working for Adidas. And Sonny said, "Young man, do you want a tip on who's going to win tonight?" And I said sure, and he said, "Kansas." I said, "Kansas? Kansas is going to beat Mookie Blaylock, Stacey King, and Harvey Grant?" He said yes. "Home court advantage." I said, "You trying to tell me a team with names like Piper, Pritchard, Newton, Berry, Maddox, is going to beat Oklahoma?" And he said, "Home court advantage."

I should have known Oklahoma was doomed because they had already played for the national championship in football. They'd lost to Miami in the Orange Bowl and finished third in the final polls.

They were tied at 50 at halftime, and I figured this was the pace that Billy Tubbs wants for the Oklahoma Sooners, that their depth, that their talent, would eventually wear Kansas down. I forgot to take into consideration just how good, how versatile, Danny Manning was. He went 13-of-24, 5-of-7 from the line, 7 rebounds, 31 points, and every time his team needed a big hoop, big block, big rebound, he supplied it. Kansas defeats Oklahoma 83–79. Kansas, with eleven victories, finishing third in the Big 8 that season, wins the national championship.

One of the last people I see as I leave Kemper Arena that night was Sonny Vaccaro, and I walked out shaking my head and he said, "Young man, three words: home court advantage." I said, "No, Sonny. Two words: Danny Manning."

9. **Game Three, National League Championship Series, October 7, 1983:** I was covering for CNN and the National League media department had no idea what or who we were, so they sat us as far out in left as humanly possible. I thought I could see the curve of the earth between my seat and home plate. And again, this wasn't much of a series. There were only three noteworthy events. Early in the game, the Philly Phanatic, Dave Raymond, who I later came to know pretty well and who remains a consummate improvisational performer, is walking along the ledge of the auxiliary

press box where we're sitting and I do my best invisible act. I just know I'm his target. And I was right. I get the full Philly Phanatic snout-in-your-face kiss. On national TV, apparently.

Later on, Mike Schmidt goes after a Dodger pop-up behind third and he basically has to shove a spectator out of the way, permitting me to say in my report that "the Schmidt Has Hit the Fan." And best of all there was Gary Matthews. Remember, I felt so far away from the action that I figured beings on other planets had better views. And Matthews turns on a pitch and I manage to follow it from the moment it leaves his bat. And the ball is hit so hard that it appears to be past the infield before we hear the **crack** of the bat out in left. And this thing is accelerating, and growing larger, and larger, and larger. It is at this point that I realize the damn thing is going to hit me. And kill me.

It hit you. You died. End of story. Thanks for reading.

Well, he came close. The ball smacked off the front of the auxiliary press box and made a sound like an explosion at a goiter clinic. The reverberation was so strong that I thought the ball had actually gone through the facing and hit me in the feet. An amazing home run. That and the long, lingering memory of a Philly Phanatic Phacial.

9. **Rick Wise No-Hits Reds, June 23, 1971:**

The Phillies make the list three times!

I was able to attend this game through the generosity of my younger brother Dave. That year the Reds held a promotion where if you got straight A's, you received tickets to upcoming games. As it turned out, Dave and I received our tickets on the same day. Dave had two tickets to the Pirates, two tickets to the Cardinals, two tickets to the Phillies. I had two tickets to the Dodgers, two tickets to the Padres, two tickets to the Phillies.

So, I was thinking if I could convince my brother to relinquish his tickets to the Phillies, I would have **four** and I could double-date. So I tried to convince Dave—not exactly your most knowledgeable baseball fan—that the Padres, who were at the time twenty-two and a half games out of first place, were on the verge of a breakthrough season.

Well, the Phillies were only fifteen and a half games out of first, so it was not like they were lighting up the National League East. So Dave coughed up his two tickets to the Phillies in exchange for two tickets to the Padres. I could really care less about seeing the game: I was on a double-date.

You and Elle MacPherson, and Michael Jackson and Lisa Marie.

Well, no. But as it turned out, Rick Wise hits two home runs, no-hits the Reds. The fourth no-hitter in Philly history, the first pitcher ever to throw one **and** hit a pair of homers. And I got home at about one in the morning, and the first person to greet me at the door was not my mom, not my dad, but my brother Dave. He had this long, sad look on his face because he had listened to the game on radio. And I said, "Dave, if you think Rick Wise had a good night . . ."

You're lying. Lying lying lying.

No comment.

10. **Milwaukee Brewers at Baltimore Orioles, October 3, 1982:** Could've been one of the greatest games in history. It wasn't. Six weeks earlier, the Orioles had been seven and a half games behind the Brewers in the AL East race. Then they started winning. The season was to end with a four-game series in Memorial Stadium with the Orioles three games out. They won a doubleheader Friday, 8–3 and 7–1. I was in Washington covering the damned football strike when on Saturday morning, my boss Rick Davis calls and says, "If the Orioles win today and tie it, forget the stupid strike—you're covering the game." So after spending all day Saturday dozing in the pressroom at some hotel in DC, I get the word: Orioles 11, Brewers 3. They're tied, and the final game of the season decides the division.

But there was even more to it than that. Earl Weaver had long before announced that he was retiring as the Orioles' manager. So this was it: Either they won the game and they went to the playoffs, or they lost, wasted the incredible comeback, and Weaver was gone. And Jim Palmer was pitching. Fifteen and four going in. He'd pitched the first World Series game I'd ever seen on TV. And the O's had this punk shortstop who everybody was talking about even though he'd been hitting .117 on May 1 and they were thinking he wasn't ready yet. The third base coach's son. Ripley or Ruskin or something. And the Brewers were going with Don Sutton, whom they had brought in like a Prussian mercenary in a trade with the Astros just before the deadline. I didn't know it, but between just

Palmer and Ripken, I was seeing guys play who span my entire history as a fan.

So with all this buildup, what happens? The Brewers vivisect Palmer. The game's over in the **second** inning. No drama. Nothing. Brewers 10, Orioles 2. And what's worse, my producer, Phil Griffin, had already imposed on the Orioles' staff for credentials the morning of the game. Bob Brown was the publicity director and he stuck us in the auxiliary football booth, a little basket hanging from the first base deck that you could only reach by ladder. We were stuck in there with Mike Hegan and the Brewers' radio crew. So now, by the sixth inning, Phil gets the idea that we have to be **on the field** the moment the game ends so we can get the shots of the Brewers whooping it up. So he has to go to Bob Brown, who is watching his team's comeback being ruined, and seeing all his plans for the playoffs against the Angels go down the tubes, to arrange this for us. And Bob Brown does the most gracious thing I've ever seen in baseball. He tells Phil, "Well, you can't wait in the tunnel to the dugout. You can't sit in the seats. You can't sit in the aisles. I guess you'll have to wait on the field."

And Phil and I look at each other and I look at Brown and I say, "Excuse me?"

"Yeah, take this note," and Brown starts scribbling on Phil's press credential. "Go down during the seventh-inning stretch and tell the cop at the gate to let you on the field. Stand at the far side of our dugout. You're less likely to get hit by something." And as we're staring there, jaws agape, he says, "Thanks for being so understanding about the auxiliary football booth."

So Phil Griffin and I and our two-man camera crew spend the last three innings of the decisive game of the 1982 American League East pennant race **in play**, on the field, cowering behind the Oriole dugout, praying there wouldn't be a pop-up or a line drive. And we got our shots of the Brewers and followed them into the clubhouse and caught Sutton, and Ted Simmons, and Rollie Fingers singing—again and again—"California, here I come, right back where I started from." And that's all they could remember of the song. The rest of it was "Nah nah nah, nah nah nah, nah nah nah nahhhh . . ." Again and again. And the four of us drive back to the CNN bureau in Washington and we've heard them singing this so much that every time there's a lull in the conversation somebody involuntarily starts singing "California, here I come . . ." until we're all ready to scream.

We edit the tape and do two pieces—including the singing Brewers—and pack it in for the night. And Phil and I fly back to New York the next day and we talk for a little while and I start to doze off and all of a sudden I hear him mumbling, "Nah nah nah, nah nah nah, nah nah nah nahhhh . . ."

The last time I talked to him was three years ago. Damn but we didn't start singing that stupid song again.

10. **Game Seven, Stanley Cup Finals, June 14, 1994:** A hot, muggy Tuesday evening in Manhattan. The New York Rangers are on the verge of putting down the curse, and picking up the Cup, for the first time in fifty-four years. I was asked by the ESPN hockey crew if I'd like to be a part of their telecast. I said sure; I always felt a kinship with the Rangers, having worked for CNN in New York when our offices were right across from the Garden, when it was very easy for me to get through with work and go see a Ranger game. The first Ranger game I saw in person, April of 1984, Ken Morrow has an overtime goal for the Islanders, beating the Rangers in the play-offs in game five.

You understand this gives you very little credence as a Ranger fan. Ratelle, Hadfield, and Gilbert losing to the Bruins. J. D. shutting out the Flyers. Listening to some guy in the cheap seats bellowing out at Phil Esposito as he took a face-off against a diabetic Bobby Clarke, "Hey, Espo, feed him some sugar." **That's** being a Ranger fan, Ohio boy.

I know, I know. That's what I was thinking: I thought, if I could be a part of Ranger history—that's one of the big reasons I got into this business: being some part of sports history. So, I asked what my assignment would be. Well, there was a little bit of hesitating on the part of the producer, and then he finally broke the news to me: I was to go to the Polo Grounds bar on the Upper East Side of Manhattan, and do live reports from the game. I was there to add some flavor, to gauge how Ranger fans were feeling, as they were on the verge of winning—or losing—the Stanley Cup.

Well, I thought, not exactly a choice assignment; not exactly Al Michaels doing that U.S.-Russia Olympic game Keith was at, but I figured, I'll survive. And my mind-set was to try to find all the interesting stories, because I was at a decided disadvantage. Everybody in the bar was drinking, I was not.

Disadvantage? You never tried that before? You want to learn stuff about people, go drinking with them. You have seltzer while they have beer. Works especially well with Ranger fans.

You're right. During the course of the evening I found one guy who was actually on his **honeymoon** who had decided he had to see the Rangers win. He'd offered a thousand dollars to get tickets; couldn't get in, and ended up at this bar. And I said, "What's your wife think about this?" And he said, "Well, I don't think she had a problem until I said 'I can sleep with you any night; I can only sleep with The Cup tonight.' "

I think I sat next to that guy in the blue seats one night in 1973.

There was also a woman who in the course of the celebrating, actually had somebody take a bite out of her arm.

I was in Bristol that night.

Once the celebrating was over with, I walked outside and I was told by some Ranger fans that Mark Messier would bring the Stanley Cup out to a bar. They gave me directions to where it was; they said he might not be there until three or four in the morning, because he's got a few other stops along the way. So I went back to the hotel and got changed; I figured I better get ready for combat, because this could get ugly. And we waited for Messier. And we waited. And we waited.

And then he finally arrived. I later found out that he'd had to make a pit stop at a strip club because, as he would later say, "The Cup doesn't get out very often." Everybody's taking their drink out of the Cup, and it finally came around to my turn. I figured, all right, I got my tetanus shot, it's safe to drink. But I ask Messier, "What exactly did you **put** in the Cup?" And he said, "If you have to ask, you're not a Ranger fan." So, I grabbed the holy chalice and took a big gulp, and then Messier let out this devilish laugh that just echoed through the bar. And I asked him, did you **do** something to what's in the cup? And he said, "If you have to ask, you're not a Ranger fan."

To this day, I don't know what I drank. I **do** know, I'm not allowed to ask Mark Messier.

Keith's Top Ten Prominent Baseball Players' Names (Submitted Without Dan's Approval)

1. Anthony Keith Gwynn.

2. Wallace Keith Joyner.

3. Eric Keith Davis.

4. David Keith Stewart.

5. Keith Hernandez.

6. Keith Anthony Phillips.

7. Bobby Keith Moreland.

8. Keith Virgil Lockhart.

9. Keith Lavarne Smith (1979 Cardinals).

10. Patrick Keith Smith (1984–85 Yankees).

★ ☆ ★ ☆ ★ ★ 15 ★ ☆ ★ ☆ ★ ☆

PUT YOUR BASEBALL CARDS IN YOUR BICYCLE SPOKES, NOW!

The kid was about six or seven, and he was thumbing through the small stack of 3-D baseball cards with the seriousness and the fastidiousness of an art expert examining van Goghs.

He had come to the table I used to set up at the then twice-a-year baseball card "conventions" we had in New York in the 1970s, and his earnestness pleased me. There were only a couple of thousand of us collectors in the entire country then—and at seventeen I was still one of the youngest ones, so this little boy represented the next wave. Whatever money I would make at one of these three-day shows selling my extra 1976 Topps cards or the odd single from the late '60s would be plowed right back into my collection: I could turn the modern "junk" into the cards for the '50s and '30s and '10s that the older guys were selling across the aisle. There were a couple of these men who tried to make a living selling cards but almost nobody who sold them didn't also collect them on the side. The dealer charging me a bean for every 1940 Play Ball would always ask me if I'd seen any 1947 Tip Top cards at any of the other tables. It was a **hobby.**

Anyway, back to the kid. He had finished looking through the

A young Keith and his baseball cards. *(Theodore C. Olbermann)*

plastic-coated images of Bobby Grich and Willie Stargell, and now he was neatening up the stack and trying to place it back exactly where he'd found it on the table. The look on his face was so serious, so reverential, that it's with me still. He put his hands in his back pockets, then took the right one out, pointed at the stack of cards, and looked at me for the first time. And that's when he said it.

"Do these have any investment potential?"

Uh-oh. Beginning of the end, huh?

I'd love to be able to give you the exact date. I'm thinking it was 1976 and the Thanksgiving weekend show, probably at the Hotel Roosevelt in New York. We should put up a plaque or something: "Here began the End of the Meaning of Baseball Card Civilization As We Knew It." And there's lots of people to blame for the fact that there are still only a couple of thousand true collectors now, drowning in a sea of millions of speculators—the speculators themselves, the manufacturers, the athletes, the ex–coin dealers who now stick a card inside a hermetic plastic case and charge you to tell you your Excellent card is in Excellent condition, the publishers of the sports memorabilia magazines. But Dan, basically, it's my fault. I made this happen.

You know I'm here for you, KO. I'll testify at the trial and everything. I'll visit you in prison. Do you need a hug?

I'm guilty, but I'm not **that** guilty. You have to realize that the memorabilia phenomenon all started because a bunch of us in the early '70s enjoyed collecting old baseball cards so much that we used to hype it to people. We started monthly magazines and wrote analytical articles on the variations in the 1915 ZeeNut Candy Pacific Coast League cards, and we started having these three-day shows in Detroit and New York over big holiday weekends. I can remember, clear as a bell, the day Walter Cronkite showed film of the card collectors' convention in Michigan in 1971 on the *CBS Evening News*. I can't think of any other analogy: It was like we were being welcomed out of the closet. We—the adults especially, but also any kid who didn't throw his old cards away once school started— had been treated like nutburgers by our friends and our families. Here we were on **the news.** Hell, the first time I was ever on TV, I was interviewed by Charles Crawford of WCBS-TV in New York at the card show in the District 65 Union Hall on Astor Place in Manhattan. I was fourteen. Ten years later Charles Crawford was sitting there introducing me on CNN and I told him all about it.

I bet he was **delighted** by that.

He laughed. Not convincingly, but he laughed. Kind of like how we laughed when the Yankees signed that kid Jackson Melian last year and I told you that if he was really sixteen, that meant he'd been born in 1980. Anyway, back to the cards. We wanted people to know that there was real joy to these old cards: that it was a kick to look at a 1909 cigarette card—not just the scarce, valuable ones like Honus Wagner ($250! Who'd spend $250 on **one** baseball card!)—but the ones from the same set of the obscure guys like Jimmy Williams and Jean Dubuc and Harry Krause. In 1973, a 1952 Topps Mickey Mantle was worth $50. A 1952 Topps **Bob Borkowski** was also worth $50. The player **on** the card didn't dictate the value of it—its scarcity did. The fact that you needed Borkowski

(#328) and you already had Mantle (#311) meant you spent your $50 on Borkowski and left the Mantle for somebody else.

And the cards themselves—from whatever era: You were holding history in your hand. There were people a hundred years before who'd loved the same game, who'd had the same hopes for their favorite teams and their favorite players, who collected the new cards of 1888 the way we collected the new ones of 1972! And here were objects that were themselves intrinsically worthwhile and even beautiful—and they'd survived two world wars and lord knows how many presidents!

And there was another thing. I'd see adults come to my table and sort through some extra cards I had from the '40s or '50s, and they'd come across a card—one card—and they'd stop. And you'd see the smile come across their face and then maybe the eyes film over with tears. Some goofy $2\frac{1}{2}$ inch by $3\frac{1}{2}$ inch photo of Jim Finigan of the 1957 Detroit Tigers had transported them back in time. It was a summer day. It was the first trip to a ball game. It was childhood. It was perfection. And just watching **them** get so nostalgic made **me** more appreciative of what I was seeing then, and of what it would mean to me later.

So we tried to tell people: sports history and your own private history. And a lot of fun. And the problem was, we did such a great job of telling everybody, that a lot of people came into our cozy little naive world, bought our treasured cards from us at twice what we usually sold them for, and then sold them back to us for a hundred times what we usually bought them for. And then other people came into this slightly-less-cozy little world and began to scarf up all the cards of the star players and before we knew it the '52 Mickey Mantle was "worth" $50,000 while Bob Borkowski still hovered around $50. And finally came the manufacturers to create artificially scarce cards, and the magazines to hype the investment potential and how you never knew if an '88 Gregg Jefferies might turn into the next '52 Mantle and it was over. It was all over.

Let the High Council of the Planet Krypton speak: "Guilty!" "Guilty!" "Guilty!" We meant well. We tried. We screwed it all up.

Who's this "we," Kemo Sabe? I started collecting baseball cards in 1964; that was also the same year I saw my first game in person. My father took me and two of my brothers to see the Cubs and Giants in spring training, and I remember before we left the house, I went search-ing through my cards trying to find any members of these two teams, because I figured while we were there, we were going to get some auto-graphs. Two of the cards I treasured were Ernie Banks and Willie Mays, but that didn't stop me from finding a Jesus Alou card, a Jim Ray Hart—I figured I might as well get all of these guys to sign their cards. As it turned out, I probably got eight or nine autographs that day, including Willie Mays and Ernie Banks. And it never fails: When I tell people about getting those future Hall of Famers to sign those cards, the first reaction is: "Do you know how much those cards are **worth?**" It was insignificant.

Exactly. Even those of us at those card shows didn't think in those terms. The price we attached to the cards we were selling was just a means of establishing relative value. If I wanted a card you had, but you didn't need any of mine, I sold some to somebody else and then came back to you with cash. Then you took the cash and bought the cards you needed from somebody else. It was money-as-barter. Nobody looked at a '52 Mickey Mantle and said, "Fifty dollars!" They said, "Mickey Mantle!"

Those Banks and Mays cards are long gone. Probably destroyed in the spokes of my bicycle or perhaps tucked away as a bookmarker in my mom's attic. But the memories are still there, of those cards, that day, watching a game with my father and my brothers. I think that's what is lost nowadays with younger kids collecting cards. It's a value attached to it—not memory value, but monetary value.

It's not just kids, Dan. It's afflicted everybody. I remember hav-ing a conversation with a friend of mine who owned a card store. And he wasn't your traditional slick operator who just saw some quick money. He was in it for the profit, sure, but he loved the games, and he liked the cards, and he had a small collection of items in a beautiful display case in his home. And during the '94–'95 base-ball strike, he and I were talking about Cal Ripken, and something Todd Jones of the Astros had said about how if the owners actually started the '95 season with replacement players and the games ac-tually counted, none of the striking guys would hold it against Rip-ken if he crossed the picket line to keep his games-played streak alive. And Cal, of course, said he'd never do that. Never. And my friend was outraged. "What about his fans?" he asked me. "What about them?" And I thought, he's got a point, a lot of people besides

Cal cared about whether or not he broke Lou Gehrig's record. Then my friend said it: "Doesn't he realize how many of his fans have **invested in his cards?**"

That was a breaking point for me. The idea of being a fan was now intertwined with a cash payoff. You didn't **admire** Cal Ripken. You didn't **root** for him. You **bet** on him by buying his cards.

Five years ago, I turned the last remnants of my baseball card collection over to two of my nephews, and I told them: "Feel free to do whatever you want to with these cards—all I ask is: If you sell them, you get money back to buy **more** baseball cards." They rummaged through the cards and came back to me two weeks later and said, "Do you realize how much those cards are worth?" And I said no, what did you find? And they said, "Well, we found six Mike Schmidt rookie cards." And I said they could have the cards. Now instead of them saying, "Boy, that's great, we can treasure this card of a Hall of Fame player, a player that you looked up to and admired when you were growing up," their reaction was, "We can sell this card and make a lot of money!"

"Guilty!" "Guilty!" See you later, Dan. The big interplanetary mirror is swooping down here toward Krypton to suck me up and send me careening across the galaxy.

So I told them: Remember, you can sell the cards, but you have to buy more cards in return. It was kind of disheartening to hear their reaction, because I used to engulf every bit of information on those cards—whether it was what Vic Davalillo did in his spare time, or what Sonny Jackson's real name was.

Roland. I don't even have to think twice. Roland Jackson. I think I learned to enjoy reading, in part at least, because of cards. I know they taught me the rudiments of baseball history, of getting some sense that stuff had happened in the world before I was born. Roland Thomas Jackson.

Nowadays, I don't know if the kids really absorb the information that's on there and learn about the players—**treasure** the cards.

How about just **looking** at them? Trying to guess which ballpark they were taken in, or if the guy had been traded and they'd blacked out the logo on his cap, trying to guess what uniform he was really wearing? When I was eight years old, I was utterly baffled by one thing on one card in the 1967 Topps set. Now, 1967 was the first year I collected cards and I swear I must have spent an hour looking at each new one. You say to me "John Boccabella 1967" and I can probably tell you what number the card is. I can tell you what the picture looks like, where it was taken, what color "Cubs" is on the front. We **memorized** the cards. Now to the bafflement. Tommie Reynolds is a coach with the Cardinals now, but back then he was just this twenty-five-year old outfielder trying to stick with the Mets. And all the cards in the 1967 set had the player's name and position at the top of the card. And the lettering is always spaced the same way: a blank space between the first and last names, just a little narrower than the average letter. But on Tommie Reynolds's card—number 487, by the way—he's looking just to the right of the photographer, and his batting helmet is reflecting either the sun or the photographer's flash—there's enough space between "Tom" and "Reynolds" to put in two or maybe three letters. All the others: short space between first name and last. His? A mile wide. It just looked **wrong.** Apart from the fact that he's "Tom" on the front of the card and "Tommie" on the back.

I'll say it simply: This drove me nuts, for years. That space. Why? I could never see the card without wondering. Who screwed up? These meticulous, almost anally retentive proofreaders at Topps and here's this space between "Tom" and "Reynolds" big enough to throw a fastball through. I asked other collectors. I wrote articles about it. I asked friends who worked for Topps. Nobody had a clue.

In 1989, Topps went through its warehouses and offices and did what it had never done before: It sold its secrets. They trotted out hundreds of uncut sheets of cards, and, better still, hundreds of uncut sheets of "proof" cards—the first print run that they did just to check for little things like spelling and colors and the spaces between a guy's first and last names. And I had a field day: I found and bought cards I'd never seen before—Bob Gibson tricking the photographer and throwing lefty instead of righty, and a sheet from 1980 with two cards on it that were never issued because the players retired. And there, hanging from an easel in the auction room, was a proof sheet from the 6th Series of the 1967 Topps baseball card, and as soon as I saw it, the face of Tommie Reynolds just jumped out at me, and I had my answer. The proof card read "Tommy Reynolds." Only **he** spelled his first name "Tommie." At the last minute, some alert proofreader removed the "MY" from "Tommy" on the front and figured a space was better than a misspelling: Bingo—"Tom (Space) (Space) Reynolds."

Twenty-two years of wondering were over. If I tripped over an explanation for the eighteen-minute gap in the Richard Nixon Watergate tape, I couldn't have felt a greater sense of closure. Now, I had to buy that sheet. But there was nothing else on it that interested me, and I was spending enough on the Lefty Gibson and the unissued 1980s that I had to stay within reasonable budget. But some other guy didn't. I think there was a Pete Rose and a Roberto Clemente on the same sheet, so this guy, who couldn't give a damn about Tom, Tommie, or Tommy Reynolds, finally wore me out and he won the auction. And I've been kicking myself ever since. Because what the guy did was **cut the sheet up** and sell the star cards at exorbitant prices. And I actually tracked down what happened to nearly all the cards on this sheet, but nobody knows what happened to this one and only "Tommy" Reynolds that I'd still pay through the nose for. Could've thrown it away, for all I know.

That's what the cards meant then. Nowadays, it's just, "Ooh, a Griffey. Better put that in an album before I dent a corner and it's worth $2.75 instead of $3."

It's "I've got two of these, that means I can probably get one of those." Or, "If I sell this one, do you realize how much more it's going to be worth if I get two of **those** rookie cards?" Maybe I'm being naive as a businessperson, but that's why I collected cards in the first place.

No fourteen-year-old today would ever have done what I did in 1973. Back to the New York "convention." A fellow comes in from Chicago for this and he has a small van full of 1950s cards. He's got probably two thousand 1953 Bowman Gum cards—a beautiful set of cards, with just photos on the front, no artwork, and at least half of the pictures taken in Yankee Stadium, the Polo Grounds, Ebbets Field. Gorgeous color, great biographies on the back. And I needed probably half of the set of 160 different cards. He had **two thousand of them** at a dime apiece. Not a dime in Very Good condition and a quarter for Near Mint. Not a dime for Larry Miggins and a hundred bucks for Mickey Mantle. One card, one dime. So I didn't have the Mantle. He had thirty of them. I looked through them all very carefully and picked out the nicest one, and left the other twenty-nine of them. Never thought twice about spending the whole three dollars. Who needed **thirty** Mickey Mantles? I still needed Larry Miggins. And there was more to it: I felt a **responsibility** to leave the other Mantles for the next twenty-nine guys who stopped by this guy's table trying to finish off their 1953 Bowman sets.

The '53 Bowman Mantles are now priced at around 2,500 fish, per. You do the math. And yes, sometimes I regret it.

You could buy and sell me right now, couldn't you?

Probably. But not even the pleasure involved in that thought makes me **truly** regret it. If I'd bought all thirty of them, my disillusionment would have begun when I was fourteen instead of when I was thirty-four. I have **good** memories of that card now. That 1953 Bowman set is a memory from my childhood the way your '64 Ernie Banks is. Besides which, what would I have done with them? I would've taken them back to my table and sold them for a quarter apiece.

Four years ago, I went to Arlington, Texas, to interview Mitch Williams for ESPN, one month after he had served up the home run to Joe Carter in the World Series, the game six game winner in Toronto. And before I left, I remembered I had been asked by a person who works for a charity, if, when I went out on the road, I could get some autographs or some things that they could auction off. I brought some baseballs with me, some 1993 World Series balls, and before I left, I asked Mitch if he would sign them, which he did. And he said something that surprised me. "You should get **Joe Carter** to sign those balls, too. Then they'd **really** be worth a lot." I never thought of it at the time, but one week later, I was going to Kansas City to interview Joe Carter, and I asked him if he'd mind signing the balls for charity. And he looked and he saw that Mitch's name was on there, and he signed them, and he said, "Those are going to be worth something someday!" It just hadn't occurred to me.

I remember. I also remember that the collector is still alive in you. You managed to save one of those balls for me. It's still up in my office. And you sold it to me for the cost of what the charity was going to sell them for.

You **did** sell it to me at **cost** didn't you?

Shut up. You know, I don't begrudge people who collect memorabilia for the sake of investments, or even trying to make a quick buck, as much as I feel sorry for them. Because they're missing what the true value of memorabilia is, and that's memories. Maybe I'm naive and maybe I'm a purist, but that's why I collected. So I would **have** memories—ten years, twenty, thirty years after the fact, of what these cards meant to me, or baseballs. I still have a foul ball I caught at Riverfront Stadium in 1970. Ron Santo hit it, and last year at Wrigley Field, I met Ron Santo, and I told him that I'd caught a foul pop-up that he hit at Riverfront. And he said, "I'll be more than happy to sign it for you." And I thought that was great. I just didn't want him to say, "Then it might be worth something"—because it already **was.**

That's it in a nutshell. But I thought you were going to say you were afraid Santo was going to say, "I'll be more than happy to sign it for you—for twelve dollars."

I'm not too fond of that idea, either.

The autograph hobby was perverted, too, and there's so much forgery—some of it deliberate and some of it from the days when the clubhouse boy used to sign the star's name to the autographed ball. Did you know that one of the top newscasters in Chicago, Walter Jacobsen, admitted to doing that when he was the Cubs' ball boy? Anyway, for all the things wrong with autographs, I really don't mind retired players charging for autographs.

Huh?

Well, follow my logic on this. Everything that has made millionaires out of the modern players came from the efforts of guys who struggled to make $10,000 a year playing big-league sports, many of whom get nothing or virtually nothing in the way of pensions or any other recognition from today's players. And even the stars of that time got nearly zip for their endorsements. With all the manufacturers making baseball cards these days, every player gets a licensing fee of around $80,000—just for the use of his likeness. You know what, say, Ron Santo, got? $125 a year, then raised to $250, and sometimes not even in cash—they used to be able to pick discounted appliances out of a catalog instead of just getting the money. Joe Boever gets $80,000. Ron Santo got a blender.

I see nothing wrong with Ron or anybody else, even an active player, going to a show and charging for his autograph—with the proviso that they'll still sign for fans at a game or in public when it's not inconvenient. I don't think I'd ever charge for my autograph—like it's **worth** anything—and fundamentally I don't think anybody should, ever. But especially for the older guys who built the financial end for today's player, this is a relatively innocuous way for them to get a little piece of the pie.

But there's still no way around it. Memorabilia as an investment, autographs as a business. The losers are the fans, and it's self-inflicted.

When I was a collector, I collected for what I thought were all the right reasons. But nowadays, they probably seem like all the wrong reasons. I just remember looking through all those cards, memorizing birthdates, just minutiae—what a guy hit in single-A ball. But that was important; for some reason, it was important. They were **my** cards. And even now, all the opportunities to get jerseys and bats—I don't know what you do with them, where you put 'em. I usually get items just so I can turn them over to charities so they can sell them. I just hate to see these little kids with ten cards hoping to get them signed, and then they turn them over to their dad, and Dad realizes how much they're worth.

It's not collecting anymore. And the other thing is, collecting and money don't have to be mutually exclusive. Like you said to your nephews—you want to sell them? Great. Buy more cards. When I was sixteen, a set of cards came out on the backs of the Hostess baked goods: Twinkies, HoHos, you name 'em. Now, you could buy these things at the supermarket, but there were 150 different cards and they came three to a box. Like I said before, do the math: even at $1.29 a box that's $65 in 1975 dollars. And, what's worse, by the time you completed a set, you had to have eaten half of the Twinkies and DingDongs and LardButts or whatever they were called. So you had a set of cards, you were out $65, and you weighed seven hundred pounds.

So one day I had a bright idea. I remembered that about fifteen minutes from my house Hostess had what they called a "Thrift Store," which was a pleasant euphemism for "Place Where We Sell Two-Week-Old Bread—Cheap." And sure enough, they would get cases and cases of these unsold Twinkie boxes with the cards on them. And one day I went in and asked to speak to the manager and I asked him what happened to the Twinkies if they didn't sell even at the Thrift Store. And he mentioned how they were stuffed in a big dumpster in the back every Tuesday and shipped off to New

Jersey as slops for the hogs. So I asked him if he'd mind if I came by once a week and went through the dumpster and salvaged the cards. I even offered him money, and he said, "No, son. If you're willing to stand waist-high in a dumpster full of old HoHo's, you must be a real collector."

So every Tuesday I would dress up in my rattiest jeans and a pair of rain boots and dive into the HoHo dumpster. And using an Exacto knife, I would wade through the crushed DingDongs and the now three-week-old bread, and cut off the backs of the boxes to get the baseball cards. And I mean I got hundreds of them. And I would think about only one thing . . .

Just how bad a month-old DingDong can smell.

Nah. That wasn't a problem. Those things had a shelf-life of a thousand years. Put one in the ground today and dig it up in 2767 and it would taste exactly the same. I would think of how I could trade my duplicates for the ones I didn't have, then sell the rest, and buy more cards. **That's** collecting.

It's not as bad as diving in to the DingDong Dumpster, but to give you an idea of what people **will** collect: When I told some friends I was going to Augusta to cover the Masters, they asked me if I would bring back . . . some divots.

So I had a piece of Tupperware, and actually brought back turf from Augusta that my friends wanted. I gave one of those pieces of turf to our old producer, Mike McQuade, and McQuade was going to bring it back and plant it in his yard. Believe it or not, somebody **stole** his piece of turf from Augusta.

I was nowhere near his desk when that happened. Besides, I can't get **any** grass to grow in my backyard. My favorite odd memorabilia story comes from personal experience. Yankee Stadium was closing in 1973, and since there'd been very few people besides my family **in** Yankee Stadium in '72 and '73, we had become friends with most of the staff: I mean, we knew groundskeepers by name. And one of them was this quiet, slight, really generous man named Moe. And on the last Friday night of the season, he comes up the runway from the groundskeepers' cave, and he comes to my seat and gives me a package. "Don't tell anybody where you got this, and don't tell anybody who gave it to you, and, whatever you do, don't open it until you get out of the ballpark." And he was dead serious about this. What Moe had given me was this two-foot-square, two-inch-high object wrapped in brown paper and yarn, with a big, thick spike sticking out of the bottom of it. I don't know how he thought people **wouldn't** know it was a base—but I sat there the whole night with the thing placed, very carefully, on my lap, and it's still one of the favorite things in my collection.

But you didn't ask for it. Harry Wendelstedt, the umpire, collects hats from championships. Just hats, just from championships. 1986 World Series, towards the end of game six, Harry asked Wade Boggs if he could have his hat after the game, figuring there would not be a game seven. Then the ball was hit to Bill Buckner. I don't know if Harry Wendelstedt ever got Wade Boggs's hat.

Harry's **son** got my hat, of course. It was Hunter Wendelstedt who threw me out of my only game in a professional baseball uniform, last year in the Eastern League. I threw my cap at him. The day will come when Hunter makes the big leagues. And I'll get something of his—in revenge. But anyway, you can collect hats, or bases, or autographs, or cards, or whatever. We both know a sportscaster of sorts who has, or had, George Brett's jockstrap, bronzed and hanging from a plaque. But the point is that the line used to be between the large number of collectors who didn't care how much something was worth or who was on it, but only what it meant to their collection or their memories, and the small number of collectors who would also sell stuff. Now the line is between the small number of collectors who actually get something because of what it **means** to them, and the vast number of speculators who simply hope to resell it later at a profit.

And we'll close this with my favorite warning to collectors: Never buy anything you won't be happy to keep forever. In Holland in the seventeenth century, the big hobby was collecting varieties of tulips. The thing grew just like the baseball card hobby, only faster. Within a few years, you could trade tulip futures on the Dutch stock market. In every town there were tulip banks, tulip grading experts, tulip catalogs. You could get a mortage **on** a tulip; you could get a mortgage **to buy** a tulip. Calculating four hundred years' of inflation, somebody once paid about $82,500 for **one** tulip. And then one day, somebody figured out that nobody was keeping the tulips anymore. Never mind the beauty, never mind the smell, never mind the intrinsic worth of the plant. It was only Tulip Cash Flow. They had **all** become speculators, and the moment everybody realized this, the whole market came to a grinding halt. Thousands were bankrupted, the government had to establish special tulip commissions to handle all the tulip lawsuits, and the Dutch economy crashed into ruins.

So keep that in mind the next time you're about to buy a card or a jersey or an autograph not because you want it but because you think it's going to be "worth something someday." And if you ever see any card manufacturer announce it's got a special set of Tulip Baseball Cards—sell everything and run for the flipping hills.

BUT ENOUGH ABOUT US, WHAT DO <u>YOU</u> THINK OF US?

The following are unsolicited testimonials about our intrinsic talent, skills, and basic human goodness, sent in by prominent viewers. And, of course, when we say they're unsolicited, we're lying. We asked for each and every one of them. On the other hand, we didn't pay a dime for any of them, and yet we've made them into an entire chapter! If we'd thought of this earlier, we could have had other people write **the entire book.** The mind boggles at the concept: Ultimately, is this not the dream of American business? We write the book, only **we** don't write a word of it?

Well, maybe for the sequel (Ha!). For now, we could only milk them for one chapter.

Charles Barkley, Forward, Houston Rockets, and the next Governor of Alabama:

When I watch sports, I want to watch great athletes, and enjoy myself. It takes me away from reality. Dan and Keith make me laugh; they bring joy to sports; they make the absurd seem funny. I'm tuned in every Sunday to see those two 'cause they make me laugh.

Michael Jordan, Guard, Chicago Bulls, Four-Time Most Valuable Player, NBA, Owns His Own Continent:
What show? **Who** are they?

Rebecca Lobo, 1995 NCAA Player of the Year, Olympian, Author, Forward, New York Liberty, WNBA:
I watch "The Big Show" to get my update on President Polk drooling his drool of regret. I watch just in case Dan has learned any new Spanish besides "En Fuego." Basically, I watch these two goofs on *SportsCenter* for a simple reason—they make me laugh.

They make the uneventful seem eventful and the ordinary, extraordinary. They not only report the scores and show the highlights, but bring fun to watching any sport.

So even though Keith uses words that make people scramble to their dictionary, and Dan truly believes he could beat any woman basketball player in a game of one-on-one, I watch *SportsCenter* as much as possible.

Besides, it's the only alternative to the 11 o'clock news.

Gene Siskel, Cohost, Siskel & Ebert; Film Critic to the World:
What I like about "The Big Show" is that it is hosted by a couple of smartasses. I like smartasses; I think I play one on TV.

Keith seems like a biker smartass. Remember the awful leather jackets he wore when he switched over to ESPN2? Dan is more of an altar-boy smartass, the kind who would put peanut butter on holy wafers. As I write this I just heard Dan, in an NFL highlight, refer to "Leslie Shepherd of the Washington Redskins getting the sheep knocked out of him."

Hey, if you want bland highlights, watch your own local sportscaster. "The Big Show" is for Big Boys.

Dennis Rodman, Forward, Chicago Bulls, Author, Professional Fashion Risk:
Dan and Keith would both be better off wearing a dress.
I know I'd watch more often if they did.

George F. Will, Baseball Fan, Baseball Author, Syndicated Columnist (excerpted in part from his column of 10/17/96):

Were someone to render my television set incapable of receiving anything but ESPN, it would be weeks—months, maybe—before I noticed. . . . There already is the jewel in ESPN's crown—*SportsCenter*. It is, as everyone knows, the thinking person's "World News Tonight with Peter Jennings." . . . My heart, and what remains of my mind, belong to ESPN, especially at 11:00 P.M., when it, even better than sleep, "knits up the ravell'd sleave of care."

Darius Rucker, Lead Singer, Hootie & The Blowfish, "Cracked Rear View" selling 13,000,000 CDs:

I was sitting in our bus, early in our tour, and there were a couple of us watching the show. And Dan said something about Dick Trickle, and Keith said something else about Dick Trickle, and I looked over at Gary Green, our percussion player, and I said, "Gary, how did we ever watch sports highlights before Dan and Keith?"

"The Big Show," to me, is what's sports is about. It's when you're a sports junkie, and you need to get all you can, but you want to be entertained by it, because then it can just command your undivided attention. I don't know why everybody didn't do "The Big Show" years ago. I don't know why it took them so long.

The one thing we miss the most when we're touring in Europe is "The Big Show."

Barry Sanders, Running Back, Detroit Lions:

Dan "The Human Highlight Film" Patrick: great outside jump shot, but does not pass the rock. I can't tell you how many times he has looked me off cutting to the lane. I am honored to be in his list of top ten athletes, since he is on my list of top ten playing big white stiff basketball players.

I empathize with Keith Olbermann and hope his medical insurance is paid up, since his back must be killing him from having to carry Dan for all these years on the show.

P.S.: The "Human Highlight" reference has nothing to do with Dan's athletic ability, just the videotape on The Big Show.

Rush Limbaugh:

"The Big Show" with Keith and Dan is just the best program of its kind on the air. You get every salient fact of every story covered.

And you get some of the funniest commentary to video highlights you'll ever hear; sometimes juicily subtle, other times audaciously loud. And if you listen closely, you will hear solid lessons of life expressed, in the form of fearless criticism of depraved behavior by some of our nation's most celebratedly disturbed athletes. Let your kids watch, by all means! They will learn right from wrong. And one other thing: "The Big Show" with Keith and Dan is one of the few things in life in which you can invest total passion without consequence. You'll never need a PSL to watch these guys.

Mel Kiper, Draft Expert:

I watch "The Big Show" every night, and I think every real sports fan does. Anybody can do highlights, but it's the extra perspective from the guys **doing** the highlights that makes the difference. Dan and Keith use humor, use insight, use creative writing, use perspective, use their great size, speed and agility—and about **every** sport.

And this is what amazes me: I cover college and pro football from an analytical viewpoint. But on "The Big Show": Football, Baseball, Basketball, Hockey, Horses, Auto Racing, Tennis, Soccer, Golf, Skiing—no matter what the sport is, these guys have some level of expertise about it. You feel like these two guys never talk down about a sport, and always show the knowledgeability of a sport. Thusly a fan of that sport is served, and someone who doesn't care about that sport is entertained and informed.

And I've never seen two cohosts in any sports broadcast complement each other the way Dan and Keith do. When you have two cohosts who communicate, who banter back and forth, sometimes conflicting, sometimes on the same page, that's the only way a team can be successful in the long run. That's their durability—a command of what they're talking about—that's their strength.

Jim Harbaugh, Quarterback, Indianapolis Colts:

It used to be that "The Big Show" meant playing in the NFL. Now it has taken on a whole new meaning. "The Big Show" is Dan and Keith on ESPN—and I need my fix at least twice a day.

(Authors' Note: At least sixteen times a year, Mr. Harbaugh is thrown bodily to the ground and often lands on his head. He once

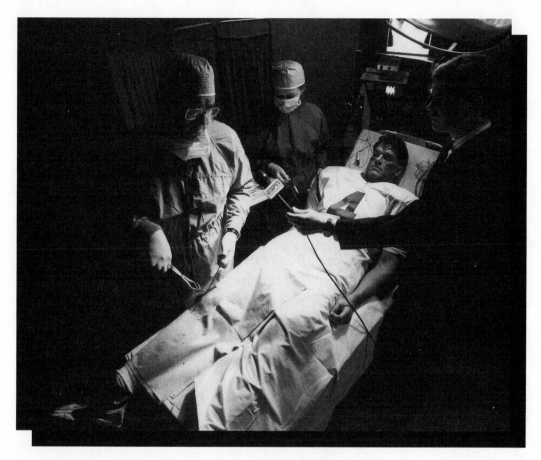

Jim Harbaugh gets his wish. *(photo by Scott Clarke)*

*stated that if an MRI of his knee revealed the need for surgery, he
wanted Keith to do it. We worry for him.)*

**Marv Albert, Play-by-Play Announcer, the NBA and NFL on
NBC, Who Has Announced Everything in the World Except New
Zealand Rugby League:**

I really enjoy "The Big Show" since Keith and Dan took over. I
think it has the right mix of commentary and video, the latter of
which has improved tremendously over the past few years. Sometimes, however, I still miss the original host. What ever happened
to that Bob Saget guy, anyway?

One key to the success of the show is that Dan and Keith prepare for their telecasts as diligently and intensely as any profes-

sional athlete getting ready for a big game. They arrive early. They look at video. They go over the game plan. They get dressed. And then they scream at everybody within earshot to get the hell out of the studio!

Of most significance, Keith and Dan have really taken this ESPN gig to an extreme. I understand that they often go out to eat after the show, but it's never anything fancy. You've heard of TV dinners? They have "cable TV dinners." You may not have heard of them because they are still only available in about seventy percent of the country.

Nancy Lieberman-Cline, Basketball Hall of Famer:

I knew that I did not have a balanced life style when my two-year old son T. J.'s first words were "Dah dah dah, dah dah dah." I guess he knows Dan and Keith just like he knows Barney and Big Bird. Besides, he thinks "The Big Show" is funnier and more informative. He sets his schedule by going to sleep once the show's over. Most parents put their kids down at a more decent time, but as long as "The Big Show" is going to be on that late, my boy's going to have to stay up and watch it.

Mike Lupica, *New York Daily News*, "The Sports Reporters," Author and Raconteur:

I would call "The Big Show" the only town meeting we have going in sports, but Olbermann and Patrick are much too hip for that. And they don't need any help for the audience. They'll do all the talking, thank you, handling both the questions and the answers. They give us the news and they gave us their commentary, their take on the whole thing, with the sharpest writing you will find anywhere on television. Somehow, they manage to do all that and separate the good guys from the bad guys and get laughs while they're doing it. Believe me, this is the one show everybody in the business most hates to miss.

In the end, here is the best part about Olbermann and Patrick, tag-team partners. They show up every time as if they've just taken over the principal's office. Don't just put me down as a fan, put me down as a member of "The Big Show" fan club.

Martina Navratilova, Winner of Nineteen Wimbledon Titles and Thirty-Three Other Grand Slam Events:

If the book is as funny as Keith is on TV, I'll buy it. I love that guy.

Dick Trickle, the Greatest Name in NASCAR:

All I know is evidently there's a lot of people watch that "Big Show" because I get a lot of feedback from the fans. I'll be walking down pit row or in the garage area or something, and people up at the fence'll say "There goes *SportsCenter*'s Dick Trickle." A lot of fans ask me why they always bring me up and I always tell them I'm not sure how and why, but it's all been a positive from this end. Sometimes if it ain't broke, you don't fix it. It works for me, and evidently it's working for them.

It's done more for me than Tom Cruise did, for sure!

Richard Lewis, Actor, Comedian, Writer, Bon Vivant, AKA "The Prince of Pain":

I'm real glad that the Mormon Tabernacle Choir fell out so there was room for me in this chapter. Aside from the obvious, slightly embarrassing penis-envy title of their broadcast, "The Big Show," it is still, even on off-days, the most orgasmic summing up of the world of sports ever.

I'm a tad conflicted writing this because of a close, personal relationship with Mr. Olbermann (a man who, thankfully, listened to me when after finally shaving his mustache, he panicked backstage and had to be restrained by Dan and me not to quickly greasepaint a Groucho look-alike), particularly in the area of women. Sadly, the both of us—unlike Dan—have led a tortured life off-camera in our daily search for a nurturing woman to have a child with, and whose friends and family generally aren't involved in some sort of satanic cult. But, hey, as long as you have your health.

In any event, being a sports "junkie," I was never quite satisfied with a sports newscast until their pairing. Why? Well, to be frank, some of those reasons I will have to take to my grave. But for openers, what other team on the air, I ask you, instantly reminds you of your favorite Abbott & Costello routine? None; who would have the "balls" to? Which show in the history of broadcasting would ever, on occasion, sacrifice the final score of an important game in favor of getting self-serving laughs? None.

Their amazing knowledge and grasp of almost all sports, except for their obvious, slightly retarded take on soccer and auto racing, coupled with their flair and healthy narcissism make them a lock for the "Hall of Fame."

Eddie George, Running Back, Houston Oilers, 1995 Heisman Trophy Winner:

I love The Big Show and Keith and Dan. However, I am miffed that it was only after I won the Heisman that they paid me any attention. They clearly jumped on the bandwagon. I am happy that these two bigwigs are on the bandwagon now, but why did it take so long?

*(Authors' Note: While winning said Heisman, Mr. George played nearly all of his games on Saturday. We wish to point out that we are **off** on Saturdays and thus had no opportunity to praise Mr. George's work until after his professional career commenced, and he began working Sundays like we do. Helen Hunt could be playing college football for Florida State this year, and we wouldn't be able to say a word about it.)*

Jason Kidd, Phoenix Suns, 1995 NBA Co-Rookie of the Year:

In the history of sports in America there have been a number of great duos: Gehrig & Ruth, Rice & Montana, Jordan & Pippen. Well, add Patrick & Olbermann to the list.

Arturs Irbe, Goaltender, Dallas Stars:

Keith and Dan are Sports Addicts! They're hilarious. I just wish ESPN's "Big Show" could be seen in Latvia, because half of my family and friends don't believe I'm an NHL goaltender. They think I'm either a KGB spy or partners with Maxwell Smart in the greeting card business.

Brad Faxon, Winner of Four PGA Tournaments:

Trying to remember what life was like before *SportsCenter* is like having to live again with Baggies that don't zip-loc! The Big Show is a ritual before bed that includes brushing and flossing.

My most memorable moment was during a trip to ESPN when Keith walked past me fresh from makeup and with blue jeans below his double-vested navy sportscoat. That really put a spin on my thought process that says maybe they don't take the show that seriously after all! Anyway, in the PGA Tour locker rooms we replay their comments just like we relive our completed rounds.

I look at The Big Show as a marriage-saver because I don't **have** to watch all the sports I want to; I just turn to ESPN at 11:00 P.M.!

Mike Fratello, Head Coach, Cleveland Cavaliers, the NBA's Erstwhile Tsar of the Telestrator:

"The Big Show" with Dan and Keith reminds of other classic TV shows. In the '50s, it was *Your Show of Shows* with Sid Caesar and Imogene Coca. In the '60s it was Ed Sullivan's *Really* Big Show. In the '70s, who can forget *The Gong Show* and Johnny Carson's *The Tonight Show*. And of course, the Coz led the way with *The Cosby Show* in the '80s. But for my money, the '90s will always be linked with "The Big Show" and Keith Olbermann and his tag-team partner, Dan Patrick.

Valeri Kamensky, Left Wing, 1996 Stanley Cup Champions Colorado Avalanche:

These days, I just hope to "put the biscuit in the basket," then rush home to watch the highlights on "The Big Show." Those guys should be put away in a Prophylactorium.

(Authors' note: Mr. Kamensky explains that in his native Russia, a "prophylactorium" is a mental institution. You thought he meant something else, didn't you? Shame on you.)

Wayne Gretzky, Forward, New York Rangers, NHL All-Time Leading Scorer:

I'm sure it will be a surprise to everyone, including Keith and Dan, to learn that they had a very big influence on my decision to come to New York this year and play for the Rangers. Having played in Los Angeles for the previous eight years, I had certainly seen Keith Olbermann on television in that market. I'm not sure what station he was on or even if he was doing sports, because, really, at that stage in his career, I don't think he could even get arrested. But I do remember the mustache.

Dan Patrick is not a broadcaster that I recall seeing before he arrived at ESPN, but my sources tell me that he anchored the sports desk at both Channel 5 in Brainerd, Minnesota, and Channel 7 in Rancho Cucamonga, California.

Knowing that they come from backgrounds of anonymity and then watching them team up on "The Big Show," it became obvious to me that working in the New York area can make anyone a star. As a result, it became obvious to me that the lucrative offers I was receiving from NHL teams outside New York paled in comparison to the opportunity for me to play and work in the same city as Dan and Keith. It's a decision that I have never regretted. Things are going well and will only get better once my mustache grows in like the one Keith sometimes has.

Actually, I know that Dan and Keith really work in Bristol, Connecticut, but they try to tell everyone that they are "based in New York," and I won't argue with them. Besides, Bristol doesn't have an NHL franchise, so I couldn't play there.

Mike Mills, Lead Bass Player, Award-Winning Group R.E.M.:

I have loved "The Big Show" since the first time I saw it. The perfect blend of irreverence, wit, and respect—or, to paraphrase Pete Townshend, "From you, I get opinions. From you, I get the story."

Joe Magrane, Pitcher, Broadcaster, National League ERA Champion (1988) and Leader In Hit Batsmen (1987):

I've enjoyed watching Dan and Keith's *SportsCenter* blossom into a true event. "The Big Show" has changed the way we get sports. There have been many imitators, but *SportsCenter* has blitzkrieged them all and left them in their wake.

I look forward to "The Big Show" taking us into the twenty-first century; maybe by then, Keith's clothes will be back in style.

TOM

I had been on *SportsCenter* for four days when he came over to my desk.

"Keith, I wanted to apologize," he said. I looked back at him blankly. I'd known him professionally for eleven years and all that time flashed through my mind and this one was real easy: There wasn't one thing he needed to apologize **for.**

"I said something to somebody about you." This was chewing him up. His usually pale face was a little flush, and I was a little worried. "About how you do the show. I'm sorry. I shouldn't have said it and not only that, I didn't mean it. I was just frustrated about something here and I took it out on you and I'm sorry." I was still in the dark. Whatever he'd said—Lord, we cut each other all the time in this business and 99 percent of the remarks represent only the pressure finally eating through the shell we build around it—I'd never have taken it personally. Moreover, whatever he'd said, nobody had said it to me, and I told him so.

"Doesn't matter," he said. "I just wanted to make sure that if you **did** hear it, you knew I was sorry and I didn't mean it and I think it's great you're finally here."

And that, in the short, slice–of–life, anecdotal form, should tell you exactly who Tom Mees was.

We lost him on a beautiful Wednesday in August last year. We lost him an hour after he'd been in the office he helped to build, in the parking lot shooting the breeze with one of the twenty or thirty or who knows how many *SportsCenter* anchors he helped to break in, Charley Steiner. We lost him in a swimming pool not two miles from the ESPN complex that, quite frankly, couldn't possibly be standing, nor standing so tall, if he hadn't slugged it out all those years when ESPN was not only **not** the monolith it seems to be today, but was something that the rest of us in sports media looked at with, at best, sympathy.

Tom Mees was one of the originals at *SportsCenter* and in the coverage of virtually every sport ESPN has ever televised. When the company logo still looked like the sign in front of a cut-rate service station and the background on the *SportsCenter* set was made out of swatches and carpet remnants, Tom Mees was laying the ground-work for all that followed. But even acknowledging this truth— Tom Mees **was** ESPN when ESPN **wasn't** cool—somehow demeans his contribution to what goes on here.

I used to run into him at games, and strike negotiations, when his network and my old one between them weren't worth the price of basic cable. I had strong doubts about my longevity in this busi-ness but he didn't. "Nice work on that . . ." was usually his greet-ing, even before the handshake. Football talks in 1982. Dodgers-Mets play-offs in 1988. The unnecessary, never-to-be-forgotten apology in 1992. The last time I saw him, not a month before he died. "You said something six weeks ago about the Pirates and I laughed my butt off. . . ."

We didn't do all that many *SportsCenter*s together ("You talk faster than I do!" he said during a commercial break once. "How are we ever going to fill a whole hour?"), but there were a couple of tough times for Tom during the year we overlapped on the show, and I just happened to be there and managed to make myself useful to him, maybe by just listening, and he never forgot it. And I don't just mean he was pleasant or warm or supportive—all of which he was. I mean he used to remind me of this trifling thing I'd done and made me feel like it had been the grandest thing in the world. "Hey, how are you and Dan holding up? I was watching in San Jose the other day and you guys looked beat. The shows are great—but are you holding up?"

Tom lived literally ten minutes away from me, but the opportunities for socializing were few, and as odd as this sounds, I was delighted that this was so. This meant he was on the road most of the winter doing hockey games—NHL, college, pickup on a frozen pond if they'd have let him—that crisp, even delivery bursting into genuine enthusiasm at every goal, at every brilliant save. The NHL had always been his dream, and for three seasons he did as many national telecasts of it as anybody on the continent. And the true benefit of that, of course, was that it meant days on end in the winter, and virtually complete summers, at home with his wife and his two daughters. One of the off-air originals here saw him the night before he died and said Tommy had said it again that evening, just as he always did: Every game he broadcast, every dollar he made—those were for his daughters. In an industry of transients, this was a stable family man. He went to the zoning board and knew about the noise codes. There were people in our town who didn't know what ESPN was. But they knew who Mr. Mees was.

These last few years Tom Mees probably got the closest anyone in this business could get to having the perfect job. Enough money, enough work, enough fame, enough satisfaction from—finally—enough hockey. And all that time with the family.

He should have had more time. After all, he had **two** families to spend it with. Just how true that was we learned and felt at the occasion of his wake. Dan and I like to kid each other about needing hugs. We weren't kidding that night. And it wasn't because they had worked together for a time with Tom that brought Greg Wyatt up from Florida or Alan Massengale in from Los Angeles to say good-bye. And almost as sad as his passing was this simple fact: The way people come and go here, there have already been generations of production assistants and sportscasters and executives who never saw Tom Mees host *SportsCenter* or do more in the studio than stop by and shoot the bull with old friends—a task that by itself could take hours. There will be many more such generations who will never know his laugh, or even the bite of his caustic wit. There have been, and now there will be, generations of sportscasters who get to work at ESPN or ESPN2 or ESPNews or ESPNext rather than in a small town somewhere because Tom Mees took the risks and took the hits and built the place. There will be many more such generations who will lean on the network name to get some interview arranged or throw some weight around, and will never realize that the particular brick they're leaning on was put there, with great sweat and great toil and great love, by Tom Mees.

Nothing ESPN did, nothing ESPN ever became or ever will become, did not feel his skilled, direct, and professional touch. But moreover, Tom Mees was our friend and our colleague and no words can describe his value to us as individuals.

And nothing and no one here will ever be the same without him.

———

There are two charitable funds which we mention here in Tom's memory. The Mees Children's Trust will support his daughters' educations. It's located at P.O. Box 6811, East Brunswick, New Jersey 08816-6811. Five percent of what Dan and I are receiving from this book is going to this fund.

Tom's favorite charity helped children with cancer. It's the Valerie Fund at 1878 Springfield Avenue, Maplewood, New Jersey 07040.